P9-CLD-800

WELFARE IN TRANSITION

WELFARE IN TRANSITION

A Survey of Living Conditions in Sweden 1968–1981

Edited by
ROBERT ERIKSON AND RUNE ÅBERG

HN
577
.V3313
1986

CLARENDON PRESS · OXFORD
1987

WITHDRAWN
Library
Fort Wayne

Oxford University Press, Walton Street, Oxford OX2 6DP
Oxford New York Toronto
Delhi Bombay Calcutta Madras Karachi
Petaling Jaya Singapore Hong Kong Tokyo
Nairobi Dar es Salaam Cape Town
Melbourne Auckland
and associated companies in
Beirut Berlin Ibadan Nicosia

Oxford is a trade mark of Oxford University Press

Published in the United States
by Oxford University Press, New York

© Swedish Institute for Social Research
Stockholms Universitet 1987

All rights reserved. No part of this publication may be reproduced,
stored in a retrieval system, or transmitted, in any form or by any means,
electronic, mechanical, photocopying, recording, or otherwise, without
the prior permission of Oxford University Press

This book is sold subject to the condition that it shall not, by way
of trade or otherwise, be lent, re-sold, hired out or otherwise circulated
without the publisher's prior consent in any form of binding or cover
other than that in which it is published and without a similar condition
including this condition being imposed on the subsequent purchaser

British Library Cataloguing in Publication Data
Welfare in transition: a survey of living conditions in Sweden 1968–1981.
1. Sweden — Social conditions — 1945 -
2. Erikson Robert   II. Aberg, Rune
948.5'057   HN573.5
ISBN 0–19–828516–7

Library of Congress Cataloguing in Publication Data
Välfärd i förändring. English
Welfare in transition.
Translation of: Välfärd i förändring.
Bibliography: p.
1. Sweden — Social policy.   2. Sweden — Economic policy.
3. Sweden — Social conditions — 1945 -
4. Welfare state.   I. Erikson, Robert, 1938 -
II. Aberg, Rune 1942 -   III. Title
HN577.V3313   1986   361.6'1'09485   86-16485
ISBN 0-19-828516-7

Set by the Castlefield Press, Wellingborough.
Printed in Great Britain
at the University Printing House, Oxford
by David Stanford
Printer to the University

WITHDRAWN

Foreword

This is a report on living conditions in Sweden, prepared by a group of
Swedish social scientists and based on the results of a research
programme which originated in a distinctively Swedish political
situation.[1] Why, then, should it be thought that the report is of
sufficiently wide interest to merit an English edition? Two main reasons
may be given.

In much current political and economic debate, Sweden represents a
critical case — even though, as a result of misrepresentation or simple
neglect, its significance has not received the recognition it deserves. The
report prepared by Erikson, Åberg, and their colleagues is then of value
in the first place in helping us to appreciate the full relevance of the
Swedish experience — and also, perhaps, to understand why this should
have been so often obscured. For in the light of the data and analyses
that are presented, Sweden emerges not only as a critical, but in fact as a
decidedly *awkward* case for many theorists of contemporary capitalism,
and not least for those who have of late been most assertive on both the
Right and the Left.

Thus, for exponents of the 'new *laissez-faire*', a country such as
Sweden — with an ambitious system of social welfare, based upon
ramifying public bureaucracies, demanding high levels of personal
taxation, and supported politically by a highly organized labour
movement — should display distinctive symptoms of economic and
social malfunctioning: for example, sluggish labour markets and
declining employment opportunities, an unresponsive workforce lacking
adquate incentives, a population at large whose members are prevented
from controlling their own destinies and become increasingly passive and
dependent upon the 'nanny state'. However, while it will be apparent to
any reader of the pages that follow that Sweden is certainly not without
its economic and social problems, it should be equally apparent that the
foregoing cannot count as a particularly accurate characterization of
them, at least in the period from the late 1960s through to the 1980s. For
instance, as regards employment — which for Swedish governments
(Social Democratic and 'bourgeois' alike) has been a concern of social as
much as of economic polity — the record can only be described as
enviable. While participation rates have steadily risen from levels that
were already comparatively high, unemployment has been vigorously
combated and is at present below 3 per cent. More Swedes are now
actually working for pay than ever before in the nation's history. Nor is

evidence of increasing unresponsiveness or inactivity any more apparent in political or social life. Unusually high levels of organizational membership have been maintained, various more active forms of political participation have become more common, a growing number of people believe that they are capable of defending themselves against the decisions of public authorities, and fewer appear to live without supportive social networks of relatives and friends.

From a Marxist standpoint, on the other hand, Sweden, as a country in which control of the economy remains largely in private hands, should show characteristic features of 'late-capitalist' development: for example, persistently wide class inequalities in economic resources and basic life-chances and an unremitting 'degradation' of labour as technological advance is constrained within exploitative property relations. Again, however, the empirical evidence is disobliging. For example, in the course of the 1970s an appreciable reduction occurred in inequalities in personal incomes, the influence of class origins on educational attainment declined, mobility between classes increased and, to judge by employees' own reports, the number experiencing boredom or a severe lack of autonomy in work decreased, although more found their jobs mentally exhausting. It is, moreoever, apparent that these changes were in some large part politically determined. Greater equality in incomes was promoted by the governmental commitment to full employment, by pension reform, and by the unions' 'solidaristic' wages policy, while a series of measures were enacted to improve employees' working conditions and to extend their rights within the workplace. Whether or not, then, it is impossible — as Marxists would claim — to 'legislate socialism into existence', the Swedish experience would confirm that action via the institutions of liberal democracy can at all events modify the outcomes of capitalist relations, in labour markets and production units alike, and in ways that prove highly consequential for the everday lives of substantial sections of the population.

The second reason for presenting *Welfare in Transition* to a wider readership — and, it might be said, to a British readership especially — is of a rather different but no less important kind; namely, that it stands as a powerful reaffirmation of a particular tradition of relating social enquiry to the political process. This is the tradition of what, in the British idiom, would be called 'political arithmetic', and it is indeed one to which the British contribution was for long outstanding. It is not accidental that when in their introductory chapter Erikson and Åberg set out the basic assumptions and objectives which have guided their work, the name most often invoked is that of Richard Titmuss; and they could have well traced back the spirit of their enterprise further to Lancelot Hogben's splendid 'Prolegomena to Political Arithmetic' of 1938.[2]

This tradition is one which, it must be said, has clearly declined in favour within the sociological community, at least since the upheavals of the 1960s — and, by a sad irony, to a greater extent in Britain than elsewhere. Research which has sought to inform public opinion with a detailed quantitative account of 'the condition of the people' has frequently been disparaged as merely descriptive — or, worse, 'positivist' — as having only 'administrative' significance, or as being insufficiently 'theoretical' and 'critical'.[3] However, there are now welcome indications that the tide is once more turning. Among a new generation, recognition would appear to be growing of the rather hollow pretentions of the 'committed sociology' or 'critical theory' of the post-1968 period — and of the narrowness of their political appeal — and, at the same time, of the importance of social analysis with a sound quantitative grounding to both policy formation and political argument alike. The availability of the impressive exemplar that has been provided by Swedish colleagues can only encourage this trend. So far as British sociology is concerned, the best indication that 'political arithmetic' is being restored to its former pride of place would be an early start on the long research process which would mean that, by the year 2000, a British equivalent of *Welfare in Transition* could be produced.

John H. Goldthorpe

Nuffield College, Oxford
October 1985

Notes to Foreword

1. See further Sten Johansson, 'The Level of Living Survey: a Presentation', *Acta Sociologica,* 3 (1973).
2. See Lancelot Hogben (ed.), *Political Arithmetic,* London, Allen and Unwin (1938) pp. 13–46.
3. As an early but still fairly representative example, see John Rex, *Key Problems of Sociological Theory,* London, Routledge (1961) chap. 2.

Preface

In the international discussion of social welfare Sweden has often been held up as a prototype showing the effects that follow when the ideas of the welfare state are implemented, sometimes even as an ideal where several aspects of utopia have been realized. More recently, however, it has been presented increasingly as a warning against the frightening consequences of sweeping social policy. To some of us who have followed this discussion from the vantage point of Sweden, both sides have often appeared to be misinformed about the living conditions existing here. As the Swedish case still seems to attract a lot of attention, our hope is to give both friends and foes of the welfare state the basis for a more well-grounded discussion — through our attempt to describe how living conditions in Sweden have actually developed. At best, we may make a contribution to the general debate on the ways and means of welfare politics as well as to research on the welfare state, by making facts about Sweden more readily available and comparisons between Sweden and other countries more feasible.

Our aim is descriptive. It is to give an account, as accurately as possible, of the levels and trends in welfare and living conditions in Sweden over a period of thirteen years, for which we have data from three sample surveys. We have tried to achieve our goal be describing (i) average changes, (ii) differences with regard to class, sex, age, and type of community, and (iii) changes in these differences for a large number of welfare indicators. In order to keep the book down to a reasonable size, we have tried to adhere quite strictly to this descriptive goal. Thus, analyses of causes of the observed conditons and trends or of the effects of various policy measures, have been kept for later publications.

We have tried to explain various Swedish peculiarities in order to make the text comprehensible to non-Swedish readers. The list of common abbreviations which follows the preface should help in this respect.

The development of living conditions is difficult to portray, as several processes are interwoven in a complex manner. A major problem in describing societal trends, therefore is to illustrate complicated processes in a lucid way. We have tried to show the main trends by means of regression analysis and to make the results of these analyses easily accessible, we have presented them diagrammatically. In Chapter 2, Jan Selén explains how these diagrams should be interpreted. *To understand many of the other chapters, it is necessary to read Chapter 2.*

The currency used in the text is the Swedish crown, abbreviated to SEK. To ease interpretation of information on incomes, the exchange rates between the Swedish crown and the British pound and the US dollar, respectively, are given here for the three years for which income data were collected and for the latest available year. The figures show how many pounds and dollars, on average, were equivalent to 100 Swedish crowns for each year. In most cases, income figures for 1967 and 1973 have been corrected for inflation to the price level of 1980. We have, therefore, also given the correction factors, which show the amount which each year corresponds to 100 crowns to the 1980 price level.

	£	$	PL
1967	7.1	19.2	37
1973	9.3	22.7	50
1980	10.1	23.8	100
1985	9.0	11.6	156

Again, in order to limit the size of the book, the English translation is somewhat shorter than the original Swedish version. Two chapters have been omitted in their entirety, one on victims of crime and accidents, and one on childhood conditions. In addition, three chapters have been cut down, those on working conditions, housing conditions, and leisure.

Many people have assisted us in the preparation of this book. Our gratitude to most of them was expressed in the Swedish original, but there are some whom we would specially like to acknowledge here. Sten Johansson headed the work on the first Level of Living Survey in 1968, and was responsible for the project until 1982. He thus conducted much of the groundwork, and has continued to offer help as well as constructive criticism. Miljan Vuksanovic has been responsible for the computer work and programming since 1974 and his work has been performed excellently.

Paul Lappalainen and Karen Leander translated our text into English. We worked in close co-operation with them, a rewarding experience both for us personally and for our language skills. As many times before the secretaries at the Swedish Institute for Social Research, Eva Carlsson, Ulla Carlstedt, Anne-Maj Folmer-Hansen, and Eleanor Rapier, managed, quickly and accurately, to transform a messy stack of papers into a neat typescript. The advice and help of John H. Goldthorpe enabled us to present our book in a British context. Oxford University Press has suggested many editional changes to the text which have improved its style and clarity.

The Ministry of Education and Cultural Affairs, the Swedish Delegation for Social Research within the Ministry of Health and Social Affairs, and the Ministry of Labour have supported our work through generous research grants which made it all possible. The Swedish Institute has contributed to making the translation possible. The Swedish Institute for Social Research, board and staff, has encouraged us, offered help and criticism, and most of all, created an ideal research environment.

All these and many others have made this book possible. We hope that they and other readers will find their and our efforts worthwhile.

The Authors
Stockholm, June 1985

Contents

List of Abbreviations

LNU	Level of Living Survey
LO	Swedish Trade Union Confederation (of manual workers)
LRF	Federation of Swedish Farmers
N	Number of Observations (in tables)
SACO/SR	Swedish Confederation of Professional Associations
SAF	Swedish Employers' Confederation
SCB	Statistics Sweden (formerly Central Bureau of Statistics)
SEK	Swedish crowns
SFS	Swedish Code of Statutes
SOFI	Swedish Institute for Social Research
SOS	Official Statistics of Sweden
SOU	Swedish Government Official Reports
TCO	Swedish Central Organization of Salaried Employees
ULF	Survey of Living Conditions at Statistics Sweden

Contributing Authors

Rune Åberg   is Professor of Sociology at the University of Umeå and was previously employed at SOFI. He has researched in issues concerning the labour market, social stratification, and political sociology.

Christina Axelsson is a sociologist and is employed as a research assistant on the Level of Living Project at SOFI.

Robert Erikson   is Professor of Sociology at the University of Stockholm. Specializes in welfare research and studies of the social structure and social mobility.

Tofte Frykman   is a Bachelor of Science (econ.) and is employed at the National Price and Cartel Office.

Janne Jonsson   is a sociologist and is employed as a research assistant on the Level of Living Project at SOFI.

Sven-Åke Kjellström is a sociologist and was associated earlier with the Level of Living Project at SOFI.

Olle Lundberg   is a sociologist and is employed as a research assistant on the Level of Living Project at SOFI.

Jan Selén   has a Ph. D. in statistics and works at SOFI. He has specialized in econometrics and problems in methodology in survey studies.

Ryszard Szulkin   is a sociologist and is employed as a research assistant at the Level of Living Project at SOFI.

Henrik Tham   has a Ph. D. in sociology and works at SOFI with primary research in the fields of criminology and social problems.

Michael Tåhlin   is a sociologist and is employed as a research assistant on the Level of Living Project at SOFI.

1

The Nature and Distribution of Welfare

ROBERT ERIKSON AND RUNE ÅBERG

Developments in Swedish society have been painted in increasingly sombre colours in recent years; conditions are hardening and things in general are getting worse, it is often claimed. There are many signs which lead credence to such a view. Unemployment has gone up and real wages down. The national budget has a large deficit, and Sweden has experienced serious imbalance in foreign trade of goods and services.

In other words, the economic crisis is real. But if we look at different aspects of Swedish society over a 10–15-year period the picture becomes a subtler one. There have also been positive changes. The findings of the Level of Living Surveys reported in this book, show that from 1968 to 1981 improvements occurred in several spheres. Housing conditions have improved and the economic resources of the inhabitants of Sweden have grown. People have become more active in their leisure time and in politics. The numbers suffering from impaired mental well-being seem to have dropped, although the health of the Swedish people has not improved otherwise. Working conditions have been ameliorated in some ways, such as in the broadening influence workers have over their own working conditons. But here too there are some signs of deterioration — the number of workers exposed to poisonous substances, noise, vibrations, and inappropriate work postures has increased.

In 1965, the Swedish government set up a Low Income Commission whose task was not so much to put forward suggestions on how to solve the problems of low incomes as to consider the information needed to give the discussion on low incomes an acceptable base. To do this, the Commission set out to describe the conditions of the Swedish population — not only the low income earners — in three respects: income, purchasing power, and level of living. For the final tasks, a sociologist, Sten Johansson, was asked to make a survey of adult Swedes. This survey was conducted in 1968. In 1974, the then newly-opened Swedish Institute for Social Research was commissioned by Parliament to conduct the survey anew, and the same assignment was repeated in 1981. It is primarily the results from these three surveys that form the basis for the description of developments in Swedish welfare in this book.

When the findings from the first Level of Living Survey were published in 1970 and 1971 — a period characterized by optimism about the future — they received a lot of attention. To the surprise of many, the survey showed that large groups of the population had been left behind during the expansion of the welfare society. Then, as now, these results seemed in conflict with what most people believed had been happening in our society. It was the description of conditions that provoked the most reaction, as the inequality reported was so much greater than people expected. Today, it is the description of the developments in welfare that is in conflict with prevailing conceptions.

We have chosen to use the term 'level of living' although it may sound curious to some readers. It was introduced in Sweden in the first of the surveys analysed in this book and has since become accepted usage in Swedish. Taken originally from UN publications in English, it is an expression which has a wider connotation and less materialistic ring than the more familiar 'standard of living', with its reference mainly to standards of consumption. The distinction between the two seems as relevant in English as it was in the original Swedish and we have therefore continued to use 'level of living' as our basic concept in this British edition.

That the point of departure in this book is the first Level of Living Survey means that we are bound to define and measure the level of living largely in the manner developed in that survey. Although this does imply a limitation, we do not consider it a real drawback. On the contrary, fifteen years' research has proved the fruitfulness of the approach chosen then, as well as its usefulness in describing key elements in the welfare of people.

Theoretical starting points

The level of living is assumed to be determined by the choices people have in making decisions which concern their own lives. A high level of living then means that people have a wide scope of action within which they can shape their lives and living conditions according to their own values and needs. An important source of inspiration for the 1968 survey was social policy research in Great Britain, especially that designed by Richard Titmuss (S. Johansson 1970, 1979). The central concept used by Titmuss is 'command over resources'. By basing the definition of level of living on command over resources, stress is put on the nature of men and women as beings of action. Placing the emphasis here is deeply rooted in sociological theory (see, for example, Boudon 1979).

Using Titmuss as a starting point, level of living was defined as 'the individual's command over resources in the form of money, possessions, knowledge, mental and physical energy, social relations, security, and so on, through which the individual can control and consciously direct his living conditions' (S. Johansson 1970, 25). One limitation of such a definition is that it does not take into account the context in which the resources are to be used. Education, for example, is undoubtedly an important resource, but if no labour market exists where a particular type of education is useful, its value would be limited. The definition therefore should be broadened to read: The level of living is the individual's command over resources in a given context to control and consciously direct his living conditions.

Resources include items such as income, wealth, knowledge, skills, and health. The context refers to conditions that reflect the labour market, the housing market, the educational system, and the health care system. Individuals' resources and the conditions for making use of them together determine the scope of individuals for directing their own lives.

In many cases, conditions are not measured or discussed directly. Instead, they are presented only indirectly as assumptions. An important one, whose applicability is fundamental if the overall approach is to be meaningful, is that democracy prevails. In other words, we assume that within the political system, there is no condition that functions as an effective hindrance to people's use of their resources.

The actual nature of the level of living is not easily or immediately determinable using this definition. If we follow it, level of living will encompass the most important resources and the most important conditions, which, combined, determine the individual's range of action. In making a selection of such factors, therefore, we must rely upon rather general arguments and considerations. They will then not only be based on conceptions about what the most important resources are, but also on assumptions about what constitutes the central conditions of life and essential needs.

A group of experts at the United Nations has attempted to base the level of living concept on such grounds (United Nations 1966). The working group divided the level of living into components, an approach that was further developed for our first survey (S. Johansson 1970, 1979). This led to a concept constructed from nine components:

1. Health and access to care
2. Employment and working conditions
3. Economic resources
4. Knowledge and educational opportunities
5. Family and social integration
6. Housing and neighbourhood facilities
7. Security of life and property
8. Recreation and culture
9. Political resources

Similar lists of the elements of the welfare concept have been developed in several countries for the purpose of compiling social statistics. As pointed out by S. Johansson (1979, 54 f.), the lists are remarkably uniform, regardless of the political systems or levels of economic development. Some components such as health, employment, and education appear on all lists. We believe that the central elements which make up the level of living are covered by these components. On the other hand, we do not claim to cover all aspects that could be of significance. The level of living concept is limited to factors that, at least in part, are regulated through collective decisions and are the object of collective political responsibility. This explains why factors such as talent and climate are not included in the level of living concept.

After limiting the range of the level of living with the help of nine components, the problem remains of choosing indicators or measures that accurately represent actual circumstances. The selection of indicators is an attempt to find a number of valid indicators among all the possible ones. For the construction of the questionnaire, expertise in the different areas enabled us to choose indicators which would incorporate the intended components as much as possible. The technical quality of the indicators was tested in different ways, and we avoided using those appearing to be defective.

The level of living relates to people's actual circumstances. For the purpose of measuring these, we asked the interviewees to describe their circumstances. We have used so-called *descriptive indicators*. The alternative was to use evaluative indicators, that is, allowing the interviewees to express the level of their satisfaction with different aspects of their situation.[1] The valuation by individuals of their situation is not only influenced by the actual situation, but also by their aspiration level, what they consider rightfully theirs or what level they think they ought to reach. Descriptive indicators are not without problems, but they are not influenced by variations in the aspiration level to the same degreee as are evaluative indicators, and are thus preferable for our purposes.

One problem with studies of change is that the selected indicators may indeed cover important aspects of the component they are meant to measure at a specific point in time, but be less relevant at another point in time. Over a long period, for example, it has been extremely helpful to measure housing standards by access to running water, sewer drainage, toilets, and central heating. However, when there is almost universal access to these basic conveniences, it is no longer possible to measure the distribution and change in the housing standard with these indicators. But for such a relatively short period as is covered by our measurements, we are of the opinion that only one indicator, in fact that of housing standard, has decreased in relevance.

Principles for description

The first Level of Living Survey was conducted in the spring and early summer of 1968. About 6000 Swedes between the ages of 15 and 75 were interviewed. Methods previously used for measuring opinion were used for collecting information about actual living conditions of the population. A similar approach had been applied earlier within single areas such as the level of unemployment, but not so comprehensively.

In 1974, The Swedish Institute for Social Research conducted what was, for most purposes, a replication of the first Level of Living Survey. After adding six cohorts of young people and newly-arrived immigrants, the remaining people under the age of 76 were interviewed again using essentially the same questionnaire as before. Another similar survey was conducted in 1981.

In these surveys, the people selected have been asked to describe their living conditions by answering a series of questions in standardized interviews. The questions concerned the nine Level-of-Living components, as well as occupation and other conditions.

A starting point for the presentation in this book has been that the developments we describe are to be in some way or another assessed by the reader. The question then arises of how to formulate a description which is relevant to most people in their assessment and evaluation of Swedish developments. This requires a criterion against which the element to be evaluated can be measured.

As a rule, no such criterion appears in the form of a predetermined desirable development or a specific desirable condition. Perceptions about what should be striven after vary among individuals and groups in our society. Sometimes, however, these perceptions are incorporated into the political process and expressed as norms against which a condition or trend can be assessed. They then often take the form of a limit below which no one should fall. Such is the case for limits for density found in housing policies. Such norms can be seen as an expression of social policy ambitions of the type embraced in 'the social citizenship' (Marshall 1950).

Marshall viewed citizenship as a collection of rights and divided them into three groups: civil, political, and social. Civil rights constitute the prerequisites for personal freedom; the individual's independence and equality before the law, freedom of thought, expression, and religion, and the right to own property and to make contracts. Political citizenship is built on the right to participate in political decision-making. Social citizenship encompasses the right to a certain economic security, and the right to participate in social life as a fully-fledged member of society according to the norms prevalent in the society.

From the right to participate in social life and be met with regard and respect are derived the rights to a basic education, to a certain housing standard, and to a minimum economic standard. Marshall's social citizenship can perhaps be seen as a relatively modest distribution policy ambition that aims at providing all members of society with a basic level of security. This type of policy, endeavouring to raise all citizens above the minimum levels in various areas, but where market mechanisms are allowed to determine the distribution above these levels, is usually called a *marginal social policy*.

In social policy discussion since the war, the ambition, at least in Scandinavia, has been higher than merely keeping the poor out of the clutches of misery. Social policy, it has been said, should not aim merely at improving the conditions of the poorest, but rather operate as a support system for all citizens. In an *institutional social policy* (see Titmuss 1974, 30–31), an attempt is made to provide solutions that satisfy the demands and needs of all citizens. Day-care centres and schools should be so good that members of all classes will want their children to attend; public care should be of such quality that demand for private care will disappear; everyone should have access to public housing, and so on.

With this in mind, the questions of distribution gain an enhanced significance for assessing society's development: to what degree are health care and housing dispersed according to need and to what degree according to resources? Are education slots allocated according to the parents' resources, or to the pupils' needs, talent, and interest? Of importance is also how systematic the distribution is, that is, to what degree problems in different components tend to befall the same individuals, and whether individuals with problems are concentrated in certain population groups. The goals of distribution policy, however, are seldom fixed; instead, they are manifested in terms of a 'direction of movement' or in general ideas about how welfare should be transformed and how it should be distributed among different groups in society.

What the desirable distribution would be is thus unclear and disputed. Nor is there any agreement about the extent to which the actual distribution is to be determined by political interventions or market mechanisms. In other words, how people assess an existing distribution is dependent upon their political values and other interests, but also upon the causal mechanisms which they believe have brought it about. This book contributes nothing directly to these issues. We do not offer our version of the ideal distribution of resources. Moreover, the causal analyses are meagre. Our primary goal is to describe the development in the level of living by outlining the average developments for the entire population, and by describing it in such a way that it facilitates the discussion on distribution policies. For the latter purpose, we consider it be crucial to priorite a description showing the extent to which the living conditions of people are related to their place in the social and demographic structure.

More precisely, we try to answer three questions for all components: Has the level changed from 1968 to 1981? Are there differences among the sexes, classes, types of community, or different age groups? Have these differences increased or decreased over time? A specific development will be appraised differently depending on individual values. We have attempted to formulate the description so that judgements based on different ideologies should be possible to make, and have therefore described the structure by using the variables that have played the greatest role in the distribution discussion — sex, age, class, and type of community.

During the period studied, at least three of our background variables played significant roles in the public debate. At the end of the 1960s, population movements were extensive and the urbanization process was a topic of debate. Living conditions in the cities were compared to those prevailing in rural areas or in smaller towns. In the political arena, it has always been important to ensure that the regional dimension is represented.

Class is undoubtedly the most important dimension in Swedish politics. It is along class lines that interests are grouped when the crucial distribution decisions are made. The Swedish party structure, therefore, mirrors this dimension to a large extent. Class differences in society also came to occupy a central place in the public debates of the early seventies.

During the latter part of the seventies, the question of the position of women took an increasingly prominent position in discussions and in the political sphere. Equality between the sexes became a political goal as women and women's organizations fought for their interests more vigorously than before.

The variable that has not so far been of the same importance as the others in promoting particular interests and in distribution policy is that of age or generation. But with a more rapid growth in the number of elderly people and the distribution conflicts this can occasion, it is not impossible that the generational antagonisms will be pushed increasingly to the forefront of political battles.

The four background variables are dissimilar in nature. Sex is a given property that does not change during one's lifetime. In contrast, people's needs and life styles change as they grow older. Class and type of community by nature lie between these two extremes, in that it is possible to change both class and type of community; but as a rule people remain stable in both factors over long periods of time.

This difference in the nature of the variables probably influences their significance in the distribution discussion. That age differences have not before carried any ideological weight is perhaps due to the fact that all people live through different ages.

The stability referred to in the areas of residence and class is fundamental to the distribution-policy relevance of type of community and class. If a regular life for most people includes mobility between classes, for instance, this variable looses much of its significance for the distribution discussion. For this reason, it is meaningful to look at the scope of such mobility.

To describe changes in the level of living in our country that are relevant for the assessment of distribution policy making, we have described for all level-of-living components: (i) the average change since 1968; (ii) the differences between categories of citizens as defined by the variables given above, and finally (iii) how these differences have changed.

In this way, we get a picture of how the different level-of-living components are distributed in the social and demographic structure and of changes over time in that respect. We can also see whether it is the same population groups that are ill-favoured as regards the various components. On the other hand, with this approach we cannot determine whether it is the same *individuals* who have problems or are disadvantaged in several areas. Therefore, in the final chapter we will describe to what degree problems in one area are linked to or coexist with other problems. It is in principle an uncomplicated issue as to how the findings of this analysis should be interpreted from the point of view of distribution. The greater the coexistence among components, the more systematic the functioning of the distribution processes in our society.

Some findings

The findings from the three Level of Living Surveys are presented in the coming chapters component by component; one chapter will discuss the question of health, another education, and so on. The questions we have posed nevertheless require a description of the changes in the level of living according to the dimensions of the social and demographic structure. To this end, we will finish this chapter by summarizing the main trends found in the material as they emerge if we focus on changes in differences among the categories of the socio-demographic structure.

Women's increased entry into the labour market

Perhaps the most conspicuous finding is related to the impressive changes in women's living conditions. The most significant aspect of this change is that women are entering the labour market at a growing rate. This entry, however, is not taking place under the same circumstances or on the same conditons as men's. Sex differences in the length and direction of education remain. Women also display a weaker tendency than men to move upwards socio-economically during their professional career. It is uncertain whether this pattern has changed, but a somewhat declining sex-segregation among young people may be an indication of some degree of equalization evolving. Sex segregation on the Swedish labour market, however, is still extensive.

It is to part-time work in the public sector that the newly employed women have moved. Women are overrepresented in unqualified work, have less independence at the job, and are underrepresented in management and among supervisors. They are more often than men physically and mentally exhausted after work. Very small advances towards equality can be discerned. As regards income, there has been some change. Women's incomes have increased in line with the increased degree of their gainful employment but both sex segregation and the ubiquitous part-time work among women are the reasons for their lower incomes. However, even among full-time working women in the same occupational groups, women receive lower incomes than men, although these differences have somewhat abated.

Women's lives outside their jobs changed to some degree during the study period, most likely as a result of their increased labour-force participation. Women's responsibility for the household still completely overshadows that of men, but movement towards a levelling is seen. Women maintain contact with relatives to a much higher degree than men, but otherwise the scope of social relations is not different between the sexes. In one area, that of political and union activities, women have increased their activity level at a faster pace than men. Consequently, the difference in activity level between the sexes has decreased as regards degree of organization, political association, and opinion formation, but not in union work.

We have not observed any changes in the health differences between the sexes. Women have mental and physical complaints more often than men. Their utilization of health care is greater, but their lives are also longer. Moreover, the risk of death for middle-aged men has increased, whereas it continues to decrease for women of the same ages. The risk of meeting with crime or accidents has been less for women than for men for the entire period.

Class differences have decreased slightly

The size of the social classes was modified during this period. The working class decreased in size, and salaried employees, on both the middle and upper levels, became more numerous. The class boundaries have also perhaps become somewhat less distinct because more households have members working in different classes, and because mobility between classes — both between and within generations — has risen.

It has also become somewhat more common that children from working-class families receive higher education, but the educational opportunities are still quite unequally divided among the classes. This makes the opportunities on the labour market different for children from workers' homes than for children from the homes of salaried employees — they choose different occupational paths and begin working at different ages. The risk of unemployment is much greater in the working class than in the other classes. However, the differences are less for young people than in other age brackets since the risk of unemployment has increased for young people in the non-manual classes.

It is almost a truism that working conditions are not the same for members of the different classes, since occupation is the basis for class assignment. It is more common for workers than for non-manual employees that their physical workload is heavy, their independence low, their work environment unhealthy in various ways — noise, dirt, handling of poisonous substances, jolting and vibrations — their working hours inconvenient, job qualifications low, and jobs monotonous. Less common are jobs demanding heavy mental exertion. Nor are extremely long working hours common among workers. The differences in working conditions among the classes did not change appreciably during this period.

Workers have always received lower wages for their work than have the middle- and upper-classes, and their wealth is substantially lower. But considerable equalization in incomes has occurred, whereas changes are more doubtful as regards wealth. A large part of the capital formation of households has been linked to residence. Those who invested in their own residence, often small detached houses, have made capital gains, fostered among other things by inflation and tax relief. Because the tremendous growth in the number of small houses is mainly attributable to the middle class, a large share of the capital gains have also landed there. Differences in residential patterns with regard to form of tenure have more likely widened among the classes.

The differences in economic resources are reflected, not only in residences, but in disparities in access to resources for leisure enjoyment — summer cottages, boats, and holiday trips. We did not observe any change worth mentioning in the distribution of these resources. The unequal property distribution also resulted in the upper class running a greater risk of crime connected with property. The risk of being exposed to violence, however, is greatest in the working class.

For the leisure activities studied here, the level of activity is lowest in the working class and highest among the higher salaried employees and large-scale employers. This applies to cultural events as well as to entertainment and outdoor activities; it is also true for other activities such as degree of political organization. All the differences have decreased except those for political activity.

The dissimilarities in living conditions are also manifest in people's health. Disabilities, extreme pain, circulation difficulties, decaying teeth, fatigue, and impaired mental well-being, are all problems that affect the working class more than salaried employees. These differences are revealed in corresponding gaps in health care consumption and mortality. There has been no levelling off of health differences.

The young get an education, the aged get better finances

Different ages represent different stages in the life cycle and with that, differences in needs and life styles. Many differences are seen as natural. When one is young, education, entry into working life, and building families, are central activities. As is well-known, our study period saw the prolongation of the time spent in education, and the entry into the labour market occurring at higher ages. The expansion of the educational system also meant that the generational gaps in education have grown. This has not, however, led to the older generations being squeezed out of the labour market.

It is for young people that the risk of unemployment has increased. It also seems to be the case that young people are taking unqualified and dull jobs more than before. The general wage equalization in society has in any case meant that the incomes of the economically active young people are approaching those of other groups. However, the age group that has witnessed the greatest improvement in economic resources is the pensioners. The income gulfs between age brackets has thus decreased.

As was to be expected, the use of free-time is widely divergent among the age groups. Young people dominate those who make use of entertainment and outdoor activities. Political activities are fairly uniformly divided among the ages.

Single living is most common among the young and the old. Young people run a much greater risk of being victims of crime than do older people. Young people associate mainly with friends and acquaintances, while relatives dominate the social circles of older people. In these aspects, there has not been much change. Nor has there been much regarding the health dissimilarities among age groups.

Relationships among types of community are stable

The differences in the level of living among types of community are consistently relatively small and stable. One area where the differences have remained the same is on the labour market. Manual labour, physically heavy work, and jobs with low qualifications are overrepresented in rural areas, and underrepresented in urban areas. We also know from other studies that the risk of unemployment is high and the level of employment lower in the country than in the larger and more differentiated labour markets in the big cities. Educational opportunites are also better there, which is why people who have grown up in cities have higher levels of education than those from the country. Socializing with friends is similarly widespread in all types of community, but city-dwellers have small family circles and live alone more often. People living in rural areas are more often active in their political parties. Union activity is also lowest in the big cities. People's health is about the same everywhere. One exception to this is the metropolitan areas where fatigue and impaired mental well-being are more prevalent than elsewhere. Those who live in big cities run a greater risk than others of crime. None of these differences in the level of living among types of community show any tendency to change over time.

Coexistence of problems

There is a general tendency towards coexistence of problems in the welfare components, indicating that a person with problems in one area runs a higher risk than other people of having problems in others. However, the proportion of individuals in the population with multiple problems dropped sharply from 1968 to 1981. The nature of the coexistence is unchanged although in so far as a person with problems in one component has a stable greater *relative* risk than others for having further problems.

At the same time, the risk of having problems in several areas is relatively high for older people, for women, and for members of the working class. Obviously, the person fitting into all three categories at the same time runs a particularly high risk, that is older working-class women.

The absolute differences among classes, sexes, and age groups in the proportion with multiple problems decreased from 1968 to 1981. The relative differences were reduced only between the sexes — and then rather moderately.

Are we heading towards fewer differences?

This survey has shown that people's living conditions are quite disparate depending on their position in the social and demographic structure. But the changes we have observed move mainly in the direction of diminishing differences. Expressed in a different manner, the level of living has tended to become somewhat less dependent on sex, class and age. Accordingly, the level of living within the areas we have dealt with is increasingly becoming more equitably distributed.

This has all occurred in a period of general amelioration within many level-of-living areas, but at the same time we know that the years just before the latest survey were characterized by declining real incomes and a lower demand for labour power. Also in recent years, we have seen signs of increased wage differentials. Growing imbalances in the economy seem to make cuts in public expenditure unavoidable. Conflicts in distribution policy discussions have become sharper. This might imply that the rise in level and the equalization of the economic resources established here for the seventies will not continue in the eighties. Whether this is the case and, if so, what the effects are on the remaining level-of-living components will determine the developments in welfare for the remainder of the century.

Note

1. Descriptive and evaluative indicators are often referred to as objective and subjective indicators respectively.

2

Regression as a Tool for describing Variations in Level of Living

JAN SELÉN

'The regression approach' is the designation used in this book for regression analysis adapted for summarizing and describing differences and their changes over time among various population groups. Examples are differences in average income or in the proportion of people with various types of difficulties, such as physical disabilities. The population groups are defined in this book according to the socio-demographic factors of sex, age, type of community, and social class. There are three levels for each factor except sex and three years of observation: 1968, 1974, and 1981. Two examples of population groups are: young working-class women living in rural areas in 1968 and upper-class older men living in big cities in 1981. The total number of population groups is $2 \times 3 \times 3 \times 3 \times 3$ or 162 with the given subdivisions. With the regression approach, we are able to assess how the results for these groups can be summarized, and make a description.

The findings of the regression adjustments are presented in diagrams. The diagrams have been constructed to illustrate the answers to three questions (i) Has any change occurred over time for the population as a whole? (ii) Are there any differences among the sex, age, type of community, and class groups? (iii) Have the differences among these groups changed over time? The questions refer to the average changes and differences.

Let us take a look at the diagram used for the description of the proportions of disabled people in the population groups. People who responded in the negative to at least two out of three of the following questions were coded as disabled: Can you quite briskly walk 100 metres without difficulty? Can you run 100 metres without too much difficulty? Can you climb and descend stairs without difficulty? Figure 2.1 illustrates the responses to these three questions on the basis of the proportions of the 162 population groups.

The diagram is divided into sections that correspond to the various factors. The rows on the lower edge contain the divisions within the

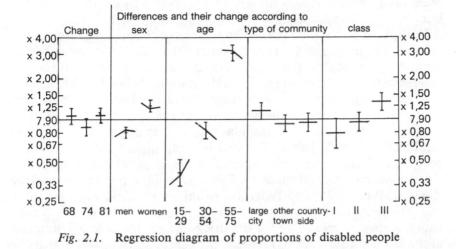

Fig. 2.1. Regression diagram of proportions of disabled people

factors, that is, the levels. The thick lines reflect the relative differences and how these change, while the thin vertical lines represent interval estimates for the different levels. The long horizontal line in the middle is a reference line for the assessment of the differences.

As an initial interpretation, the relative differences between the levels within each factor, such as the differences in sex or age, are large if the distance between the thick lines within each respective section is great. If the thick lines within one section are horizontal, this means that no change in the differences can be established over time. If the lines are not horizontal, the relative differences decrease over time if the lines approach the horizontal centre line, read from left to right. If the lines diverge from the centre line, the relative differences increase. A spontaneous reaction to the diagram would be that the differences between the three years seem to be very small, that there are sex differences but they tend to decrease, and that the relative age differences are large with a tendency towards equalizing. The differences in type of community seem to be small, while the differences in class are somewhat larger. We are not able to establish any tendency towards change among types of community or classes.

For a more exact interpretation of the diagram, the following should be kept in mind. The vertical lines within each field are interval estimates for corresponding factors. These estimates have been computed as 95 per cent confidence intervals. Corresponding point estimates consist of the points at the centre of the intervals.

When all of a factor's confidence intervals cross the centre line, it is a preliminary indication of the inability to establish any differences, preliminary because the confidence level applies to sex on two levels, but only as a rough estimate for the remaining factors.

Within each factor, the estimates have been standardized in relation to the horizontal centre line, so that the mean value of the former is identical to the latter. The actual values of the estimates emerge with the help of the scale on the diagram's borders. (Note that the scale is logarithmic.) Values above the centre line represent raised proportions, while values below represent the opposite. We estimate that 8.4 per cent of the population, for example, had physical disabilities in 1968. This is obtained by multiplying the value for the centre line 7.96 by the scale value for 1968, approximately 1.06. For elderly people, the estimate is $7.96 \times 3.0 = 23.9$ per cent. For the eldery in 1968, 1974, and 1981, the estimates are 25.8, 21.2, and 22.8 respectively. They are computed as 7.96 times the respective year's value times the scale value for the thick line for the elderly, obtained at the left end of the scale (1968), at the centre point (1974) and at the right end of the scale (1981).

The conclusions from the diagram can now be extended. It is among the aged that the highest proportion of disabled people is found. Women are more often disabled than men, and the working class more often than other classes. Neither year nor type-of-community differences are established. Because the diagram presents relative and not absolute changes and differences, the proportion of disabled people among the aged is about seven (3/0.4) times higher than it is among younger people.

Let us look at another diagram. It is taken from the chapter on political resources and gives the proportion of active individuals according to an index of opinion-forming activities. The diagram in Figure 2.2 shows that the proportion of active individuals increases over time, that men are more active than women but that the relative sex differences decrease over time, that the proportion of active individuals is lowest among young people and highest among elderly people, but that this difference levelled off from 1968 to 1981, that the differences among different types of community are small with a complicated pattern of development, that the differences among the classes are to the advantage of the highest class and to the disadvantage of the working class, with no tendencies towards equalization observed.

Observe that it is not possible to see immediately from the diagram whether the proportion of active men has decreased or increased. To make a judgement of that kind, it is necessary to look at the results

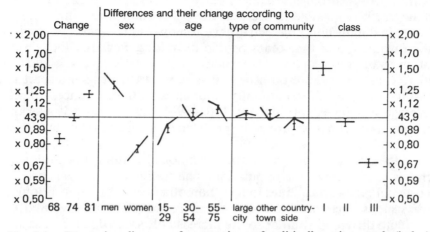

Fig. 2.2. Regression diagram of proportions of politically active people (index)

for year and sex simultaneously. The proportion of active men in 1968 is estimated at about 54 per cent ($43.9 \times 0.85 \times 1.45$), and the proportion of active men in 1981 at about 61 per cent ($43.9 \times 1.20 \times 1.15$). Accordingly, the proportion has increased despite the fact that the sex differences have decreased and the thick line for men slopes downwards. In a similar manner, the proportion of active people has increased in all population groups.

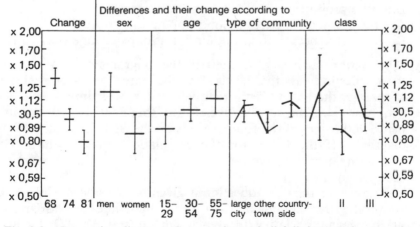

Fig. 2.3. Regression diagram of proportions of all full-time employees with a gross working time of at least 50 hours per week

The diagram in Figure 2.3 is taken from the chapter on leisure and recreation, and presents the proportion of all full-time employees with a gross working time of at least 50 hours per week. From the diagram, it is possible to see that the proportion with long working hours is diminishing, that men have long working hours more often than women, and that older people have long working hours more often than young people. No change in these relative sex and age differences has been established. It is more difficult to interpret the results for type of community and class. No differences on the average can be established for 1968–1981, but as regards working hours, class III has improved its position over time in relation to class I.

In the diagram, we can see the conditions for full-time employees, that is, a segment of the population. The confidence intervals become larger and the vertical lines longer than otherwise, the latter as long as the scale is unchanged. Because the diagrams show relative and not absolute differences, an absolute increase of, say, 10 per cent is seen more distinctly if it is from 10 to 20 per cent (a relative doubling) than if it is from 80 to 90 per cent (a relative increase of 12.5 per cent) on an unchanged scale.

A more detailed description of the regression approach is given in Appendix B.

Easy guide to interpretation of regression diagrams.

The diagrams are constructed in order to answer three questions for a level-of-living indicator:

1. Does the proportion or level change over time?
2. Are there any differences among population groups?
3. Do the differences among population groups change over time?

A. The section farthest to the left in the diagrams responds to the first question. If the levels for the three years are clearly disparate, there has been a relative change over time.
B. The answer to the second question is found in the relationship between the lines in the four sections on the right-hand side of the diagrams. If the levels for the population groups within one section are clearly disparate, there are relative differences among these groups.
C. The answer to the third question is given by the slopes of the lines within the four sections on the right. If these lines are horizontal, no change in the relative differences can be established. If the lines are sloping away from each other, the relative differences have increased; if they incline towards each other, the relative differences have decreased.

3

The Class Structure and Its Trends

ROBERT ERIKSON

The distribution of the classes and occupational groups

Sociological analyses of society have often pointed out how people's relationships, opportunities, opinions, and activities, are determined by the class structure and social stratification. No society has been found which has no stratification, that is, a hierarchy within which some people are better off and some people are worse off. This hierachy is institutionalized in all more developed societies. This means that it has a certain legitimacy, a relatively set structure and that benefits in society are at least partially connected to positions rather than to individuals.

In industrial societies the hierarchy is basically structured on the manner in which the production of goods and services is organized and the structure can best be described with the help of occupations, which constitute the positions in the system of production.

As early as 1911, a classification system was constructed in Sweden in which different occupations were combined into a number of groups, which were combined, in turn, under three main categories that later became well-known as classes I, II, and III. When the classification system was constructed they were known as 'the upper class', 'the middle class', and 'the working class'. Three civil servants at the Central Bureau of Statistics, as it was then, put together the classification system during a few short summer months.[1] The intention was to use it for the statistical analysis of the general election in 1911. The classification system, with various modifications, was used for election statistics for about fifty years. It was also used in a series of other investigations both within and outside the Central Bureau of Statistics.

No criteria were specified for how individual occupations were placed in the different occupational groups, nor any guiding theoretical principle. It seems that the classification system was constructed on the basis of the three civil servants' conceptions of the structure of Swedish society.[2] They succeeded in constructing a classification which obviously reflected relatively well the main characteristics of this society's stratification. This indicates how apparent the stratification was and the use of the classification system for over fifty years shows how stable it has been.

When the classification system was used in the Level of Living Survey in 1968, only two major changes in the definitions and placing of the different occupational categories were made. One was that shop assistants were moved from class II to class III, because of the character and conditions of their jobs, indicated by them being organized by LO, the trade union confederation of manual workers. The other change meant that independent farmers with less than 10 hectares of arable land *and* less than 100 hectares of forest were moved from class II to class III. Such a small farm cannot yield enough to support a family. Smallholders must therefore, as a rule, seek outside employment as, for example, forestry workers, and it therefore seemed more appropriate to place them in class III. Independent farmers could thereby appear in all three classes: as smallholders in class III; as landed proprietors in class I if they owned more than 100 hectares of arable land or more than 400 hectares of forest and; as farmers in class II if the size of their farm was between that of the landed proprietors and the smallholders.

Other than landed proprietors, class I consists of large proprietors (with more than 20 employees), professionals with an academic occupation (lawyers, architects, doctors, dentists) and higher-grade salaried employees in the public and private sectors. In most cases proprietors and self-employed professionals in class I are included among the private employees within this class. Of the groups in class I the two groups of salaried employees are clearly the largest and they have also grown substantially in recent years.

Class II consists of, in addition to farmers, small proprietors and businessmen and lower-grade salaried employees in the public and private sectors. Wives who work on the family farm or in the family business are included among farmers and small proprietors respectively. Regarding salaried employees in the private sector, foremen are placed in a separate category. It can be of interest to keep them separate since their work environment is often the same as that of workers and they are also often recruited from the working class.

The dividing line between classes I and II is not very precise, but one can say that those occupations which previously required higher education and other occupations on the same level have been placed in class I. This does not mean that everyone with an academic education is automatically placed in class I. It is the occupation and not the education which determines the breakdown into classes.

Class III is made up of workers and smallholders including wives working on the farm. There are eight different occupational categories in class III. Other than smallholders, forestry workers, and other agricultural workers, who together make one group, there are three groups of manufacturing workers (metal workers, other manufacturing workers, and construction workers), two groups of private employees in different service industries, and two groups in public workers who are employed by either the state or local government.

The entire population must, however, be covered by the classes; the structure of society covers everyone and not just those who are gainfully employed. Those who are not gainfully employed have been divided into three groups within each of the classes, namely pensioners, housewives, and students. In addition, there is another group in class III which is not gainfully employed, namely the disabled.

Pensioners and housewives are placed in classes according to their previous occupation and their husband's occupation respectively. The classification of students have been problematic, they do not quite fit into any group. The principle chosen has been that they shall be placed in the class to which their education can be expected to lead them. Those who have undertaken academic studies (studies at a university or its equivalent) have been placed in class I. Previously this would have been self-evident and it still seems reasonable even though university studies no longer lead to occupations in class I with any certainty.

Those following the three-year secondary school and those studying in higher level vocational schools, for example, nursing schools, were placed in class II. Elementary school pupils and those with two years of secondary school were placed in class III. It is obvious that the classification of elementary school pupils and pupils taking three years of secondary education was arbitrary, since many of them will continue their studies at higher levels. However, we found that these groups were so small that there was no reason to deal with them separately.

Those who have been judged as being unable to support themselves through gainful employment have been placed in the disabled group. If they have received a pension after many years of gainful employment, they have, however, been classified as pensioners. Most of the disabled have been sick their whole lives, but some may have become handicapped through, for example, long-term alcohol abuse. Placing them in class III may have been questionable for some, but in the majority of cases this classification was definitely the correct one.

Table 3.1 shows the distribution according to occupation and class in the three surveys and the percentage of women in each group is shown. From the table it can be concluded that fairly large shifts in occupational distribution occurred between 1968 and 1981.

If we start by considering the relative size of the three classes, we find that class II and especially class I increased during the period, while class III's percentage of the population decreased. In absolute figures the number of people in the adult population in class I increased from about

Table 3.1 Percentages of the population and percentage of women in different
classes and occupational groups in 1968, 1974, and 1981

	Percentages of population			Percentage of women in class		
	1968	1974	1981	1968	1974	1981
Prof., exec. in private employment	2.0	2.3	2.8	11.7	11.9	11.4
Prof. in public employment	1.9	2.6	3.2	20.0	25.5	30.0
Housewives	1.4	1.1	0.8	100.0	100.0	100.0
University students	1.2	1.5	1.5	37.1	40.1	46.3
Pensioners	0.6	0.6	0.8	47.9	41.9	36.6
Class I, total	7.2	8.2	9.1	38.7	36.1	33.4
Farmers	3.0	2.5	2.1	32.1	31.9	32.4
Small proprietors	4.7	4.4	4.7	24.8	27.6	27.2
Foremen	2.3	2.1	1.6	8.2	8.6	11.1
Priv. technical, clerical	8.1	8.8	8.9	43.8	51.0	50.6
Public lower salaried	6.3	8.5	10.5	66.3	68.0	71.7
Housewives	5.5	4.2	3.2	100.0	99.2	98.9
Secondary school students	2.8	2.2	2.2	43.9	36.7	50.8
Pensioners	2.6	3.2	3.9	57.8	44.8	42.3
Class II, total	35.2	35.9	37.1	51.7	52.6	54.1
Agricultural workers	3.7	2.5	1.8	34.9	28.0	26.2
Metal workers	6.1	6.6	5.6	10.2	13.0	17.2
Other manufacturing workers	6.7	5.8	4.9	32.0	34.0	31.5
Construction workers	3.7	3.2	2.7	2.3	2.7	3.3
Manufacturing workers, all	16.5	15.6	13.2	17.2	18.7	19.6
Workers in commerce	3.6	4.1	3.8	61.8	73.5	64.8
Other service workers	4.2	4.4	2.9	59.1	55.4	41.5
Service workers, all	7.8	8.5	6.7	60.4	64.0	54.5
Workers in local govt.	5.0	6.8	9.8	75.6	76.1	77.3
Workers in state govt.	2.5	2.6	3.0	26.4	29.8	34.9
Workers in public employment, all	7.5	9.4	12.8	59.1	63.3	67.5
Disabled	1.5	1.6	1.3	44.2	41.8	56.8
Housewives	9.5	7.0	5.0	99.8	99.3	99.2
Pupils	4.1	3.8	5.3	48.9	54.5	50.3
Pensioners	6.9	7.5	7.8	51.9	46.3	41.5
Class III, total	57.5	55.9	53.8	50.4	50.4	50.0
Population 15–75 years	100	100	100	50.0	50.0	50.0
Number 1000s in population	5,922	6,077	6,239			

426,000 in 1968 to about 568,000 in 1981. Class II increased even more in absolute figures, from about 2,085,000 in 1968 to about 2,315,000 in 1981. The relative decrease in class III corresponds with a minor increase in absolute numbers, from about 3,310,000 in 1968 to about 3,357,000 in 1981.

The increase in class I is quite substantial. In 1981 the group was about 25 per cent larger than in 1968. At the same time, the percentage of women in class I decreased. This is because each person with gainful employment is classified accordingly. In 1981 fewer women with husbands in class I were housewives and more were gainfully employed. However, in many cases their occupations were placed in class II which ,explains the decreased percentage of women in class I. This and other similar movements explain the increased percentage of women in class II.

The occupational groups which have increased most clearly in all three classes are those in public employment. In total, they increased from 16 per cent of the population in 1968 to slightly more than 26 per cent in 1981. In class I they increased from about 2 to more than 3 per cent, in class II from 6 per cent to over 10 per cent and in class III from about 7 per cent to almost 13 per cent of the population. Within class III one can also see that the percentage of state employees increased only slightly while local government employees almost doubled their percentage of the population. These results are in accord with what we know from other sources. The increase in the number of gainfully employed, which occurred during the 1970s, is a result of the increased number of pubic, and especially local government employees (SCB 1981c). The percentage of people gainfully employed outside the public sector decreased, from 48 per cent of the population in 1968 to 42 per cent in 1981. The percentage of employees as a whole increased from 64 per cent to 68 per cent during the same period as a result of the increased percentage of public employees.

The increase in the public employees' percentage of the population is connected to the increased percentage of women in this category. The percentage of female public employees increased from 57 per cent in 1968 to 65 per cent in 1981. Among other occupational categories the percentage of women was essentially constant, 31 per cent in 1968 as opposed to 33 per cent in 1981. As indicated, the percentage of women was much higher in public employment than in the rest of the labour market during the entire period. In two categories of private employees, the percentage of women increased more noticeably during the period. This was among salaried employees in class II and among metal workers in class III.

In two occupational categories the percentage of women decreased during the period. This was among smallholders and forestry workers and among those working in other service industries. Smallholders, and thereby smallholders' wives, probably decreased more in number since 1968 than forestry workers, a group which is almost entirely made up of men. On the other hand, there does not seem to be any simple explanation for the decreased percentage of women in other service industries.

If we examine the individual occupational categories we find that all categories of salaried employees increased in size, and not just those in the public sector. The percentage of small proprietors was unchanged during the period at about 5 per cent of the adult population. On the other hand, the number of farmers continued to decline, which is a well-known trend for this entire century. Even the foremen category decreased in size, which probably reflects the decrease in many groups of workers.

Small proprietors in contrast to others, became younger between 1968 and 1981.[3] It may, therefore be of interest to take a closer look at which occupational categories the small proprietors of 1981 belonged to in 1968 and 1974. They were, naturally, to a great extent small proprietors in 1968 and 1974. Those who were small proprietors in 1981 were also, both in 1968 and 1974, relatively often foremen, construction workers, or workers in other service industries. In addition, we found a certain overrepresentation among small proprietors of immigrants who came to Sweden after 1968. Small proprietors were also relatively often metal workers in 1968, but this tendency did not reappear for 1974. Furthermore, another tendency is that small proprietors were *not* public employees, either in 1968 or in 1974.

If we look at the non-gainfully employed, the trend among housewives is especially worth studying. This is a female category which, if the current trend continues, will soon disappear. The percentage of men who were coded in these categories increased very slightly between 1968 and 1981, but it was miniscule even in 1981. However, the percentage of the population in these categories decreased substantially during the period. The percentages in 1981 were about half of the corresponding percentages in 1968. On the other hand, the percentage of housewives in the population is affected by the number of people who are married. Table 3.2 shows the percentage of housewives among cohabiting couples in different classes in each respective year.

Many of those who were pensioners and took care of the household at the time of the interview were coded as housewives. To avoid having the results affected by the size of the pensioners' groups, couples in which the woman was over 59 years old were excluded from the table. The table shows that the percentage of couples in which the woman works as a housewife decreased dramatically, from 46 per cent to 14 per cent.[4] In

Table 3.2 Percentages of cohabiting couples in different classes in which the woman was a housewife in 1968, 1974, and 1981. Only couples in which the woman is under 60 years old

Class of spouse	1968	1974	1981
I	46.5	24.8	9.7
II	43.6	26.6	11.8
III	47.2	30.3	16.3
All	45.8	28.3	13.8
Number	1,583	1,605	1,601

1968 the percentage of couples in which the woman was a housewife was approximately the same in the three classes. Thereafter, the percentages decreased faster in classes I and II, so that in 1981 men in class I were least likely to have a housewife while men in class III were relatively often married to a housewife. This differentiated trend can have several different explanations. Women who are married to men in classes I and II generally have a higher education than those who are married to men in class III. And women with a higher education can be expected to retain their connections to the labour market to a greater extent than women with a lower standard of education. It is also possible that they return to their jobs more quickly after having a child than women with a lower education. As will be shown later in this chapter class I also lives in large cities more often than others where it is probably easier to retain, or establish, connections to the labour market.

The average age among housewives changed from 1968 to 1981. From one survey year to the next the average age among housewives increased by almost the same number of years as had lapsed between the surveys. This should mean that very few women are becoming housewives. If we consider what the housewives of 1981 were doing in 1968 and 1974 (table not shown), we find that about 47 per cent were already housewives in 1968 and about 53 per cent were housewives in 1974. Most of the rest belonged to various occupational categories in the earlier survey years. This should then involve women who got their pensions in 1981, but who take care of the household and their husbands themselves and were therefore classified as housewives. If this trend continues, housewives will occur almost entirely in the pensioner's category in a few years.

If we look at what category women who were housewives in 1968 and 1974 belonged to in 1981, we find that large percentages were still housewives or pensioners. But a large group also entered the labour market. Those who were housewives in class I had obtained jobs, above all, as salaried employees in the public sector in class II and also, to some extent, as private employees in class II. Those who had been housewives in class II became salaried employees in the same class, but they also got jobs as municipal workers in class III. Finally, housewives from class III became, above all, municipal workers.

The number of pensioners increased in all three classes, a trend which is connected with the increased percentage of older people in the population and the decrease in the pension age from 67 to 65 in 1976. That men make up more than 50 per cent of the pensioners, despite the well-known sex distribution among older people, is because pensioners who take care of a household for more than one person were coded as housewives as has already been mentioned.

If one examines the extent to which those who belonged to a certain class in 1981 belonged to the same class in the two earlier survey years, one finds that this is most often the case in class III whereas it applies least often in class I. However, if we examine recruitment to the different occupational groups in a similar manner, we find that the percentage who belonged to the same group during the earlier surveys was, if anything, smaller for the occupational groups in class III than for the others. This should mean that people change occupational groups relatively often *within* class III. In other words, those who get jobs in different groups in class III relatively often come from other occupational groups within the same class.

Class and community type

One important aspect of people's living conditions is the type of community in which they live. Classification into geographic areas can be done in many different ways. In the Level of Living Surveys we chose classifications based on the degree of urbanization. These classifications were already used in the 1968 survey and are based on the county classifications of that time. In the first place the large cities of Stockholm, Gothenburg, and Malmö, along with their suburbs, were separated as one group.[5] Next came cities which had a population of at least 30,000 inhabitants at the time. The last groups were made up of the towns and villages with less than 30,000 inhabitants and finally the then existing rural communities. The classifications were used in an unchanged form, with essentially the same geographic boundaries, in 1974 and 1981. In other words, the 1968 community boundaries were also used during the later years.[6]

In 1981 about 16 per cent of the adult population lived in the Stockholm area, about 7 per cent in the Gothenburg area, and about 5 per cent in the Malmö area. Approximately 20 per cent lived in each of the two types of smaller cities while about 30 per cent lived in the countryside. The distribution between the community types did not change much during the period. Between 1968 and 1974 the percentage of the population living in rural areas decreased while there was an equivalent increase in cities with less than 100,000 inhabitants. The percentages of the population in three large cities remained practically unchanged during the period.

Class distribution according to community type varies appreciably. The Stockholm area in particular has a deviating class distribution. The percentage of the population belonging to class I is about twice as large in the Stockholm area as compared with the rest of the country. In 1981, 17 per of Stockholm's inhabitants belonged to class I. Even the percentage which belongs to class II is larger in the Stockholm area than in the other community types. Accordingly the percentage of Stockholm's inhabitants belonging to class III is relatively small. This circumstance has various consequences on the distribution of different social welfare indicators based on community type. In Stockholm, for example, the average income is higher than in the rest of the country and the fact that Stockholm's residents devote themselves more to various cultural activities is probably not only a result of the greater availability there, but is also partially a consequence of greater demand in the area.

Table 3.3 Percentages of the population in different community types who belonged to classes I and III in 1968, 1974 and 1981

Class	I			III		
Year	1968	1974	1981	1968	1974	1981
Type of community						
Greater Stockholm	15.1	15.3	17.1	43.6	42.9	40.5
Greater Gothenburg	9.2	12.1	14.5	56.9	53.3	52.6
Greater Malmö	10.1	8.8	11.0	59.3	48.9	50.6
Cities 30 000–100 000	8.5	8.4	7.5	54.2	54.9	54.3
Other cities and towns	6.1	5.8	7.5	58.3	61.5	57.9
Countryside	2.8	4.9	5.4	65.1	61.3	58.2
All	7.2	8.2	9.1	57.5	55.9	53.8

The deviating class distribution in Stockholm should be seen as a result of the special character of a capital. Almost the entire central administration of the country is concentrated there as well as the main offices of many large companies, which leads to a divergent distribution.

In the Greater Gothenburg and Malmö areas as well, the percentage belonging to class I is relatively large, even if it is not as large as in the Greater Stockholm area. In both these cities there has been a noticeable decrease in the percentage belonging to class III.

The class distribution in cities other than the large cities seems to have been relatively stable between 1968 and 1981, while the distribution in the countryside became more like that for the rest of the country. Thus the percentage in class I increased while the percentage in class III decreased. It seems probable that this is less a result of the jobs in the countryside changing character and more a result of salaried employees at different levels moving to the countryside and commuting fairly long distances.

Has the working class become smaller?

How the working class will develop after the industrial society turns into what is known as the post-industrial society, that is, a society in which most people are employed in the service sector, is a question which has been focused on by many social scientists. The answers they have given have varied greatly. At least partly these different answers seem to be a result of ideological differences.

Daniel Bell (1973), an American sociologist, expects the working class to decrease greatly in size because of continuing productivity increases in industry. Another American sociologist, Harry Braverman, believes that the working class has increased in size because increasingly larger groups have ended up in proletarian types of work (Braverman 1974). In Sweden Göran Therborn investigated the changes in the class structure since 1930 and in a recently published book (Therborn 1981) he asserts that the working class constituted a constant percentage of the population from 1930 to 1975.

If we consider class III and the working class to be equivalent, the data we have presented indicate that Therborn's conclusion cannot be stretched to cover the later part of the survey period. The working class appears to have decreased in size during the 1970s. Therborn's conclusion is based on the gainfully employed only, but even if we do this as well, our conclusion remains the same. Class III has decreased from 56 per cent of the gainfully employed in 1968 to 50 per cent in 1981.

It has, however, been asserted that even if the working class in its classical meaning decreases as a percentage of the population, this does not reveal the essential elements in the trend. Namely, salaried employees with routine tasks and no managerial responsibilities enter into an increasingly proletarian situation. The increase in this group is assumed to outweigh the decrease in the working class in its classical meaning. Therborn also found that the traditional working class had decreased among the gainfully employed, but when he included lower-grade salaried employees the percentage which the proletarian wage-earners constituted of the gainfully employed has been extremely stable since 1930.

To investigate the changes in size of this more broadly defined working class, we can add the public and private salaried employees in unqualified positions, which seldom include any managerial duties, to this class.[7] At the same time we can remove certain supervisors who have been coded as part of class III as well as certain groups, such as policemen, which Therborn placed in what he called special categories because of their role in the relations between the classes. The trend among the gainfully employed in regard to this broadly defined working class is shown in Table 3.4

Table 3.4 Percentages of gainfully employed men and women with occupations in the different classes in 1968, 1974, and 1981

Class	Men			Women			All		
	1968	1974	1981	1968	1974	1981	1968	1974	1981
Class I	8.8	10.3	12.5	2.5	3.6	4.2	6.5	7.5	8.8
Middle class and small proprietors	35.8	35.3	36.3	23.7	28.0	36.1	32.5	32.3	36.2
Working class in broad sense	55.4	54.3	51.1	73.2	68.5	59.6	62.0	60.2	54.9
Total	100.0	100.0	100.0	100.0	100.0	100.0	100.0	100.0	100.0
Number	2,304	2,325	2,344	1,277	1,630	1,923	3,581	3,955	4,267

The table shows that from 1968 to 1981 this broader working class decreased among gainfully employed men and even more among gainfully employed women. The decrease seems to have been faster during the later part of the period. As indicated previously, the percentage of small proprietors did not increase in size. The increase which is connected with the decrease in the working class is the increase among salaried employees. For men it is above all the higher-grade public employment group in class I which has increaded in size, whereas for women it is the salaried employee groups in the middle class which have increased.

The above analysis seems incomplete because it only includes the gainfully employed while the class structure presumably includes the entire population. The increase is gainful employment among married women which has occurred in recent years cannot be assumed to have been neutral in relation to the sizes of the different classes.

Before we continue, however, we must discuss which factors determine an individual's class affiliation. For a single, gainfully employed person, it is quite simple. It is his or her employment position which is decisive for class affiliation. But a woman who is a shop assistant and married to an engineer; does she belong to the working class? What if she is a metal worker? If the woman is an engineer and her husband is a metal worker, which class does she then belong to? What about the husband?

In this report we have allowed individuals' class affiliation to be determined by their own employment position, if they have one. It seems reasonable, perhaps obvious, to do this in a study of the individual's conditions with regard to central welfare components such as health and working conditions. But in a field where an important question is how an individual's consciousness of his class affiliation is formed, the situation is far from being as obvious. We would claim that families rather than individuals make up the units in the class structure. The interests and experiences which are attributable to an individual's employment are important, but the interests and impulses that are provided through other family members' positions in working life are at least as important. Married couples should therefore be assumed to belong to the same class, even if their respective occupations would place them in different classes. That one of the spouses is at least a middle level salaried employee or a proprietor tends to mean more in relation to both spouses' consumption, behaviour, and opinions, than if one of them is a worker (Erikson 1981, 1983).

Therefore, people whose occupation would normally place them in one of the other classes, but whose spouse belongs to class I, has been placed in class I. In the same way we placed people with working class occupations who were married to people with middle level occupations in the latter group. Students under 20 years old were placed in their father's class. The adult population's class distribution, in accordance with these principles, is shown in Table 3.5.

Table 3.5 Class distribution of the adult population in 1968, 1974, and 1981. Percentages

Class	Year		
	1968	1974	1981
Class I	10.0	11.9	12.3
Middle class and small proprietors	36.4	37.4	41.4
Working class in broad sense	53.6	50.7	46.3
Total	100.0	100.0	100.0

As is apparent from the table, the working class decreased in size from 1968 to 1981 while the other two groups we have defined increased in size even when we included the entire population. Our conclusion must consequently be different from Therborn's conclusion; the Swedish working class decreased in size during the 1970s. How then can one explain the differences in our results?

The differences in the data are actually relatively small, even though there is no reason for total correspondence. Therborn found that the group he called proletarian wage-earners, which should essentially be equivalent to what we described as the broader working class, made up 61 per cent of the gainfully employed in 1965 and in 1975. These figures can be compared with the ones we presented in Table 3.4, which show the broader working class as constituting 62 per cent of the gainfully employed in 1968 and 60 per cent in 1974. Other than different sets of data and definitions and the fact that we are dealing with a sample, these insignificant differences could be a result of the fact that we included all of the gainfully employed, whereas in the census which Therborn used, only people who worked at least half-time were counted. Furthermore, the crucial differences between Therborn's results and ours appear to be that Therborn did not include the entire population in the class structure and that the trend seems to have accelerated in the later part of the 1970s.

The data presented here clearly indicate that the working class decreased from 1968 to 1981, both as a percentage of the gainfully employed and as a percentage of the population. Only if we make an assumption which is directly the opposite of the one made earlier about family affiliation do we get a working class which does not decrease in size. Thus if we assume that everybody in a family belongs to the working class if one person in the family belongs there because of his employment, 63 per cent of the population belonged to the working class in 1968, 66 per cent in 1974, and 65 per cent in 1981. However, such an assumption hardly leads to a picture which accurately reflects reality, which is why it should be rejected.

The groups that increased in size were the higher-grade salaried employees and the middle-level salaried employees. We can see two tendencies which together explain this trend. On the one hand, the public sector has increased its relative size. Since the percentage of middle-level salaried employees and higher is greater in the public sector than in the private sector, the public sector increase, with no change in organization, means that the percentage of salaried employees at these levels will increase. On the other hand, the employment organization of the private sector seems to have changed in such a way that increasingly large percentages of the employees have relatively qualified tasks at the salaried employee level. If we think of the class structure as a population pyramid in which the various strata are placed on top of one another with a breadth which is equal to their size, then the class structure has changed in the same manner as the population pyramid — the strata higher up have become somewhat broader while the base has become somewhat narrower.

Social mobility

Social mobility seems to be a topic which has always attracted people's fantasies. Stories about people who have worked their way from the bottom to the top of society and people born in luxury who end up as paupers seem to arouse feelings of hope, envy, and sometimes malicious pleasure. Social mobility is of interest here because it touches upon a central goal of society. Both the liberal and the socialistic ideologies propound the idea that a person's living conditions should not be dependent on his class origins. Talents and interests should influence the development of people's lives, and not the circumstances into which they were born.

We shall examine social mobility in terms of the extent to which people change classes. We will concentrate on mobility between the generations. This means that we will examine what class people belong to in relationship to their father's class. In other words, the father's occupation is used to determine the class affiliation of the home. In the examination of social mobility, class II has been divided into two groups, farmers and others within the class, which have been labelled as II F and II O respectively. The reason is that these two groups differ substantially in the resources they receive from their parental homes.

Table 3.6 shows the percentage of men and women in different age groups, in each respective year, who have been socially mobile in relation to their fathers. The percentage of both men and women who were socially mobile increased from 1968 to 1981. About half the population belongs to a class other than the one their father belonged to. Thus the other half belongs to the same class and has not changed class in relation to their father. Of course, the size of this percentage depends on how many classes we distinguish. If we divide the population into more classes, we will find more mobility.

Women have been slightly more socially mobile than men. Men and women in the 30–54 age group, however, have been socially mobile to about the same extent. That women tend to be more socially mobile is mainly because the occupation distribution among women deviates more from their fathers' than the distribution among men, a result of our sexually segregated labour market.

Mobility does not vary with age in the same manner for women as for men. Among women we found the least mobility in the older age group and the most in the younger age group. At the same time we found that mobility increased within each age group in each of the later survey

Table 3.6 Percentages among men and women in the adult population, in different age groups, who had been socially mobile in relation to their class of origin in 1968, 1974, and 1981. Primary and secondary school students excluded

Age	Men			Women		
	1968	1974	1981	1968	1974	1981
55–76	42.8	43.9	45.4	43.8	46.4	46.9
30–54	48.1	49.8	52.3	47.9	49.7	52.5
15–29	44.4	45.0	41.6	49.3	53.9	54.1
All	45.4	46.7	47.9	46.9	49.6	50.9

years. Thus, mobility increases over time. This increase seems to come about because, as each new generation of women reaches working age, social mobility tends to be greater than in previous generations. The simplest explanation for this increase is that social mobility among married women is greater if one compares a woman's occupation with her father's than if one compares the husband's occupation with her father's occupation (Erikson 1976). The results then follow as a consequence of the increasing percentage of married women with gainful employment.

This does not, however, have to be the entire explanation since we also found an increase in social mobility among men. On the other hand, we found the pattern in age groups among men different from those among women. Young men displayed less mobility than men in the middle age group. At the same time, as stated above, mobility increased during the later survey years for men as well. Therefore, the lower mobility rate among young men seems to be an age-related phenomenon. Accordingly, to a certain degree young men begin their occupational careers in the same class as their fathers and then later become socially mobile during their working lives.

Previous studies have shown that social mobility increased among men in Sweden during the period of 1950–1974 (Erikson 1983). Based on the results in Table 3.6 the increase appears to have continued after 1974. The previously observed increase in social mobility was mainly explained by the fact that the deviation between the class distribution of men in 1950 and the distribution of their fathers was less than equivalent deviations in 1968 and 1974.

The entire increase in mobility between 1950 and 1974 could not, however, be explained by the increased differences over time between occupational distributions for different generations. After 1968 the observed increase in social mobility certainly cannot be explained by increased differences between occupational distributions because of the simple reason that no such increase has been observed. If any change at all has occurred during the period, it is that occupational distributions of fathers and their children have become more similar. We shall return to the issue of an increase in social mobility but before that we shall discuss the inflow to and outflow from different classes.

Inflow to the classes

In Table 3.7 we show how different classes are recruited with regard to the class origins of their members, that is, how members of the different classes are distributed according to their father's class.

As can be seen in the table, the various classes have very different compositions with regard to class origins. If we first concentrate on the situation in 1981, we find that about two thirds of the men in two of these classes, farmers and workers, had fathers who belonged to the same class. The two other classes did not have anything like the same high rate of internal recruitment. In fact, the internally recruited members of these classes did not even constitute the largest group within their respective classes. The largest group in class I were sons of men from class II O. Class I is clearly the most heterogeneous in its recruitment, only slightly more than every fifth man has his origins in the class and more than one out of four has his class origins in the working class.

The situation is similar among women. Only one group, farmers (including farmer's wives), has a clearly different recruitment pattern among women than among men. Among men in this group, as indicated above, two thirds were farmer's sons, while among women about half were the daughters of workers (including agricultural workers) and only a third were farmers' daughters.

If the trend over time is examined, the percentage with origins in their own class seems to have decreased among both men and women in class I, and the same relationship applies to class III. In class II O, however, the opposite trend seems to apply, internal recruitment has increased somewhat during the period.

The men who belonged to the same class during all three survey years constituted 64 per cent of class I in 1981, 60 per cent of class II O, 84 per cent of class III and 76 per cent of class II F (figures not in the table). Even though we do not know the entire occupational history of the people we interviewed, it is probable that very few of those who belonged to the same class during all three survey years had had jobs in another class. This should mean that about five of six men in class III have no experience of working in another class. The similar proportions are thus somewhat less than two of three men in classes I and II O and about three of four men among farmers.

Table 3.7 Men and women in different class in 1968, 1974, and 1981 distributed according to their class of origin. Percentages

Class of origin	Men					Women				
	1968									
	Class of destination					Class of destination				
	I	IIO	IIF	III	All	I	IIO	IIF	III	All
I	27.0	4.8	0.0	1.1	4.5	31.1	5.6	0.0	1.2	4.4
IIO	38.0	30.0	6.7	16.0	21.6	39.1	32.5	9.5	16.6	23.1
IIF	6.6	12.6	68.1	12.8	14.8	8.9	13.3	53.6	14.9	15.1
III	28.5	52.6	25.2	70.1	59.1	20.9	48.6	36.9	67.3	57.4
Total	100.0	100.0	100.0	100.0	100.0	100.0	100.0	100.0	100.0	100.0
Number	259	768	128	1,552	2,707	166	915	74	1,580	2,735

Class of origin	Men					Women				
	1974									
	Class of destination					Class of destination				
	I	IIO	IIF	III	All	I	IIO	IIF	III	All
I	21.6	5.2	1.5	1.8	5.0	28.5	6.1	1.8	1.7	5.0
IIO	40.6	35.2	7.4	18.3	25.3	37.3	34.1	12.3	20.0	26.1
IIF	7.7	10.5	56.6	10.8	12.2	9.5	13.3	32.9	13.8	13.8
III	30.1	49.1	34.5	69.1	57.5	24.8	46.5	53.0	64.5	55.2
Total	100.0	100.0	100.0	100.0	100.0	100.0	100.0	100.0	100.0	100.0
Number	318	830	115	1,569	2,832	180	1,036	59	1,569	2,844

Class of origin	Men					Women				
	1981									
	Class of destination					Class of destination				
	I	IIO	IIF	III	All	I	IIO	IIF	III	All
I	21.5	7.0	2.0	2.0	6.1	26.2	7.7	3.6	3.0	6.4
IIO	41.0	38.1	5.1	20.5	28.1	37.6	36.2	12.4	21.2	27.9
IIF	7.6	8.8	66.0	10.4	11.5	10.4	11.9	33.6	13.4	13.1
III	29.9	46.1	26.9	67.1	54.3	25.8	44.2	50.5	62.3	52.6
Total	100.0	100.0	100.0	100.0	100.0	100.0	100.0	100.0	100.0	100.0
Number	376	891	103	1,502	2,872	188	1,113	69	1,491	2,861

We can expand our perspective to examine how many people in different classes appear to lack any experience of the conditions in other classes. This can be done by determining how many people indicated that not only did they themselves belong to the same class during the three surveys, but that their fathers belonged to the same class as well. In this case we found greater differences between the classes. In class I about 16 per cent of the men had never belonged to any other class according to this definition. Among men in class II O the percentage was similar, 21 per cent. Among farmers and especially among workers, the percentages were much higher, 52 per cent and 61 per cent respectively.

The inflow to class I may be used to illustrate the influence of education on social mobility. Almost all men who belonged to class I in 1981 and whose fathers also belonged to the same class were already members of class I in 1968.[8] It could be that most of them received some form of higher education and immediately thereafter received employment in class I. On the other hand, of the men in class I in 1981 whose fathers belonged to another class there were a substantial number, more than one third, who belonged to classes II O or III in 1968. Thus they probably did not receive a higher education or if they did they did not immediately get a job in class I. They probably, at least in part, moved up socially through their working life. Therefore, with regard to today's adult generation in Sweden, a substantial percentage of the men in class I have arrived there through an occupational career rather than through a higher education. One question is how common such careers will be in the future considering the huge expansion of higher education which has taken place since the middle of the 1960s. From being a sufficient but not a necessary condition for a job in class I, a higher education may now have become a necessary but not a sufficient condition.

The percentage who belonged to the same class during all three survey years was somewhat lower for women than for men, except in class II O which contains many of the typical 'women's jobs'. The percentages among women in 1981 were 54 per cent in class I, 64 per cent in class II O, 77 per cent in class III and 61 per cent in class II F. The equivalent percentages for men were, as mentioned previously, 64 per cent, 60 per cent, 84 per cent, and 76 per cent respectively. Accordingly, women seem to be somewhat less stable than men in their class affiliation. If the percentage of those who appear to have belonged to the same class their entire lives (which their father belonged to as well) are considered, there are differences between men and women only in class III and, especially, class II F. The percentages for women in 1981 were 15 per cent in class I, 24 per cent in class II O, 53 per cent in class III, and 16 per cent in class II F. The equivalent figures for men were 16 per cent, 22 per cent, 62 per cent, and 52 per cent.

Outflow

Thus far we have looked at social mobility percentages through the years and the sources and manner of recruitment to the various classes. We shall now examine another aspect of social mobility, namely, what happened to people from the different classes. This is usually called a study of the outflow from different classes. Table 3.8 shows the distribution in the classes of origins, during the three survey years, of men and women according to their class destinations.

Table 3.8 Men and women of different class origin distributed according to class of destination in 1968, 1974, and 1981. Percentages

	Men						Women					
Class of origin	1968											
	Class of destination						Class of destination					
	I	IIO	IIF	III	Total	N	I	IIO	IIF	III	Total	N
I	56.8	29.8	0.0	13.3	100.0	123	42.7	42.3	0.0	15.0	100.0	121
IIO	16.8	39.4	1.5	42.4	100.0	586	10.3	47.1	1.1	41.5	100.0	632
IIF	4.3	24.2	21.8	49.7	100.0	399	3.6	29.5	9.7	57.2	100.0	412
III	4.6	25.3	2.0	68.1	100.0	1599	2.2	28.3	1.7	67.7	100.0	1569
All	9.6	28.4	4.7	57.3	100.0	2,707	6.1	33.4	2.7	57.8	100.0	2,735

Class of origin	1974											
	Class of destination						Class of destination					
	I	IIO	IIF	III	Total	N	I	IIO	IIF	III	Total	N
I	48.6	30.5	1.3	19.7	100.0	141	36.0	44.5	0.8	18.7	100.0	142
IIO	18.0	40.7	1.2	40.1	100.0	717	9.0	47.6	1.0	42.3	100.0	742
IIF	7.1	25.2	18.8	48.9	100.0	347	4.4	35.2	5.0	55.5	100.0	391
III	5.9	25.1	2.4	66.6	100.0	1627	2.8	30.7	2.0	64.5	100.0	1569
All	11.2	29.3	4.1	55.4	100.0	2,832	6.3	36.4	2.1	55.2	100.0	2,844

Class of origin	1981											
	Class of destination						Class of destination					
	I	IIO	IIF	III	Total	N	I	IIO	IIF	III	Total	N
I	46.1	35.5	1.2	17.2	100.0	175	26.9	46.9	1.3	24.8	100.0	183
IIO	19.1	42.1	0.7	38.2	100.0	806	8.8	50.5	1.1	39.6	100.0	799
IIF	8.7	23.7	20.5	47.2	100.0	331	5.2	35.3	6.1	53.4	100.0	375
III	7.2	26.3	1.8	64.7	100.0	1560	3.2	32.7	2.3	61.8	100.0	1504
All	13.1	31.0	3.6	52.3	100.0	2,872	6.6	38.9	2.4	52.1	100.0	2,861

If the distributions for all men and women are compared first, we find a substantial difference in the class distributions of men and women.

To a much greater degree men belong to classes I and II F, while women belong to class II O to a greater extent. The differences increased between the sexes in this regard from 1968 to 1981. The change is connected to the increase in the number of salaried employees during the same period. The increases in these jobs in class II went to women in most cases.

Table 3.8 shows the manifest differences in life chances, the probabilities of ending up in different classes for people of different class backgrounds. The men whose fathers belonged to a particular class have a much higher probability of joining that class than men from other backgrounds. This applies especially to the sons of farmers. It is ten times more likely that they, as opposed to anyone else, will become farmers. Almost 50 per cent of the sons of men in class I will eventually belong to that class, a figure which is substantially higher than that for sons of men in class II O, the class which comes closest in this regard. Sons of workers are clearly much more likely than others to become workers. Only sons of lower-grade salaried employees and small proprietors deviate from the pattern in that the differences between themselves and others regarding the likelihood of joining this class are relatively small, even if they are noticeable. Because of other studies we know that it is the sons of lower-grade salaried employees, rather than the sons of small proprietors, who take on their fathers' occupations to a relatively small extent.

We found the same general pattern for women as for men, but the differences in life chances between daughters from different classes tend to be smaller than the differences for men. The only deviation in this regard was among daughters of men from class I. They have a much greater chance than other women of ending up in class I. The relative differences in this regard are, if anything, greater among women than men. If we assume that the positions in class I are the most advantageous and those in class III are the least advantageous, then the percentage of children from a particular class who end up in these classes gives us information about the relative advantages of the life chances of children from different classes. The order in which the classes are placed in Table 3.8, I, II O, II F, and III, also is the order of the relative advantages of the life chances of children.

If we now look at the outflow distributions in each of the survey years we find that some levelling off of the differences in life chances seems to have occurred during the period. The relative differences in the percentages of the different classes that have ended up in class I decreased from 1968 to 1981, and the same applies to those who have become members of class III. This applies to both men and women. This means that the range in the class structure — the distance between class I and class III — decreased during the 1970s. In other words, the class structure became somewhat more open during the period.[9]

We can only speculate about the causes of this change. It is possible that the investments made in the education system during the 1950s and 1960s resulted in a more open class structure during the 1970s, but it is doubtful that they have had much of an effect on our data since so few cohorts have been affected thus far. It is also possible that the conditions of life in the different classes have levelled off during the post-war period, and that this is showing its effects in that the differences in children's life chances have levelled off to some extent. A closer analysis of this levelling off must, however, be put off until a later date.

Career mobility

How then have the occupational careers of men and women developed? In Table 3.9 the most usual career paths of men and women born between 1918 and 1947, who have been included in all three surveys, are shown. Each combination of class membership during the years which includes more than 1 per cent of the men or women is included in the table.

Table 3.9 Class membership in 1968, 1974, and 1981 for men and women born 1918–1947. Percentages

Class membership in			Sex	
1968	1974	1981	Men	Women
I	I	I	10	3
I	I	IIO		1
I	IIO	IIO		2
IIO	I	I	2	
IIO	IIO	I	2	
IIO	IIO	IIO	22	27
IIO	III	IIO		3
IIO	IIO	III	1	4
IIO	III	III	2	4
III	IIO	IIO	6	4
III	III	IIO	6	4
III	IIO	III	2	2
III	III	III	36	38
IIF	IIF	IIF	3	2
Total			92	92

The most usual combinations concern those who belonged to the same class during all three years. About two thirds of both men and women have been stable in their class membership between the three survey years. High rates of stability were naturally found mainly in the numerically large classes III and II O. A larger percentage of men than women were stable in class I while a somewhat larger percentage of women were stable in class II O.

Within these classes, stability among men in class I is especially great. It is obvious that if a man has entered class I in virtue of his occupation, he tends to continue his membership in that class. A similar result has also been found for England and Wales (Goldthorpe 1980, 136).

The number of patterns which indicate mobility between the years is fairly limited. There are 64 possible combinations of class membership in the three years. Eleven combinations for men and twelve for women include 92 per cent of the entire population.

Among men who have been mobile during the period, an ordered career is relatively common. If it is assumed that classes I, II O, and III constitute a hierarchy, most of the mobility among men during the period 1968–1981 was upwards.

Women have apparently experienced more mobility between the surveys. It is especially between classes II O and III that women, regardless of class origin, have been mobile. To some degree, the mobility noted can probably be explained by women changing between being housewives, when they were classified according to their husband's class, and their own gainful employment when they were classified accordingly. Another partial explanation could be that women, with a weaker connection to the labour market, change jobs between classes to a greater extent than men. On the other hand, if one only considers the mobility among women who were gainfully employed during each survey year, there is a high degree of stability, even higher than among men. If the weaker connection of women to the labour market has any effect in this regard, it is that they change between gainful employment and other activities more often than men, not that they change jobs between classes more often.

Women also do not stay in class I, after entering, to the same extent as men. This can involve women who are married to men in class I who leave their roles as housewives and enter the labour market, in which they often obtain a job in class II O. This can also involve women, especially from 1968 to 1974, who studied at a university during the first year and were therefore classified in class I, but who did not get jobs in this class once they entered the labour market.

Among women, we did not observe any equivalent pattern in the upward social mobility trend during their occupational career which was noticeable among men.

Summary

The picture presented by the data in this chapter is that the class structure seems fairly stable — the internal relationship of the different positions seems to have changed only insignificantly. However, the structure has apparently changed fairly significantly regarding the placement of people in it — both in that there have been fairly large shifts in the distribution of individuals across the positions and in that so many individuals change positions one or more times during their lives.

The change which is perhaps most notable for the thirteen-year period studied is the altered position of women. In 1968 almost half of all married women under 60 years old were housewives, whereas in 1981 barely one in seven were housewives. The percentage of women has especially increased in the public sector, at the same time that the number of people with state and municipal jobs has increased substantially.

There have also been shifts between the classes, class I increased in size while class III in 1981 constituted a smaller percentage of the population than in 1968. Even if lower grade salaried employees are included, the working class has decreased as a percentage of the population.

Many people changed occupations during the thirteen-year period. It is especially common that people change occupations between different categories within the working class.

Social mobility from one's class origins to one's own position in adult life has increased. This is mainly a result of the substantial changes in the sizes of the classes. However, mobility also increased independently of these changes. We found that the structure itself changed; it became more open during the period or, alternatively the distance between the different classes decreased.

During their adult lives, women move between classes more than men. Men in particular remain in class I once they have entered it. Class I thereby becomes fairly homogeneous regarding its members', especially its male members', occupational experiences in adult life. On the other hand, class backgrounds vary in the most in class I. It is recruited to a great extent from each of the different classes. It is workers and farmers who are the most uniform in regard to class background.

Notes

1. The former general director Ernst Höijer, who was one of the three civil servants, explained this background to the classification system at a Statistical Association meeting in 1967.

2. However, in a coding instruction from the 1950s it was stated that 'the emphasis is not always on the person's position within the occupation but more on the person's relation to the class which he can be considered to belong to from a social perspective.'

3. This also applies to smallholders. For them it is almost certainly a result of the shifts in the group mentioned earlier, from smallholders to forestry workers.

4. The decreased percentage of housewives could be explained by the fact that women previously left the labour market when they had children and then returned later, whereas in later years they have only taken a leave of absence. In the latter case they would be registered in an occupational category and not as housewives. We can check this for 1974 and 1981 by placing the women on leaves of absence who take care of the household in the housewife category. The percentage of couples in which the woman is a housewife increases then from 28.3 per cent to 30.0 per cent in 1974 and from 13.8 per cent to 14.7 in 1981. Therefore, the behaviour discussed cannot explain the decreased percentage of housewives. The decrease in the housewife category is also examined in Chapter 6.

5. Each large city area includes the city itself as well as the neighbouring communities which fulfil the following three criteria:

   1. 50 per cent of the population lives in a densely populated area,
   2. at least 15 per cent of the gainfully employed commute to the city centre area and
   3. a maximum of 33 per cent of the gainfully employed work in the agricultural sector.

   Also see S. Johansson 1970, 83f.

6. This attempt to keep the classification constant between the years led to slight problems in 1981. The spread of housing into peripheral areas during the 1970s means that some city inhabitants living in the outer areas of the city are classified as living in the countryside. The percentage of persons improperly classified in this manner should, however, be quite small.

7. Those placed in the working class are salaried employees with codes 5 and 6 in the socio-economic classifications used by the Central Bureau of Statistics 1975–1981 (SCB 1981 d.). These salaried employees have jobs which normally require a maximum of two years' education after primary school.

8. The results refer to men born 1918–1947. They were therefore more than 20 years old in 1968. Thus, even then, they already had a realistic possibility of belonging to class I.

9. A log linear test shows that a signficant change occurred between 1968 and 1981. The relation between class I and class III has thereby changed so that the difference between them has decreased.

4

Disparities in Mortality

ROBERT ERIKSON

Mortality is the classic indicator of social ills. By studying variations in mortality, we have been able for a long time to see how health and general living conditions have changed. Sweden experienced almost continuous reduction in mortality rate from the early 1800s until the middle of the 1900s, reflecting a corresponding improvement in people's living conditions.

Mortality can be used as an indicator for changes in welfare over time as well as a means for studying disparities in health and general conditons of segments of the population. In comparisons over time and among groups, age distribution is usually taken into consideration, so that observed disparities are not due to differences in age. That older people have higher mortality rates than others undoubtedly is a consequence of their worse general health, but this is a well-known and unavoidable biological truth that should not obscure other potential differences in mortality.

Sex differences in mortality

In all industrial societies, men die at higher rates than women. This difference must arise from the fact that women's biological constitution is more resistant than men's, since this difference is found in all age groups, including miscarried and still-born children. To some degree, however, the differences may also be due to the fact that the life styles of men and women are dissimilar. The differences in mortality between the sexes are greater in some ages than others and also vary among countries. The disparities are especially large for people in their twenties and those in their sixties. The risks stemming from life style and other living conditions thus seem to be particularly unfavourable for men in their youth and those in their late middle age, whereas the differences are less in childhood, in the years between 30 and 40, and in old age.

The association between sex, morbidity, and mortality could be seen as a paradox of sex. Despite their higher mortality, men are healthier than women. No matter how we measure morbidity, and almost regardless of

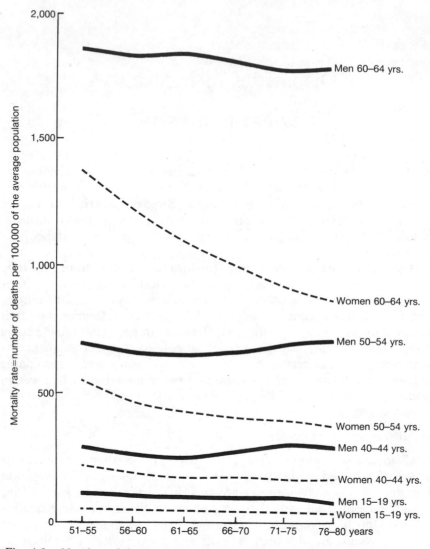

Fig. 4.1.   Number of deaths per 100 000 of the average population for men and women in different age groups, by year

which disease we study, women tend to have more health problems than men (see next chapter). The paradox would be explained if the higher mortality of men was due to causes of death that were not related to illness, such as injuries and accidents, violence and so on. Indeed, men die from these factors to a much greater extent than women, but they far from explain the entire difference in mortality between the sexes. There is no generally accepted explanation for this paradox of sex. Explanations may range from the claim that women are more willing than men to accept a sick role and therefore more often describe themselves as ill, thereby also raising the possibility of early detection of serious illnesses to explanations based on biological differences between men and women.

To the extent that differences in mortality between men and women are due to contrasting life styles, it seems reasonable to expect that they would have decreased in recent years. For several of the types of behaviour that we are sure, or think we are sure, influence mortality risks, differences between man and women seem to have diminished. These include smoking and drinking alcohol. This also applies to risks connected with gainful employment.

Mortality figures since 1950, or the number of deaths per 100,000 in the population, are shown in Figure 4.1 for men and women in some age groups. As is seen from the diagram, the expected convergence in mortality rates for men and women did not appear. On the contrary, the relationship is the opposite. Mortality rates for women in all age categories drop steadily throughout the period. For men, the developments are much less favourable. Mortality among older men decreases slightly during the period. For younger men, the death rate is largely constant, while for middle-aged men, it rises after 1960. The development for middle-aged men is remarkable. The increased death rate marks a break in a very long trend of diminishing rates.

The ratio between the mortality figures for men and women is shown in Figure 4.2. As mentioned above, men between the ages of 15 and 19 have a much higher mortality rate than women — from Figure 4.2, we can see that it is twice as high. This has been more or less the case since 1950. For the age groups from 20 to 75 years, women's mortality has dropped substantially in relation to men's. In the early fifties, about 130 men died for every 100 women who died between these ages. By the end of the seventies, the corresponding relation was 190 men for 100 women.

A deeper understanding of this development is reached if we divide the deaths according to principal groups of causes of death.[1]

Figures 4.3–4.6, show the development from 1950 to 1978 for four types of fatal illness for men and women between 50 and 54 years old. Even if the mortality trend is not identical for different age groups, it has been similar enough to enable us to describe the main characteristics for all adult groups with the trend for one group. Therefore, only the development for 50–54 year olds is given here.

As is shown in the diagrams, the relationship between men's and

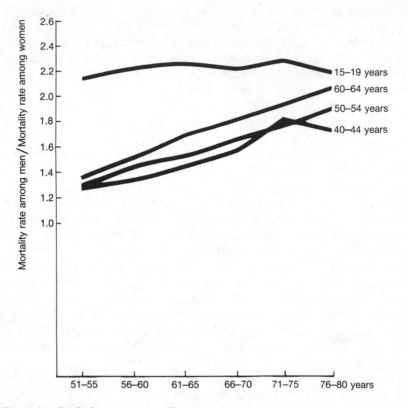

Fig. 4.2. Ratio between mortality rates for men and women in different age groups and years

women's mortality varies widely in the different groups of fatal illnesses. The relative increase in men's mortality seen in Figure 4.2 is explained by one group in particular, that of death from heart and cardio-vascular diseases dealt with in Figure 4.3

Men's mortality in heart and cardio-vascular diseases in these age groups has risen since the early sixties. In other age groups, deaths of men from this cause also either rose or remained constant during this period. Women's deaths from cardio-vascular diseases, on the other hand, have declined in all age groups. For the age groups shown in Figure 4.3 (50–54 years), the difference in the trends for the two sexes was particularly pronounced. At the beginning of the 1950s, men's mortality from cardio-vascular diseases within this age group was about 1.5 times larger than women's. By the middle of the seventies, the corresponding relationship was about 3.5.

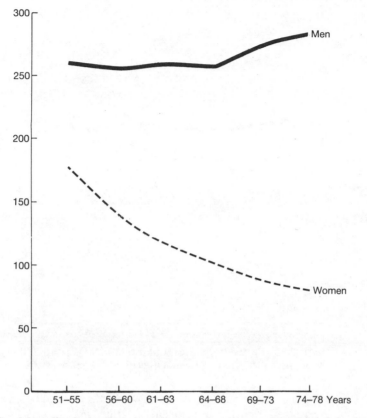

Fig. 4.3.   Mortality in heart and cardio-vascular diseases (number of deaths per 100 000 in the population) for men and women aged 50–54 years during the period 1951–78

   This trend is mostly due to more favourable shifts in women's mortality from cardio-vascular causes. There is, however, another factor involved. For both men and women, the developments have been more unfavourable for mortality from what are called the ischemic heart diseases than for other cardio-vascular diseases (Valkonen 1983, 9). As ischemic heart diseases are relatively more common among men, this tendency reinforces the disadvantageous mortality situation for them.

   The other large groups of fatal illnesses is tumour diseases. In Figure 4.4, the development for this cause of death since 1950 is shown for both men and women. The picture that emerges is quite dissimilar to that for cardio-vascular diseases. First, women have higher mortality rates than men. This is true for all ages under 55 years, whereas men over 55 have a higher mortality in tumour diseases than women of the same age. Second, developments for men and women are much more similar. As is

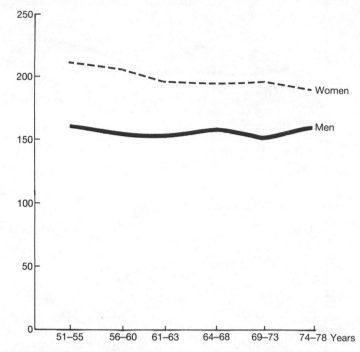

Fig. 4.4   Mortality in tumour diseases (number of deaths per 100 000 of the
population) for men and women aged 50–54 years during the period
1951–78

true for other age categories, however, women's mortality in this age
group has decreased slightly since the early fifties, while men's has largely
remained unchanged. The relative mortality of men has thus slightly
increased. This increase in men's relative mortality is nevertheless
insignificant compared with that for cardio-vascular diseases.

One example where death is almost entirely determined by human
actions, concerns deaths caused by accidents and other injuries, violence,
and suicide. The trends in mortality for this causal group for the ages
50–54 years is given in Figure 4.5. For these categories, men's mortality is
much greater than women's in all age groups. Since 1950, the deaths
from these causes have increased for both sexes. The increase has turned
out to be relatively faster for women than for men, which means that
men's mortality from injuries, and the like, has dropped in relation to
women's. Consequently, our original hypothesis about the relationship
between deaths among men and women is correct for this causal group.
The fact that women's deaths from accidents, injuries, and violence are
approaching those of men, can probably be explained by the fact that
women's conditions and life styles have become more like men's.

In Figure 4.6, the development for the remaining causes of death is

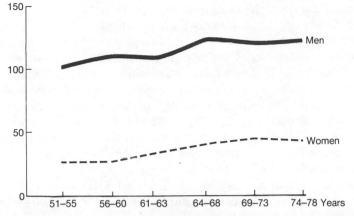

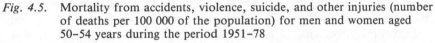

Fig. 4.5. Mortality from accidents, violence, suicide, and other injuries (number of deaths per 100 000 of the population) for men and women aged 50–54 years during the period 1951–78

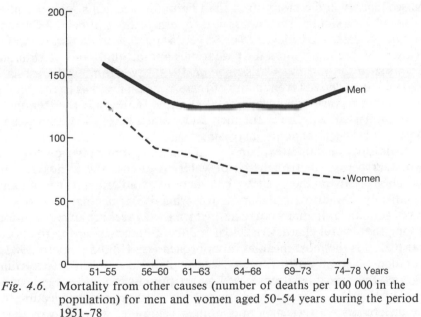

Fig. 4.6. Mortality from other causes (number of deaths per 100 000 in the population) for men and women aged 50–54 years during the period 1951–78

shown for men and women in the ages 50–54. The diagram thus shows deaths from causes other than cardio-vascular diseases, tumours, accidents, or violence. For these remaining causes of death, the pattern is similar to that for cardio-vascular diseases, although less pronounced. Men, of all ages, have a higher mortality than women, and this difference has increased since 1950. Women's mortality rates from these other causes have declined throughout the period, while men's has remained fairly constant since the beginning of the sixties.

To sum up, the trend towards a greater disparity in overall mortality between men and women, then, is due primarily to the fact that the difference in death rates from cardio-vascular diseases has risen sharply since 1950, but the difference from 'remaining' causes of death has also done so. Men's deaths from tumour diseases have also increased relative to women's, but this increase accounts for only a fraction of the increase in the total disparity in mortality. The difference in mortality from injuries and violence, on the other hand, has decreased between the sexes but so insignificantly that it cannot counterbalance changes for other causes of death.

How then should we explain this observed development? Changes in injuries and violence are easy to understand and are in agreement with our original hypothesis. Women in recent years are entering the labour market in greater numbers and appear in traffic more often. Thus, they are exposed to the risk of accidents at about the same rate as men and subsequently will die more often than before in accidents, and the like.

But why is a similar trend not found for other causes of death? Cardio-vascular diseases are believed to be largely a function of diet and amount of exercise, the consumption of cigarettes and alcohol, and of external factors such as stress (see Carlsson *et al.* 1979). Even tumour diseases are assumed to be derived from many of these factors as well as to the degree of exposure to various environmental hazards. But despite the seemingly more similar circumstances for men and women here, the disparities in mortality between them are increasing.

Obviously, we cannot explain the difference in mortality rates for the two sexes here, but it might be of value to discuss the trends and to speculate briefly on their causes. We ought to avoid attempts to find any specifically 'Swedish' explanation for what is happening. The trends have been similar in many countries, which is why seeking an explanation among the general characteristics of industrial societies during the post-war period is the most meaningful approach (see United Nations 1982). Nor does it seem worthwhile to seek explanations specific to certain cohorts; that is, explanations based on the premiss that older age groups have lived under different conditions from younger groups, leading to the differences between men and women being greater among younger cohorts than older ones. When examining the relationship between men's and women's mortality rates from 1950 backwards, one finds that there is no steady trend in the ratio between the rates for the first forty years of the 1900s (see SCB 1969, Table 40). However, in the 1940s, and even more so the 1950s, the ratio increased for all age groups. Even in this somewhat longer period, the development was parallel in Sweden and other industrial countries. In the United States, England and Wales, and

New Zealand, the disparity in mortality between the sexes declined slightly between 1910 and 1930 only to rise sharply thereafter (Retherford 1975, 46). It seems that the explanation for increasing disparities in mortality between men and women should be found among the changing characteristics of societies since World War II.

When trying to explain the dissimilarities in men's and women's mortality from diseases (we will hereafter disregard accidental deaths), it is not entirely clear whether we should focus on men or women. If we assume that the 'natural' development would have been for the earlier decrease in mortality to continue, for example with regard to advances within medicine and hygiene, we should then try to explain why men's mortality on the whole has remained constant in the post-war period. It then also becomes interesting to explain the development of mortality from cancer among women.

If, on the other hand, we assume that a normal situation would be for mortality rates not to change, it is the modified women's mortality from cardio-vascular diseases and from remaining causes that is exceptional and needs explanation. One such explanation would be if multiple pregnancies entail higher mortality risks, not only during childbirth but also from the increased strains that a pregnancy places on the body. Mortality among women would in that case have decreased with the drop in fertility in the 1900s. This explanation, however, is not sufficient if one looks at how the number of childbirths is related to mortality. Kitagawa and Hauser (1973, 112) show that mortality in the Untied States is lowest for women who have borne three children; it is not until a woman has borne seven or more children that the risk increases more sharply. Women with no children or only one have a somewhat higher death rate, which is probably mostly a function of selection — sickly women bear few if any children. Bearing children, however, may also lessen the risk for cervical cancer, so that if the proportion of women who do not bear children decreases, so will the risk of death.

Because the share of women who are married increased up until the end of the 1960s, and with it probably also the share who bore at least one child, at the same time as the proportion of women with many children decreased, we should be able to explain some of the decrease in mortality among women. However, only a small part of the total decrease can be explained in this manner since the positive effects of childbirth are weak and the proportion of women who bore many children was already quite small during the earlier part of this century. Consequently, we must seek additional explanations, and perhaps then concentrate on finding the reasons for the changes in men's mortality.

One danger to health that has received much attention in recent years is the growing quantity of poisonous substances in our environment. Even if we suppose that the changing trends for men could be explained by this increase, it is still baffling why this increase affected men and not women. One possibility is that the rise in poisons mainly affects industrial workers, of which the majority are men. As we will later see, the higher risk among industrial workers is not so great that it could explain the higher mortality rates for men.

One explanation for the long-term decline in mortality is improved diet, in quantity as well as content. On the other hand, it is possible that the increased prosperity of the post-war period has led to a deterioration in our eating habits. For example, the intake of sugar and fat has increased. In order for changes in diet to explain the increased disparity in mortality between men and women, we must assume that women have altered their eating habits differently from men.

Two health risks that have increased in the post-war period are tobacco and alcohol consumption. Tobacco consumption rose for many years, and previously men smoked much more than women. In recent years, however, this relationship has changed, which is why if tobacco consumption is assumed to account for a substantial part of the explanation we are seeking we should expect the gap betwen men's and women's mortality to become narrower. However, it has been found that women are protected to some degree against vascular problems before menopause, which is why more consumption of tobacco by both men and women would lead to increased differences in mortality, at least among younger persons.

Almost all countries have witnesses a rise in alcohol consumption in the post-war period — in Sweden, especially since the repeal in 1955 of the alcohol rationing system (a limited amount for each adult citizen). The deviating trend in mortality for men could be understood if the increased mortality risks were primarily linked to large consumers of alcohol. In recent years, alcohol consumption has become more similar between the sexes. Thus, some equalization of mortality should be expected, even if the higher level of risk among men will probably remain.

Finally, another possible explanation is related to the relations between the sexes. The traditional family has been described as favourable for men, in that they were well taken care of in the family, while also feeling indispensable as the provider of the family. Changes in the institution of the family perhaps have led to less cared for and more dispensable men. If the situation improved for women at the same time as it deteriorated for men, the observed developments would have resulted. The problem with this explanation is that it does not seem to be right in terms of time. While the disparity in mortality, as mentioned, seems to have begun as early as the 1940s, the major changes in family patterns do not seem to have occurred before the middle of the 1960s.

These attempts at explanation may be seen as speculatory and hypothetical, and in many instances perhaps as dubious. But it is possible that together they explain some of the disparity in the mortality trends for the sexes.

The explanation with most support in the literature is based on differences in smoking habits. Retherford (1975) has shown that smoking in the United States has been responsible for much of the difference in mortality rates between the sexes. Valkonen (1977) finds it plausible that the higher level of risk for men in Finland and Sweden stems from differences in smoking habits. Preston (1970) reaches the same conclusion on the basis of a broad study of the factors which might explain the increasingly higher risk among men of 40–69 years. In these studies, however, there is no mention of alcohol consumption as a possible explanation.

The changes in smoking habits observed during the 1970s should lead, as with altered alcohol consumption, to sex disparities more disadvantageous for women. It may take time before this occurs, as 20 years of smoking might be what is required for lung cancer or heart troubles to develop. The increased equality between the sexes that would result does not feel much like progress.

Disparities in mortality among classes and occupational groups

Class differences in mortality have long been the object of study in other countries, especially England (see, for example, Fox and Goldblatt 1982). It has generally been shown that mortality tends to be relatively low in the upper classes, but relatively high in the working class. People outside the labour market tend to have higher mortality rates than the gainfully employed, regardless of differences in age and sex. In Sweden, there has not been much research on class differences in mortality. Earlier studies have almost exclusively looked at a particular occupational group, and it is difficult to reach any general conclusions from them.

The level-of-living material has been linked to the register of causes of death. We are therefore able to report on mortality among people in various social and occupational classes in 1968 and in 1974. In Table 4.1, an account is given of the standardized mortality ratios for 1968 occupational groups for the period 1969–1974, for 1974 occupational groups for the period 1975–1980, and for 1968 occupational groups for the period 1969–1980. The standardized mortality ratios (SMRs) are computed in such a way that the number of people who died within a particular group is divided by the number in the group that could be

Table 4.1 Standardized mortality ratios for the 1968 sample for the periods 1969–1974 and 1969–1980 and for the 1974 sample for the period 1975–1980

	1968 sample for the period 1969–1974 (1)	1974 sample for the period 1975–1980 (2)	1968 sample for the period 1969–1980 (3)	Number of deaths in periods		
				(1)	(2)	(3)
Population 15–75 yrs.	1.0	1.0	1.0	325	335	761
Private professionals	1.3	0.7	1.1	8	5	16
Public professionals	0.8	0.4	0.7	3	2	7
Housewives	1.2	1.2	0.8	3	4	5
University students	0.0	0.0	0.0	0	0	0
Pensioners	0.8	0.5	1.1	6	4	17
Class I, all	1.0	0.6*	0.9	20	15	45
Farmers and farming wives	0.8	0.6	0.8	9	7	22
Small proprietors, wives	1.3	0.8	1.1	22	10	45
Foremen	0.6	0.2	0.6	4	1	11
Private technical & clerical	0.6	1.1	0.8	7	12	24
Public salaried	0.6	0.6	0.6*	5	7	14
Housewives	0.9	0.8	0.7	11	11	22
Secondary school students	0.0	1.3	0.0	0	1	0
Pensioners	1.0	1.0	1.0	33	44	72
Class II, all	0.9	0.8*	0.8*	91	93	210
Agricultural workers	0.6	0.4*	0.7*	9	5	23
Metal workers	1.1	1.0	1.1	12	10	34
Other manufacturing workers	0.8	0.8	0.8	14	10	34
Construction workers	0.8	0.8	0.7	7	6	17

	1968 sample for the period 1969–1974 (1)	1974 sample for the period 1975–1980 (2)	1968 sample for the period 1969–1980 (3)	Number of deaths in periods		
				(1)	(2)	(3)
Manufacturing workers, all	0.9	0.9	0.9	33	26	85
Workers in commerce	0.9	0.6	1.1	5	4	16
Other service workers	1.0	1.0	1.2	8	8	24
Service workers, all	0.9	0.8	1.1	13	12	40
Workers in local govt.	0.6	0.8	0.7	5	10	17
Workers in state govt.	1.2	0.2	0.9	5	1	10
Workers in public employment, all	0.8	0.7	0.8	10	11	27
Disabled	3.0*	2.7*	2.1*	15	13	25
Housewives	1.1	1.3	1.2	29	32	76
Pupils	0.8	2.8	0.8	1	3	2
Pensioners	1.1	1.2*	1.1*	104	125	228
Class III, all	1.0	1.1	1.0	214	227	506

* Indicates that mortality in the group deviates signficantly from the 5%-level of mortality in the general population, controlling for age and sex distributions.

expected to have died if the mortality risk for each individual was the same as that for the whole country for people of the same age (one-year cohorts) and of the same sex. If the ratio for a group is 1, mortality in that group is the same as for the population as a whole. A ratio which is less than 1 indicates a low relative mortality while a ratio greater than 1 indicates a higher level of risk.

The figures in Table 4.1 should be approached with caution. The number of dead, as the expected number, is small in many instances, which is why even rather large variations in the ratios may be due to random results. Mortality in the 1968 sample up until 1974 and mortality in the 1974 sample, however, are independent of each other, which is why a result where both of these ratios point in the same direction should receive more attention. The ratios for the 1968 sample until 1980 are somewhat more stable because they are based on a greater number of deaths. On the other hand, they are not independent of the other two ratios.

In general, there are three possible explanations for differences in mortality for various occupational groups. First, there may be different selections of employees for different occupations. If certain occupations attract unusually healthy employees, we may expect a relatively low mortality in these occupational groups; at the same time, mortality may be high in occupations which do not place heavy demands on the health of the workers. Second, the health risks may be of varying magnitude in different occupations. If workers in some occupations are subject to greater risk of accident or are often exposed to harmful substances, a relatively high mortality rate may be expected among them. Third, life styles may differ among various occupational groups. For example, if workers tend to smoke and drink more in some occupational groups than in others, we may expect a relatively high mortality in these groups.

In Sweden, as in other countries, economically active people have a lower mortality rate than those who are not. All such earners and proprietors have a death ratio of 0.87 for the period 1969 to 1980, compared to a ratio of 1.04 for non-active people. This must primarily be an effect of selection. Among those not economically active, there are some who abstain from employment for health reasons and their mortality risk is undoubtedly much higher than that of others. Similarly, one can find economically active pensioners. These people are probably much healthier than many of their peers.

There also seems to be a tendency for mortality to be lower among public employees than among people in the private sector. It is possible that the selection for public jobs is more favourable from a health standpoint than the selection for private jobs, but it is also possible that the health risks are less in the public sector.

Mortality ratios for the three social classes indicate that the risk is slightly higher in class III compared with classes I and II. Admittedly, the differences are small, at least seemingly in comparison with other countries (United Nations 1982, 53–55), but they reappear in both independent cases. The most evident result is that mortality in class II is relatively low. The ratios for 1968 compared with those for 1974 point towards an increase in class differences in mortality. In the light of the uncertainty of the figures, however, it is not reasonable to reach such a conclusion solely on the basis of these data. For now, our conclusion can only be that there are some, albeit rather small, differences in mortality between social classes in Sweden.

If we look at mortality ratios for separate occupational groups, we must proceed with even greater caution. The ratio which is undeniably greatest is that for people labelled as disabled. This group includes people of working age who are classified as unable to take gainful employment on physical and psychological grounds. It is not surprising that mortality is high in this group.

The slightly higher mortality in class III, however, is not only due to the disabled. Housewives in this class seem to have a higher mortality than housewives in class II, and the same applies to retired people. Pensioners in class III constitute the only group besides the invalids in which the members have a significantly higher risk in relation to the general population. This does not necessarily mean that a high risk is evident in this group alone, since the expected number of deaths in many of the other groups is so small that the signficance tests are not decisive.

In order to explain the disparities among the classes, we should presumably resort to all three general explanations mentioned above. For example, some disabled people belong to class III as a consequence of their physical condition or life style, which also explains that fact that they have a higher mortality risk than others. It seems probable as well that the health risks implied in the jobs held by members of social class III are greater than the health risks in other jobs. The direct increase in risks does not seem exceptionally large, since the death ratios among the economically active in class III in 1968 are not systematically high.

That retired people in class III have a relatively high risk of mortality, however, points to the long-term health risks involved in the types of jobs, common in class III. It is possible that they entail more wear and tear on the body, but that these do not take effect until retirement. The higher risk in mortality among retired people combined with the tendency towards high mortality among housewives in class III may indicate that general living standards were tougher and that the life style in class III less healthy. The latter mainly concerns diet, since alcohol and tobacco consumption were both previously lower in social class III than in the remaining social classes. It is possible that differences in consumption pattern were greater between members in class III. This would mean that there was a large group who neither smoked nor drank, and in which the mortality risks were not influenced by these factors, plus a relatively large group that perhaps both smoked and drank a lot, with the ensuing higher fatality risks.

Mortality as indicator

By using mortality as a gauge for the health of a population group, we find that women seem healthier than men (a finding that nearly all other health indicators contradict), that women's health during the post-war period has improved compared with that of men, and that members of class III seem to be somewhat unhealthier than the other two classes. The sex paradox in particular indicates that this interpretation is not adequate. But we may solve the paradox if we view mortality not only as an indicator of health, but also as one for living conditions generally. Even if men have fewer problems with their health, their overall life styles, including tobacco and alcohol consumption, are more hazardous and risk-filled, which leads to a higher mortality. Correspondingly, the results in this chapter lead to the conclusion that women's living conditions during the post-war period have been improved in relation to men's, and that the lives of members of class III are riskier and tougher than those of people in the other social classes.

Note

1. True comparability over the years is elusive because of a statistical reorganization in the 1960s. It is only through the efforts of Anne-Marie Bolander, SCB, that we were able to obtain information that is comparable for the entire period, although we have been compelled to modify the period division to some extent.

5

Health and Health Care Utilization

SVEN-ÅKE KJELLSTRÖM and OLLE LUNDBERG

Introduction

In this chapter we will examine the extent of health problems in Sweden, how various groups in society differ with regard to health problems, how the incidence and distribution of sickness changed between 1968 and 1981, and how health care services are used by different groups in society.

The most common form of health measurement is the normal doctor's check-up. The doctor, who is specially trained for this, can from (i) the individual's explanation of his/her problems, (ii) the examination itself, and (iii) the results of any test that may be performed, determine the individual's medical condition and arrive at a diagnosis. With interviews of the type used in this survey we only have the first of these three methods at our service. Our reports, therefore, have a different character from the purely medical descriptions a trained doctor can produce since we merely register the individual's perception of his own state of health.

The results of these two types of investigation also have separate uses. A doctor's investigation forms the basis for treatment of the individual's illnesses and complaints, while we intend to give a general picture of the problems in public health and their distribution within the population structure.[1]

How do health problems appear, in general terms? It seems that the extent of illness *did not change* to any real degree between 1968 and 1981. In other words, those sicknesses and problems that were used as a measure of illness were about as common in 1981 as they were in 1968. The only exception was dental health, which improved considerably. Even mental health, seems to have improved to some extent. Ailments in shoulders, back, and joints, seem on the other hand, to have become slightly more common.

Differences between the sexes indicate a generally poorer state of health for women, which has also been evident in international studies. However, certain tendencies towards a levelling off were found.

Age naturally has a strong correlation with health problems. The percentage with health problems is signficantly higher in older age groups. For certain indicators, such as circulatory problems, there was a noticeable reduction of the age differences.

The type of community that a person lives in, large city, small city, or the countryside, plays a fairly unimportant role with regard to illness. This did not change during the period.

Finally, when considering class differences, our data indicate that class III has a greater rate of illness than classes I and II. This relationship showed no signs of changing. The differences were often small in the youngest age groups, but quickly increased from the age of 30 to the disadvantage of class III. To sum up then, the extent of health problems was, in general, constant, and the tendency of women, the elderly, and class III to be at a disadvantage regarding health remained essentially unchanged since 1968.

Physical health

One indicator of physical illness is impaired mobility. As being measured by ability to walk 100 metres, ability to walk up and down stairs and ability to run 100 metres, impaired mobility also give an indication of general physical state.

The percentage of people disabled in this way[2] has decreased since 1968, but the change is very small. Of the particular limitations it was the share who could not run 100 metres that decreased most (Table 5.1). This could indicate that there was an improvement in general well-being rather than an actual decrease in movement handicaps caused by problems with, for example, knees and hips.

Table 5.1 Percentages of the population 15–75 years old with various mobility impairments in 1968, 1974, and 1981

	1968	1974	1981
Unable to run 100 metres	24.7	22.5	20.0
Unable to go up/down stairs	12.8	11.1	11.2
Unable to walk 100 metres	9.9	9.3	9.0
Impaired mobility	14.6	12.9	13.0

From the regression model (see Figure 2.1, Chapter 2) it is apparent that women were disabled to a greater extent than men, but a certain levelling off of the differences for the sexes had taken place. The percentage with impaired mobility naturally increases with age, and is especially high for the group over 55 years old. We found, however, a slight lessening of the difference between the youngest and the two older age groups, although there still remained a large difference, in particular between the youngest and the oldest age group. In 1968 the percentage disabled among the 15–29 year olds was 2 per cent, while the share among those aged 56 to 75 was 35 per cent. The corresponding figures for 1981 were 4 per cent and 30 per cent, respectively.

The proportion with impaired mobility does not vary noticeably between the community types. Marked differences did, on the other hand, exist between the classes. Class III had a clearly higher percentage with movement handicaps than both classes I and II, and no tendencies towards equalization can be reported. In addition, the differences between classes varied with age. In Table 5.2 the relationship between class and age group is illustrated through the use of rates.[3]

Table 5.1 Rates for the portion of the population with impaired mobility in different classes and age groups. Average for the entire period

	15–29	30–54	55–75
Class I	0.44	0.66	1.78
Class II	0.37	0.72	3.11
Class III	0.42	1.23	4.49

Table 5.2 clearly shows that the differences were greater in the older age groups, and that it was primarily the elderly in class III who suffered most from impaired mobility. Further analysis showed in addition that the differences between class I and III increased slightly between 1968 and 1981 in the two older age groups.

Another indicator of general physical health is fatigue during the course of the day. The extent of fatigue[4] did not change significantly during the period. Class III contained the greatest proportion of consistenly fatigued individuals. Women, residents of large cities, and the elderly had higher percentages of fatigue than their respective comparison groups. The difference between the young and the elderly was less in the large cities than it was elsewhere.

Some of the most common illnesses have been summarized in three indices based on questions about perceived problems or symptoms during the previous 12 months.[5] The first index summarizes pains in the various organs of movement, the second circulatory problems, and the third stomach problems.

From Table 5.3 it is apparent that nearly every fifth Swede between 15 and 75 years old had severe pains of some kind during 1981, and that this group had grown since 1968.

The regression analysis, whereby groups are compared rather than

Table 5.3 Percentages of the population 15–75 years old with severe pains, serious circulatory problems, and serious stomach problems in 1968, 1974, and 1981

	1968	1974	1981
Severe pains	18.4	20.4	21.2
Serious circulatory problems	11.3	12.2	10.4
Serious stomach problems	9.0	10.8	9.2

individuals, revealed no increase in the portion with severe pains. There are, however, clear differences between the sexes, age groups and social classes (see Figure 5.1).

Not shown in Figure 5.1, the sex difference was greatest among the 55–75 year olds. Both this interaction effect and the overall difference between men and women remained stable during the seventies. The differences between age groups became somewhat smaller. This is the result of an increase in the percentage of young and middle aged people with severe pains, while it remained constant among the elderly.

The classes differ strickingly with regard to the percentage with severe pains, and no change in this distribution was evident. As was the case with restricted movement ability, class differences varied with age. Among the young the differences were inconsiderable, while an unequal distribution of severe pains between classes I and III is immediately apparent in the middle-aged group, in a manner corresponding to the differences presented in Table 5.2. It should also be noted that the

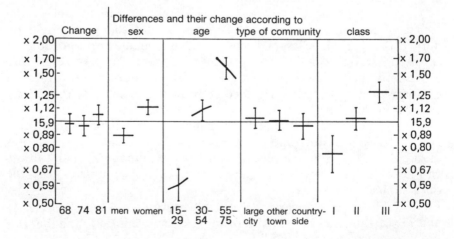

Fig 5.1.   Regression diagram of the proportions with severe pains

differences between the classes were least in rural areas and greatest in the large cities.

Another group of diseases important from a public health point of view are circulatory problems. These ailments cause a large percentage of deaths today (see Chapter 4). Approximately every tenth adult Swede had serious circulatory problems (see Table 5.3).

A regression analysis revealed no significant change in the portion with at least one serious circulatory problem. A noticeably greater proportion among the women reported circulatory problems, but this difference diminished slightly during the period. The sex difference was smaller in the oldest age group, in which men, as it were, caught up with women.

The elderly quite naturally are more subject to this type of ailment, a fact which, to a certain degree, is a result of the character of the illnesses. Many circulatory problems are typical ailments of old age. The proportion with serious circulatory problems in 1981 was 18 per cent in the oldest group, which was approximately three times greater than in the middle-aged group, and six times greater than in the youngest group. The differences between age groups remained unchanged during the period.

As was the case previously, it was class III which was most affected by circulatory problems, and the class variations apparently remained constant during the period. Also with regard to serious circulatory problems, class variations differ with age in a way that is similar to the pattern described for movement hindered (see Table 5.2). Moreover, the differences between classes were greatest in the large cities and least in the countryside.

The last illness group we shall review here involves stomach problems. About one person in ten had serious stomach problems in 1981 (see Table 5.3). Of these, approximately two-thirds suffered from stomach pains. A significant change of the proportion with serious stomach trouble was not found in a regression analysis, nor were there any differences between age groups, community types or social classes. On the other hand, minor stomach problems were concentrated in the youngest age group, and were disproportionately found in class III. This contrasts to some degree to the age pattern seen earlier, where the elderly suffered most from health problems. A greater proportion of women had stomach problems, both serious and minor ones.

Dental health improved considerably between 1968 and 1981. This may be a result of the great effort made to expand dental care and to make it less costly for the patients, in addition to the special efforts made regarding check-ups and preventive care for children and young people. Table 5.4 illustrates the trends in groups with different dental status.

We find that dental health improved most between 1974 and 1981. The share with dental problems was reduced except in one case; those

Table 5.4 Percentages of the population 15–75 years old in the various dental status classes in 1968, 1974, and 1981

	1968	1974	1981
Good natural teeth	63.6	66.7	75.4
Good dentures	26.4	23.7	18.2
Bad teeth	10.0	9.7	6.6
of which:			
Bad natural teeth	5.9	4.3	2.6
Poor dentures	3.2	4.3	3.2
No teeth	0.9	1.1	0.8

completely lacking teeth make up about 1 per cent of the population during the entire period. A regression analysis (Figure 5.2) of the portion with bad teeth[6] showed no significant sex differences, but the age differences existed and increased. This development was dependent upon the fact that practically no young people had bad teeth in 1981. In rural areas dental health was poorer, and people in class III had bad teeth to a greater degree than those in either class I or II. Neither the difference between community types nor between classes changed during the period.

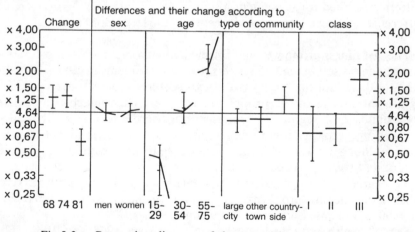

Fig 5.2.   Regression diagram of the proportions with bad teeth

Mental health

How can one assess the state of mental health of the Swedish population and how it might be changing? Is it at all possible to determine this with objective criteria? One difficulty in evaluating lack of mental well-being is that it often does not manifest itself in any outwardly measureable behaviour or symptoms.

Another problem with such an evaluation is in defining mental health and illness. The definition of mental illness employed in various societies and at various times, is the admission norms at mental institutions. These norms can at least partially be considered a reflection of the prevailing ideology and power structure. One of the methods used to estimate mental health is to compare the number of admissions or admissions diagnoses at mental institutions. This reveals information about which behaviour is considered undesirable or dangerous in society, but tells us little in fact about the mental well-being of the population, since only those admitted or under care are included in such analyses.

Another method used to evaluate mental health is a comparison of sales statistics for pharmaceuticals used for sedative or tranquilizing purposes. Such medicines are for the most part prescription drugs, and consumption is regulated, on the one hand by the doctor's willingness to prescribe the drug and on the other by the individual's own activity. A complicating factor is that not all medicine prescribed is consumed, perhaps only half is ever taken. Self-treatment with legal or illegal drugs, which according to some researchers (see, for example, Szasz 1975) is extensive and varies between different groups and times, is of course not covered by this type of testing either.

In this investigation the individual was asked about this subjective interpretation of his mental health. The interviewee was not asked to evaluate his overall condition, but just to answer a few questions about perceived symptoms or ailments.

This method, an interview investigation of a nationally representative cross-section, naturally has its weaknesses. Bearing in mind the special character of mental health, it is only proper to review some of the method's weaknesses and potential sources of error.

One such possible source of error is the point of reference. When can one, for example, begin to speak of a nervous affliction or a problem with sleep? What are slight or serious problems? It is very likely that the answers to these questions vary from individual to individual and group to group; this becomes an even greater problem when one compares different points in time.

Was the social climate more or less tolerant of mental illness in 1981 than it was in 1968? Is it, in other words, easier or more difficult for interviewees to reply honestly to questions about afflictions of a psychological nature? None of these questions can be answered on the basis of our material.

Another source of error that could distort our results is the non-response to the surveys, which included 9.2 per cent of the sample in 1968 and 17.6 per cent of it in 1981. It is possible that the group who did not respond included individuals or groups in poor mental health. However, an analysis of those who participated in 1968 but did not respond in 1981 showed that this group did not deviate from the sample as a whole as far as its mental health was concerned.

Indicators of mental health

The main part of the health section in the Level of Living Surveys consisted of 47 different questions on perceived or experienced ailments and symptoms of illness. The symptoms that are relevant to mental health, nervous trouble (anxiety, restlessness), sleeplessness, depression, mental illness, overstrain and general tiredness, are shown in Table 5.5[7] The questions on ailments and symptoms referred to the previous 12 months. Response alternatives to these questions were: none, slight, or serious problems. All the symptoms showed decreasing ratios in the population, with the single exception of sleep disturbances which remained for the most part unchanged.

Table 5.5 Percentages of the population 15–75 years old with various mental afflictions in 1968, 1974, and 1981

	1968	1974	1981
Nervous trouble (anxiety, restlessness)	19.1	16.1	12.6
of which serious	5.0	4.5	3.4
Sleeplessness	12.8	13.9	13.3
of which serious	4.1	4.5	4.2
Depression	6.9	7.5	5.9
of which serious	2.5	2.7	2.1
Mental illness	2.0	1.6	1.7
of which serious	1.3	1.1	0.8
Overstrain	7.6	6.9	5.2
of which serious	1.4	1.4	1.2
General tiredness	22.3	23.3	19.7
of which serious	5.2	5.9	4.4

The greatest decrease amongst the six symptoms is found for nervous trouble (anxiety, restlessness); from 19 per cent in 1968 to 12 per cent in 1981. All social classes were better off in 1981, but the differences between them were not eliminated. In classes I and II 10 per cent reported nervous troubles in 1981, while the corresponding figure for class III was 15 per cent. Women had a significantly higher ratio of nervous afflictions than men, 16 per cent to 9 per cent. Residents of large cities also had a somewhat higher ratio than others.

The portion of the population with sleeping problems did not change appreciably (see Table 5.5). The classes do not differ significantly, but the general tendency with class I below and class III above the sample average is also found here. The sex difference, on the other hand, was considerable, with women having twice as large a share with sleeping problems (18 per cent as opposed to 9 per cent in 1981). Residents of large cities, as well as the elderly, had slightly greater percentages reporting sleeplessness.

The percentage of the population with experiences or symptoms of depression decreased slighty during the period. Class differences existed to the disadvantage of class III. Among women, city residents, and the old, larger proportions with depression were noted.

Mental illnesses decreased during the period, but nevertheless occurred to a small degree; it was slightly more common in class III and in the older age groups. No differences were evident regarding sex or community types. Overstrain also decreased slightly, and no differences in its occurrence were evident according to sex, community type, or age.

The last of the six symptoms of mental health was a question on general tiredness. The share of the population which was subject to tiredness decreased between 1974 and 1981. The decreases occurred in class I and among women, and decreases in the differences between the various age groups and community types were also found.

A concise description of the nation's mental health

In order to give a concise description of the mental condition of the Swedish population we shall review a compilation of the six symptoms discussed above. Table 5.6 shows that mental well-being[8] remained constant betwen 1968 and 1974. By 1981 there was a slight improvement.

Table 5.6 Mental well-being: percentages of the population 15–75 years old in 1968, 1974, and 1981

	1968	1974	1981
Normal	63.9	63.1	67.7
Somewhat reduced	14.8	15.8	14.7
Reduced	21.3	21.1	17.7

Women had a somewhat higher percentage with reduced mental well-being than men. In 1981, 23 per cent of the women as compared to 12 per cent of the men had mental problems. Both women and men showed reduced percentages with problems during the test period without influencing their comparative ratios. The largest differences between the sexes are to be found in class III.

Mental well-being was poorer among the elderly. In the oldest group every fourth individual and in the younger groups every seventh individual suffered from mental problems. Inhabitants of large cities suffered from reduced mental well-being to a greater extent than those living in other community types (20 per cent versus 16 per cent in 1981). However, no change in the comparative ratios was evident during the period.

Table 5.7 Percentages with reduced mental well-being in the various social classes and in the entire population, 15–75 years old, in 1968, 1974, and 1981

	1968	1974	1981
Class I	14.8	13.6	12.9
Class II	19.3	17.4	16.1
Class III	23.3	24.5	19.7
Entire population	21.3	21.1	17.7

The largest share with reduced mental well-being was consistently found in class III. Table 5.7 lists the percentages with reduced well-being in the different classes. It is obvious that the percentages decreased in each of the groups, and the decreases in classes II and III were statistically significant. When the figures are standardized for age and sex, the decrease is statistically significant in each class. The sub-groups with a large share with impaired mental well-being were housewives in each of the classes, pensioners in classes II and III, and the disabled in class III. Increased percentages were found among housewives in class I, farmers and their wives in class II, and housewives in class III.

Another indicator of mental health is the consumption of medicines, in particular tranquillizers and sleeping pills. Questions were posed in the survey regarding medicine consumption during the previous 14 days. The questions only applied to the consumption of certain types of medicine, and not to the extent of the consumption.[9]

The percentages of the population which had taken tranquillizers and sleeping pills are shown in Table 5.8 to have decreased in the population as a whole. The greatest decrease was found in the share using tranquillizers; only half as many were using such medicines in 1981 as in 1968. Women were more frequent users of both tranquillizers and sleeping pills. Table 5.8 also illustrates the consumption rates for both

Table 5.8 Percentages consuming sleeping pills and tranquillizers in the population, 15–75 years old, according to sex, in 1968, 1974, and 1981

	1968			1974			1981		
	Men	Women	All	Men	Women	All	Men	Women	All
Sleeping pills	4.6	8.9	6.7	4.2	8.2	6.2	3.6	7.2	5.4
Tranquillizers	7.4	15.0	11.2	6.2	11.0	8.6	3.5	7.6	5.6
Sleeping pills and tranquillizers	2.8	4.8	3.8	2.1	3.8	3.0	1.4	3.0	2.2
Sleeping pills and/or tranquillizers	9.4	19.2	14.4	8.3	15.4	11.8	5.8	11.8	8.8

medicine types. Consumption decreased among both men and women, and the decrease was significant in all social classes.

Utilization of health care

To what degree does the Swedish population take advantage of the health care system? Are there any differences between the various groups in the population, and are there differences in utilization rates in the different years? In this section we shall review the use of in-patient care (hospitals and other institutions), contacts with physicians, contacts with nurses, and visits to the dentist.

The primary social purpose of the health care system is to improve public health. The second important goal is to distribute the resources available for health care, at present approximately 9 per cent of the GNP in a fair manner (Health and Medical Services Act, SFS 1982: 763). To achieve a fair distribution, health care and medical services should be distributed according to medical needs, without regard to class, sex, age economic opportunities, or community type.

To determine whether the first goal is fulfilled requires investigations of another kind. Many have expressed doubts about the health care programmes having any real effect upon the state of health of the population. The second goal, a fair distribution, will be analysed at the end of this section, in particular the distribution of out-patient care.

In models of care needs *vis-à-vis* care utilization it has been shown that certain factors can restrict utilization, among others economic status, actual availability, public attitudes to and knowledge of health care, as well as the influence of illness on daily life. The means that society employs to direct utilization are, on the one hand, fees and, on the other, the actual availability of health care facilities, doctors, etc.

In-patient care

The question concerning usage of in-patient care was given the same formulation in all three surveys. 'Have you had to stay in hospital, in a nursing home or other such institution during the past twelve months?'

The percentage reporting hospital stays was unchanged (12 per cent) since 1968. The number of places in in-patient care increased during the period studied by approximately 6,000 places, according to official statistics. The increase was for the most part in the number of long-term care places. The reason that no evidence of this increase appeared in the survey results could be that the surveys only covered individuals 15–75 years old, and those over 75 years old are the most likely to fill long-term places.

Among women a larger share were admitted for treatment, 13 per cent compared to 10 per cent of the men. The greatest share of patients was found among the oldest age group, 56–75 years old. The youngest age group (15–29 years old), had a somewhat higher percentage of patients than the middle aged, (30–55 years old.) Noteworthy differences between community types were not evident. Seven per cent of class I, 11 per cent of class II, and 14 per cent of class III had been admitted for hospital care.

Contact with a physician

Contact with a physician is here defined as an out-patient visit to a doctor. The question only referred to visits for treatment of personal health problems, and not for example, to visits for health certificates. Contact with a doctor during a hospital stay was not included. The percentage of the population that had been in contact with a doctor was 55 per cent in 1968 and 60 per cent in 1974 and 1981. Among women, a larger share reported visits to a doctor.

Ageing entails worsening health and therefore a greater need for health services. The percentages of visits to a doctor were greatest in the older group, 75 per cent of the older people and 50 per cent of the younger people had been in contact with a doctor during the previous year. Residents of large cities had the higest percentage of contacts with doctors, and no tendencies towards equalization were evident.

In 1968 class I had the most contacts with physicians (see Table 5.9). By 1974, and also in 1981, this trend had changed so that class III had the most contacts. The increase in contacts for classes II and III are statistically significant, also when the trends are standardized for age and sex.

Table 5.9 Percentages who visited a doctor during the previous 12 months in the different social classes and in the entire population, 15–75 years old, 1968, 1974, and 1981

	1968	1974	1981
Class I	57.6	56.5	52.6
Class II	53.9	59.5	58.9
Class III	54.8	61.8	61.3
Entire population	54.7	60.5	59.6

The availability of doctors increased markedly during the test period. In 1968 there were 9,840 practising doctors, or 124 per 100,000 inhabitants. In 1974 there were 13,260 practising doctors (162 per 100,000 inhabitants), and in 1981 18,300 (220 per 100,000). The number of practising doctors nearly doubled in 13 years.

The percentage increase in visits to doctors, especially in classes II and III may be an effect of improved availability. However, although the rate of increase in the number of practising doctors was the same between 1974 and 1981 as between 1968 and 1974, the increase in the percentages of visits to doctors occurred for the most part between 1968 and 1974.

The second control mechanism used by society, charges for health care, was amended in 1970 by the so-called 'Seven Crowns Reform' which was implemented to eliminate economic restraints on the usage of health care by setting the cost for all medical treatment to seven Swedish crowns (SEK). Another reason for the change in the percentages having contact with a doctor could be changing patterns of illness in different groups, and therefore a changing need for medical care. (for further discussion of this aspect, see the end of this chapter).

Contact with a nurse

The percentage of the population that visited a nurse for out-patient treatment increased substantially during the period. In 1968 13 per cent and in 1981 21 per cent of the population had visited a nurse during the past 12 months. Significant increases were found in nearly all of the occupation groups in classes II and III. The same relationship between the number of visits and the sex of the patient was evident here as with regard to visits to doctors discussed above. Women had a higher ratio of contact with a nurse, 16 per cent of the women in 1968 as compared to 10 per cent of the men. Substantial increases in the percentages with contact with nurses occurred for both sexes. In 1981, 24 per cent of the women and 18 per cent of the men had such contact during the previous year.

All age groups increased their contacts with nurses, and in 1981 the proportions were largest among the youngest and the oldest age groups. Residents in the country had the greatest share of contacts with nurses in all three surveys, which is the opposite of the trend for visits to doctors. The number of nurses more than doubled from 29,000 practising nurses in 1968 to 61,000 in 1981.

Is the increase in the percentage visiting a nurse due to the fact that groups that previously had no contact with health care services now have it? Or is it that people who previously visited the doctors now also visit a nurse? The percentage of the population that had visited a nurse but not a doctor was constant through the years at 5 per cent.

The largest increase in visits to a nurse was among people who also had visited a doctor. The largest percentage of people only visiting a nurse was found in the rural population, a fact consistent with the sparsity of doctors in these communities.

Contact with a Dentist

A rising percentage of the population visits a dentist. In 1968 55 per cent of the population went to dentists, in 1974 the figure was 61 per cent, and in 1981 67 per cent. The increase took place especially in classes II and III (see Table 5.10). However, the differences between the classes were still substantial in 1981. Among the groups that had a clearly lower than average number of visits were housewives and pensioners in class III.

Table 5.10 Percentages in the different classes and in the entire population, 15–75 years old, who visited a dentist in 1968, 1974, and 1981

	1968	1974	1981
Class I	83.3	78.1	80.4
Class II	62.7	68.4	73.7
Class III	46.2	53.2	60.5
Entire population	54.8	60.7	67.2

As was the case with visits to a nurse/doctor, women had a higher frequency of contact with dentists. No change in the sex ratios was evident. The percentages visiting a dentist decreased with advancing age, but also the differences between the age groups have been decreasing. In 1968 there was a 50 per cent gap between the oldest and the youngest age groups. By 1974 the gap had decreased to 40 per cent, and by 1981 to 35 per cent. In the youngest age group (15–29 years) 75 per cent had visited a dentist in all three survey years.

A question was also posed on the regularity with which people visited the dentist. No change was evident in the pattern as compared to that above. Those who reported visits to the dentist during the previous year also reported that visits were made regularly, that is, once a year.

A slight increase in the number of practising dentists occurred during the period: in 1968 there were 6,300 practising dentists, in 1974 7,180, and in 1981 there were 8,500 (a change from 79 to 102 per 100,000 inhabitants). A legislative dental reform was implemented in 1974 to reduce the fees for dental visits and treatment.

Is health care apportioned according to need?

Health care resources must be apportioned in some manner. The law requires that this apportionment be done in accordance with the needs of the entire population, and not according to the economic status, community, sex, or class of the patient. We have shown earlier that there were variations in the different groups' utilization of both in-patient and out-patient services, but no analysis was presented then of the different groups' actual need for health care.

No questions were asked about the individual's perception of their own health care needs in the surveys. In the following analysis we have therefore used a combined measurement of the 47 survey questions on perceived illnesses and ailments as a measurement of overall health. This can likewise be considered a rough measurement of the public's need of health care services.

A classification of this 'need measurement', where the first class included those with no symptoms and the fifth those with many symptoms or ailments,[8] revealed no major changes during the period. This is consistent with the conclusion earlier in the chapter that there was no major change in the health of the population during the period.

Table 5.11 Percentages of the population, 15-75 years old, in the respective health status classes who visited a doctor during the previous 12 months, for 1968, 1974, and 1981

	1	2	3	4	5
1968	22.7	43.9	56.1	64.8	82.1
1974	27.1	49.6	60.2	68.0	81.7
1981	27.1	48.6	57.6	70.2	83.6

The percentages of visits to a doctor in the five health classes increased betwen 1968 and 1974 in all classes except the fifth (see Table 5.11). The patterns in 1974 and 1981 were remarkably similar. The percentages of health care contacts increases slightly in each class, if contacts with nurses are included as well. It should be noted that about 30 per cent of the fourth class and 20 per cent of the fifth class had no contact at all with a doctor during the previous 12 months. This indicates an obvious need for health care that is not at present being satisfied.

If health care resources are being distributed in a fair way there should be no differences between utilization of services by different groups when their state of health is controlled for. An attempt to establish if this is the case was made with the assistance of a number of multiple regression analyses, which make it possible to control the influence of several factors simultaneously. In addition to the previously examined background factors (class, sex, age and type of community), state of health was also controlled. The state of health was measured with the combined symptom measurement mentioned above. The figures for visits to a doctor and/or nurse were used as the measure of health care utilization.[11]

Of the four background factors, sex had the greatest importance for state of health during each year, followed by age and class. Community type had little importance for general health.

When analysing health care utilization, state of health is the most important determinant. Only in 1968 was there a statistically significant difference in care utilization between the different social classes when state of health is controlled for. In this particular year class III had a lower degree of utilization than was to be expected from its state of health. Women had higher health care utilization than men in both 1968 and 1981 when health is held constant. Only in 1981 a minor difference in utilization is found between the age groups. Residents of rural areas made use of health care to a slightly lower degree in both 1968 and 1981 than was to be expected from their state of health.

The differences in health care utilization that existed in 1968 between social classes disappeared, but differences remained in 1981 between the sexes, age groups, and community types when their state of health is controlled for. The differences are, however, quite small, and the general impression conveyed is, therefore, that health care resources are being distributed roughly according to the public's actual needs.

Final comments

The most important point in this chapter is undoubtedly that the extent and distribution of health problems in the population was for the most part the same in 1981 as it was in 1968. On the basis of this result we shall, in conclusion, point out several important questions regarding the extent and distribution of health problems.

1. Why did public health not improve during the 1970s when funding for

health care increased from 6 per cent of GNP in 1968 to almost 9 per cent of GNP in 1981?

Perhaps the unchanged level of health is due to the fact that public health, unlike, for instance, education or housing, is difficult to influence in such a relatively short time span as 13 years. Another explanation could be that the efforts made in this area have been less effective than comparable efforts in other areas. A further possibility is that the additional resources have been used to increase salaries, hire additional personnel, and other such measures that have little direct influence on the percentage of sick people in the population.

It is also possible that expansion or improvement of health care cannot change the number of people who suffer from illnesses, which is what the survey examined, but can 'only' give them better care and perhaps shorter periods of sickness. One must also consider the possibility that social developments (for example, the amount of environmental pollution and toxic materials) have in practice reduced the potential for good health, and that the increased efforts in health care have merely held the number of sick people in the population at a constant level.

2. Why are there greater proportions of sick people in class III than in the other classes, and why are the differences between the classes so much greater among the elderly?

One conceivable explanation is that class III is employed in occupations that are subject to greater risks of accidents and physical strain, which after a time is reflected in a greater degree of illness. Another explanation could be that differences in the life-styles of the classes, such as eating habits, result in differences in general health. Even differences in knowledge regarding health problems and health care opportunities could be a factor.

3. Why are women ill to a greater extent than men?

One possible explanation is that sex roles control the individual's perception of health problems with the result that women have a lower tolerance to reduced health than men. This difference between the sexes could also be reinforced in the survey results if this sex role pattern were reflected in the reporting of illnesses during the interviews; in other words, if men were less likely to report and discuss their ailments. Sex roles could of course be responsible for the differences between the sexes without there being any actual differences of a purely medical type. Obviously there could also be biological dissimilarities that, wholly or partially, explain the differences in health between men and women.

Answering these questions is of primary importance if public health and well-being are to be further improved and the differences between groups are to be eliminated. Since good health is not a commodity that can be distributed from those that have it to those that do not, it is necessary instead to attack the causes of the systematic differences between the different groups. Starting from an awareness that these differences exist, society must seek to create conditions that provide all citizens with the same opportunities for good health and care, regardless of sex or class.

Notes

1. For a more complete discussion see S. Johansson 1970b, 7–11.
2. Those with impaired mobility all reported that they could not run 100 metres without great difficulty, and either that they could not walk 100 metres relatively briskly or not go up and down stairs without difficulty.
3. The higher the value of the rate, the greater the percentage of movement handicapped in the group in question. For example, if the rate for group A is 0.5 while group B has a rate of 2.0, the percentage of movement hindered is four times larger in group B. A rate of 1.0 means that the group in question has the same ratio of movement hindered as the population as a whole.
4. Interviewees were asked if during the previous 14 days they had had difficulty getting started in the morning, had felt particularly tired during the day and if they had felt extremely tired in the evening. Those responding affirmatively to all three question were labelled 'consistently fatigued'. This group represented between six and seven per cent of the population 15–75 years old during the entire period.
5. 'Severe pain' is defined as those individuals who during the previous 12 months had had serious problems with pain in at least one of the following parts of the body: shoulders, back/hips/sciatic or hands/elbows/legs/knees. In a corresponding manner those with 'serious circulatory problems' are those individuals who reported at least one serious problem of either chest pains, weak heart, high or low blood pressure, varicose veins, swollen legs, breathlessness, or dizziness. 'Serious stomach problems' are those who have responded that they have experienced serious stomach aches, nausea, diarrhoea, or vomiting. A disadvantage of these kinds of problem group definitions is that many minor ailments might be substantial. The results are nevertheless unchanged for the most even if we consider the exceptions.
6. Bad teeth is a combination of bad natural teeth, poor dentures, and no teeth.
7. Factor analyses have shown these six symptoms to be related.
8. Impaired mental well-being here means those with at least one severe or two minor ailments or symptoms.

9. The consumption of these medicines is to a large degree influenced by the doctor's willingness to prescribe them, since most of them are prescription drugs.
10. A minor ailment equals 1 point and a severe ailment 2 points. The classification was done according to the following scale: class 1 = 0–1 symptom points, class 2 = 2–3 symptom points, class 3 = 4–5 points, class 4 = 6–8 points, class 5 = 9 or more.
11. The result remains unchanged even if in-patient care is brought into the measurement of care utilization.

6

Employment and Working Hours

RUNE ÅBERG

Introduction

The importance of gainful employment for an individual's welfare is
obvious and indisputable, above all because such employment is the
basis of support. Those without employment are often, in one way or
another, dependent on other people for support. In certain cases this
dependency relationship can result in living conditions which involve a
lack of freedom, power, and fairness. For example, the demands of
women for employment have been formulated in such terms. The
individual's position in the labour market is also important during
periods of unemployment, sickness, or retirement and when the
individual for other reasons leaves the labour market. Employment is
normally the admission ticket to the social insurance system. In terms of
support, employment therefore has importance as both a direct and
indirect source of income. In addition, employment can involve
participation in a social community. By participating in working life, the
individual contributes to both his own welfare and the welfare of others.
To be unable to do this can make a person feel that he is unnecessary and
a social outcast. At best, participation can mean the opposite.
Employment can provide opportunities for self-realization through
contacts with other employees and through stimulating work. Naturally,
employment is also a resource on a collective level. The work which
people do lays the foundation for a society's material welfare and social
relations.

These ideas and similar ones have made employment a central
component of the general conception of welfare and have made it one of
the areas which people have attempted to influence through political
means for a long time. The level of ambition rose so much that in the
middle of the seventies the goal of 'full employment' had come to mean
'employment for everybody'. This is most clearly anticipated in the
government report which had that goal as its title (SOU 1975, 90). With
this definition, the rate of employment becomes an increasingly
important goal variable.

It should, however, be emphasized that employment is also a burden which takes time and energy. The more an individual's work drains his time and energy, the less is left over for other activities. Work can then become a hindrance which makes it impossible to satisfy other interests. The time an individual spends at work can also involve health risks, be monotonous, and hinder rather than stimulate personal development. A shortening of working hours is also a goal that has been striven after for many years. This goal is naturally most important for people with much to take care of during non-working hours — for example, parents of small children.

In recent years, the issue of employment for everybody has been connected with the issue of working hours. Some people claim that shorter working hours would allow more people to enter the labour market at the same time as this action would create more jobs. It is assumed that this would increase the employment level and, it is hoped, the unemployment level would decrease. An opposing point of view is that the number of jobs has no connection with working hours and that shortened working hours would not increase the scope for providing employment for everybody. We cannot determine which point of view is correct on the basis of our data but we can describe the actual trends regarding employment, working conditions, and working hours as well as how these areas changed for different population groups.

The level of employment

If one accepts the employment rate as a measure of the extent to which the goal of 'employment for everybody' has been fulfilled, then undeniably Sweden has succeeded quite well. From an international perspective, Sweden's employment rate is very high. Within the OECD it was among the highest even in 1960 and thereafter continued to increase faster than in other countries to a level of 79 per cent in 1980. During that year the average for the entire OECD was 65 per cent (OECD 1982).

The concept of the employment rate, however, is not entirely unambiguous. In the first place the employment rate depends on the basis on which it is calculated. A number of possibilities exist, and they are all to some extent arbitrary. The OECD uses the population between 15–64 years old. The census bureau and the Labour Force Surveys have used varying bases over the years, but since 1970 they have based their measurement on the population between 16 and 74 years old. Secondly, the employment rate is dependent on when a person shall be considered to be employed. Even here the definitions have changed over the years. Before 1970 the census bureau used, as its main definition, work giving rise to income or providing help in the business of the family for at least half of the normal working hours during the weeks of the measurement.

Thereafter they used the same definition as in the Labour Force Surveys, which is one hour of work for an employee or self-employed person and 15 hours for an assistant during the measurement week. (For a more detailed description of the definitions and populations used in different investigations, see SCB, *The Labour Market Statistics Yearbook)*.

In the Level of Living Surveys the individual's activity during the week prior to the interview week was charted. Everyone who, at some time during that week, was at work, temporarily absent, self-employed or an assistant was counted as employed. If this is accepted as the starting point for calculation of the employment rate of the population between 15 and 74 years old, the increase was not especially large; from 64 per cent to 69 per cent between 1968 and 1981. That the increase was not greater was due to the substantial increase in the number of pensioners. Between 1968 and 1981 their numbers increased by 366,000 or, as a percentage of the population from 15–74 years old, an increase from 13 per cent to 18 per cent (Table 6.1). If pensioners are excluded from the population base, one finds that the employment rate rose from 73 per cent to 84 per cent (based on Table 6.1). On the other hand, to look at the employment rate only according to this definition disguises the fact that many of the employed can also be classified in categories which are normally thought of as 'non-employed'. One example is an unemployed person who had a temporary job during the measurement week. Another example is a pensioner or student who worked a few hours during the week. Table 6.1 shows that these combinations of activity have increased over the years.

That some of the employed also could have been classified in other categories does not detract from the picture of the period studied as a period during which the employment level increased substantially. This even occurred at the same time as the trends in the labour market situation became worse. According to the Labour Force Surveys the total volume of work decreased from 140 million hours per week in 1963 to 125 million in 1981. Unemployment increased about one percentage point. Average participation in government labour market programmes increased from about 1 per cent of the labour force in the late 1960s to about 3 per cent in the early 1980s. Thus, the period showed both positive and negative tendencies from an employment point of view. The negative ones include increased competition for jobs and difficulties in holding unemployment down. The positive ones include the increased opportunities for employment. We shall take a little closer look at these tendencies.

Table 6.1 Employment in the adult population during the measurement week in 1968, 1974, and 1981

	1968		1974		1981	
	1000s	%	1000s	%	1000s	%
Only employed	3568	60.3	3811	62.7	3842	61.6
Employed and studying	110	1.9	140	2.3	203	3.3
Employed and unemployed	9	0.2	20	0.3	39	0.6
Employed and pensioner	101	1.7	90	1.5	199	3.2
Only studying	402	6.8	390	6.4	441	7.1
Studying and unemployed	3	0.0	5	0.1	16	0.3
Studying and pensioner	1	0.0	2	0.0	12	0.2
Only unemployed	60	1.0	77	1.3	92	1.5
Only pensioner[a]	751	12.7	909	15.0	1117	17.9
Housewives	843	14.2	576	9.5	247	4.0
Others outside the labour market	74	1.3	57	0.9	32	0.5
Population 15–74 years	5922	100.0	6076	100.0	6238	100.0

[a] This includes early pensioners but not part-time pensioners.

Unemployment

Information about the character and extent of unemployment has improved considerably because of the Labour Force Surveys which began in 1963. Continuous developments can best be studied with these measurements, issued quarterly, as a basis. Concise descriptions of the development of unemployment can be found in, for example, SCB 1981d and the *Labour Market Statistics Yearbook*. However, on certain points our data can provide complementary information. We are able to construct an unemployment measure which indicates the percentage of people unemployed at some time during the five years prior to the survey. In this way we can see long-term changes rather than short-term economic fluctuations. We are also able to examine unemployment in different social classes which is not possible with the Labour Force Surveys.

Unemployment described according to our unemployment measure reveals a picture where three tendencies appear. The first is that unemployment, at least among middle-aged and older men, seemed to decrease. We also know that their employment level decreased (SCB 1981d, 57). This is connected with, among other things, increased early retirement, which could be a result of structural economic changes and a difficult labour market situation for many older people. However, a previous study based on our material attributed limited importance to this factor (Hedström 1980). The transition to retirement has often been motivated by health reasons. The increased retirement of older men, however, probably helps to explain the fact that the number who have experienced unemployment among those left in the labour force has declined. The decreased unemployment rate among older men in class III could also be due to the fact that fewer of them are now in occupations with a high risk of unemployment, as is the case, for example, among construction workers.

Table 6.2 Percentage of those in the labour force in 1968, 1974, and 1981 who at any time were unemployed during the previous five-year period by sex, age, and class

Age	15–30			31–55			56–pension age		
Year	1968	1974	1981	1968	1974	1981	1968	1974	1981
Men									
Class I	4	4	19	8	2	2	2	0	0
Class II	8	19	9	6	8	7	8	5	4
Class III	19	26	21	16	18	13	16	14	10
Women									
Class I	4	16	12	1	3	3	0	0	0
Class II	5	14	14	2	7	4	0	4	0
Class III	9	17	18	7	9	8	3	6	2

The second tendency is that the risk of unemployment during the whole period is much higher among workers than among the other groups (Table 6.2). But among young people, the risk of unemployment has increased in classes I and II. Thus the differences in unemployment between the classes have decreased. It seems to have become harder for young people with a higher education to obtain employment without being unemployed for some time.

The third tendency is that the risk of unemployment for young women has increased substantially. This could be a result of decreased demand within the fields where women seek employment, but more likely, because they no longer choose to be housewives when there is a shortage of jobs and continue to search for employment.

The level of employment and types of working hours among women

One of the most important trends since the end of the 1960s is that the level of employment among women has continued to rise. Of all women between 20 and 64 yars old, 56 per cent were employed in 1968. By 1981 the figure had increased to 77 per cent. For men in the same age group, the employment level stayed at about 90 per cent the whole time. The employment level increase for the country as a whole is therefore due to the increased employment of women. This, in turn, is mainly because married/cohabiting women have begun to work to a greater extent. The economic motive for this became much stronger as a result of the individual tax reform of 1971. Before that year the tax base for the family was the sum of the income of spouses which gave a family with two income earners high marginal taxes. The opportunities for women to obtain employment have also been improved through the expansion of the child care system, the growth of the public sector, and the decrease in the number of children born.

In 1968 approximately 50 per cent of all married women were employed (Table 6.3). The employment level of mothers with small children was substantially less than that of women without small children. The class differences were also large. The employment level was lowest in class III, and it was especially low among mothers of small children in this class.

Table 6.3 Level of employment in 1968 and 1981 among married and cohabiting women, by household class and existence of small children. (The spouse who belonged to the 'highest' class was used as the basis of class for the household.) Percentages

	Employment level	
	1968	1981
With small children	34	78
Class I	42	83
Class II	41	85
Class III	26	67
Without small children	57	77
Class I	55	75
Class II	66	83
Class III	49	68
All	50	77

By 1981 the picture had changed. The level of employment had risen in all groups. In addition, mothers of small children were employed to the same extent as other married women. However, the class differences remained. Married women in class III still had a lower level of employment than those in the other two classes.

Another change is that the position of women in the labour market was characterized by a greater degree of permanence. Previously, women stayed at home for a longer period when they had children. It is apparent that currently the percentage of housewives only increases insignificantly among young women when reaching their most fertile years.

The rise in the level of employment among women is often assumed to be strongly related to the presence of part-time work. The idea is that part-time work makes it possible to combine housework and child care with employment. Because of demands from women, or as a way to recruit women for certain jobs, part-time employment is created. Part-time employees, that is those with a working week of less than 35 hours per week, made up 17 per cent of all employees in 1968 and 28 per cent in 1981.

There is nothing in our data which shows that the connection indicated between the increased employment of women and part-time employment is wrong, but at the same time it is doubtful whether it is sufficient as a total explanation of the increased level of employment. Among married women, with children and without, the increase in employment has occurred not only because more women entered part-time employment but also because as many entered full-time employment. Among employed, married women the share of part-time employees remained at about 55 per cent the whole time. On the other hand, among employed single women the level of part-time employment increased considerably — from 13 per cent ot 35 per cent. Their employment level remained constant at about 65 per cent of the whole time. Therefore, the increase in part-time employment seems to be only partly connected with the increased entry of housewives into the labour market on a part-time basis. It has also become more common for single women to work part-time.

Part-time employment is essentially a female phenomenon. Of all of the part-time employees in 1981, 85 per cent were women. Yet, this should not hide the fact that part-time employment has also increased among male employees. Among men the level of part-time employment increased from 3 per cent to 8 per cent between 1968 and 1981. As opposed to the situation among women, part-time employment is mainly found among older men. This is mainly a result of the part-time pension reform of 1976, which allowed people over 60 to receive a part-time pension. If special circumstances exist they can get it earlier. Among employed men over 55 years old, part-time work increased from 6 per cent to 23 per cent between 1968 and 1981.

Increased part-time employment among men has mainly occurred among the working class, both in industry and in the public sector. For women the increase has occurred within occupational fields where they have traditionally been overrepresented, that is, among salaried employees in the public sector and among service workers.

Sexual segregation in the labour market

The increased employment of women could be seen as an indication that the differences in welfare between men and women have decreased. However, the level of employment is a questionable indicator of this decrease. Increased employment of women is not, in most cases, accompanied by an equivalent decrease in housework (see Chapter 13). Also, women's participation in working life differs from that of men. The increased employment of women has, to a large extent, involved part-time work. Furthermore, women end up in different types of jobs from men. This sexual segregation in the labour market is of great importance regarding equality and will therefore be examined more closely in this section. Sexual segregation in the Swedish labour market was studied in detail by Jonung (1983). Through the use of the census data she showed that in 1975 approximately 70 per cent of all women would have had to change occupations in order to achieve the same occupational distribution as men. The occupations were classified into about 270 categories in accordance with the international standard classification (ISCO). In comparison with a number of other countries, especially the United States, England and West Germany, sexual segregation in Sweden seems to be relatively high. The report also showed that sexual segregation was even higher in 1960 (about 75 per cent would have had to change occupations) which indicates that some levelling off has occurred in recent years.

Our picture of sexual segregation differs on a number of points from Jonung's analysis, mainly because we use different occupational categories. The occupational groups we use are based on the class divisions which are useful for classifying occupations according to their character and benefits. Sexual segregation according to this occupational classification is thereby also an indication of socio-economic differences between men and women. It should also be stated that we worked with very large occupational categories, only 15 in all. This means that our measurements cannot be compared with those used by Jonung. We did not use the same measurement of inequality either. Instead of calculating the percentage of women who would have to change jobs in order to obtain the same occupational distribution as men, we determined the percentage of women who would have to trade jobs with men in order to obtain the same occupational distribution as existed among all employees at the time of the measurement. Of course, both measurements are logically related to each other.

Table 6.4 Distribution of all employed and employed women in various occupational groups and percentage of women employed in each occupational group in 1968 and 1981

	Distribution by occupational group				Proportion women	
	All		Women			
	1968	1981	1968	1981	1968	1981
Private prof. and exec.	3.3	4.1	1.0	1.1	11.7	11.6
Prof. in public employ.	3.1	4.8	1.6	3.1	19.3	28.6
Farmers	4.8	3.2	4.0	2.2	31.6	31.8
Small proprietors	7.4	7.0	4.9	4.3	24.7	27.7
Foremen	3.7	2.5	0.8	0.6	8.1	10.8
Priv. technical, clerical	12.8	13.1	15.1	14.5	44.4	50.1
Public lower salaried	10.1	15.7	17.6	25.0	66.1	71.6
Agricultural workers	5.7	2.6	5.5	1.4	36.2	25.5
Metal workers	9.5	8.1	2.7	3.0	10.6	16.7
Other manuf. workers	10.4	7.0	9.0	5.0	32.6	32.0
Construction workers	5.7	3.7	0.3	0.3	1.9	4.0
Workers in commerce	5.4	5.5	9.0	7.9	62.8	64.9
Other service workers	6.2	4.1	9.7	3.8	59.9	41.8
Workers in local govt.	7.9	14.3	16.0	24.5	76.6	77.3
Workers in central govt.	4.0	4.4	2.8	3.4	26.4	35.2
	100.0	100.0	100.0	100.0	37.8	45.2
N =	3687	4140	1392	1870		

Table 6.4 provides a description of the changes in the occupational structure between 1968 and 1981 as well as the occupational distribution of women. The table contains two opposing tendencies in segregation. The increased percentage of women in many occupations dominated by men and the decreased percentage of women in groups dominated by women leads to a decrease in segregation. We call this the 'composition effect'.

The other tendency, toward increased sexual segregation, is that occupations with an unequal sex distribution increased more in size than occupations with an equal distribution. This is referred to as the 'structural effect'.

From the standpoint of equality, it is the composition effect on which we should focus. Attempts to achieve a more equal distribution, as a rule, involve getting more women into male-dominated jobs and vice versa. The composition effect measures the extent to which this occurs. The figures in Table 6.4 (the columns on the right) show that in 7 out of

15 occupational groups the distribution became more equal — higher level public employees, small proprietors, foremen, technical and clerical personnel, metal workers, construction workers, and workers in state employment. In two groups the distribution clearly became more unequal — salaried employees in the public sector and smallholders. The more unequal distribution among smallholders and forestry workers is a result of the decreased number of helping wives in this category. Therefore, the only occupational group in which the trend has definitely been towards greater inequality is among salaried employees in the public sector.

The occupational groups which grew the most are public salaried employees and workers in local government — groups which have a substantial overrepresentation of women. Another group which grew is the higher level public employees in which there is a substantial underrepresentation of women. Such structural changes lead to increased sexual segregation.

To obtain a picture of the net changes during the period we used a segregation measure called the concentration index (CT). As already mentioned this index shows the percentage of women who would have to trade occupational groups with men so that women, and therefore men as well, would be distributed among the different occupational groups in the same manner. To provide an idea of the relative importance of the composition effect and the structural effect, we shall first calculate how the index changes if we assume an unchanged occupational distribution which provides the composition effect (CE). Then we shall calculate how the index changes if we assume that the sex distribution in each occupational group has not changed. This shows the structural effect (SE). The sum of both of these effects would be identical with the total effect if no interaction effects occurred. The interaction effect (I) means that the percentage of women changes in different ways in groups which increase in size compared with groups which decrease or stay the same size.

Table 6.5 Changes in concentration index between 1968 and 1981 and that index broken down by structural, compositional, and interactional effects

Period	CT	CE	SE	I
1968–1974	− 0.7	− 0.3	+ 5.6	− 6.0
1974–1981	− 1.4	− 1.4	+ 3.8	− 3.8
1968–1981	− 2.1	− 1.2	+ 10.0	− 10.9

Changes in the concentration index are shown in Table 6.5. In 1968

25.4 per cent of all women would have had to trade their jobs with men so that men and women, within the framework of the actual occupational distribution, would have the same occupational distribution. By 1981 that figure had decreased to 23.3 per cent. Accordingly, the index decreased 2.1 per cent, which indicates a minor decrease in sexual segregation. (The index's absolute values are shown in Table 6.6)

This relatively modest change, however, conceals changes in different directions in the structural, composition, and interaction effects. If structural changes alone had controlled the trend, sexual segregation would have increased substantially. The concentration index would then have increased to 35 per cent. But if the development had been determined solely by other patterns of choice and recruitment, sexual segregation would have decreased. The concentration index would then have decreased to 24.2 per cent. The relatively high values of the interaction effects suggest that in those cases in which occupational groups with low female representation have grown, this has meant an extra chance for women to enter the occupation, so that the percentage of women in those groups has increased.

The main tendency in our material corresponds with Jonung's results; the structural effect operated in the direction of increased inequality in sexual segregation while the choice and recruitment pattern showed increased equality. As mentioned earlier, one cannot expect direct correspondence between the two analyses because we used a different measure of inequality, a different occupational classification system with fewer categories and studied a later period. Our use of such broad occupational categories could also conceal the possibility that sexual segregation within more specific occupational groups may have changed.

Despite these differences, we are able to draw the conclusion that since the beginning of the 1960s changes have occurred in patterns of choice and recruitment in the labour market which have led toward decreased sexual segregation. It also seems that these changes increased in the later part of the 1970s. The levelling off effect has, however, been counteracted by the structural changes which occurred, for example, the considerable expansion of the public sector. However, expansion of occupations with female underrepresentation, have, in a number of cases, increased recruitment of women. This was the case, for example, among higher level public employees.

There are many different factors which help to explain male and female employment in different types of jobs. One is that they are socialised in different ways as they grow up and they therefore choose different educational paths and occupations. Another is that they have different roles in the family. Women have always had and still have the primary responsibility for child care and housework while men have been able to devote themselves to their jobs more whole-heartedly. This has led not only to differences in patterns of choice between the sexes but has also influenced employers in their recruitment decisions. The 'dual labour market theory' which has been used, especially in the United States, to explain sexual segregation on the labour market has taken these aspects into account (Roos 1981). The argument is based on the idea that there is a set of entry jobs on the labour market of which some lead to careers and some do not. The fact that women have a greater responsibility for the home results in employers preferring men for the career jobs. This leads to discrimination against women. Also, women do not succeed as well as men when they get these career jobs because of the reasons given above and because their dual roles have lowered their competitive drive. Furthermore, the occurrence of more subtle discrimination by men in the workplace is not unusual, which can make it difficult for women to assert themselves (Liljeström and Dahlström, 1981).

All these factors certainly contribute to the maintenance of sexual segregation on the Swedish labour market, but the data presented earlier indicate, nevertheless, that certain changes have occurred in recent years. Furthermore, the implication of the dual labour market theory does not, on one point, seem to fit the Swedish labour market. If differences are not only the result of unequal recruitment to entry jobs but also differences in occupational mobility during the rest of working life, then sexual segregation within each cohort should increase as time passes. This is not the case.

Table 6.6 Concentration index (CT) in different cohorts in 1968, 1974, and 1981

Age interval in 1968	1968	1974	1981
			23.0
		22.4	22.0
28–38	25.1	25.9	23.1
21–31	26.9	26.8	
15–25	31.6		
All employees	25.4	24.7	23.3

In Table 6.6 we have shown sexual segregation in several different cohorts. This means that the table is constructed so that the concentration index is calculated for 1968, 1974, and 1981 for those who in 1968 were 15–25, 21–31, and 28–38 years old. For each year the calculations have been based on all employees within each cohort. In the table, sexual segregation tends to decrease in each cohort, which indicates that occupational mobility tends to level off during working life rather than the opposite.

To sum up, our data indicate that in recent years changes toward decreased sex differences have occurred on the Swedish labour market. Many of these changes have been concealed by changes in the occupational structure which have strengthened sexual inequality. On the whole this means that sexual segregation remains substantial.

Changes in ordinary working hours among employees

Earlier in this chapter we showed that a growing percentage of employees have begun to work part-time. But even within the forms of working hours, full-time and part-time, changes have occurred in both ordinary and actual working hours. There are many factors which may have contributed to these changes, for example, changed occupational distribution, changed demand structure, changes in the labour force's composition, the individual tax reform, new laws on working hours, value changes in the labour force, a lower birth-rate, changes in child care arrangements, and changes in the pension rules. In this section we shall describe the changes which have occurred in working hours and only comment sparingly on the causes. Whether working hours really change in accordance with people's desires is also an important question. This probably presupposes that people can vary their working hours during different phases of life. Against this background, Gösta Rehn and others have stated that making working life more flexible is an important political reform. Here we shall try to describe how flexible working hours are and the extent to which people are satisfied with their working hours.

We can first conclude that, on average, ordinary working hours for part-time employees increased from 20.1 hours per week to 22.7 hours between 1968 and 1981 (Table 6.7). The average deviation from this mean decreased from 8.5 to 6.6 hours. The percentage with long part-time working hours (more than 20 hours) increased greatly. This means that part-time employees increased their working hours and that the differences between them decreased, especially because the percentage with shorter part-time working hours decreased.

Secondly, the ordinary working hours of full-time employees have decreased, which of course was the purpose of the amendments to the laws on working hours that were passed during the period studied. The law on working hours which came into effect in 1966 established the norm of a 42.5-hour working week. Two years later, in 1968, the

Table 6.7 Ordinary working hours of employees in 1968, 1974 and 1981

	1968	1974	1981
Part-time employees			
Average working hours	20.1	20.8	22.7
Average deviation in hours	8.5	7.5	6.6
Percentage with long part-time work (21–34 hours)	63%	73%	84%
Full-time employees			
Average working hours	42.7	40.3	40.1
Average deviation in hours	3.5	2.7	2.9
Percentage with more than 40.0 hours	75%	10%	8%
Percentage with more than 42.5 hours	59%	5%	1%

Working Hours Commission of 1963 proposed a law on working hours which would apply to the entire labour market, something which did not exist before. The new law meant that the working week would be 40 hours. This reduction was carried out in two stages of 1 hour 15 minutes each in 1971 and 1972. It should be noted that the law is not mandatory which means that the labour organizations and employers can make agreements regarding working hours which deviate from the law.

The first survey, in 1968, showed that many employees had longer working hours than the stipulated 42.5 hours. However, the years between 1968 and 1974 involved substantial changes in this regard. The average working week decreased. Only a small group still had extremely long working hours and the deviation from the mean value decreased (Table 6.7).

In order to gain an idea of satisfaction with working hours, the following question was posed: 'Does your normal working week of — hours suit you best, or would a shorter or longer working week suit you better? We are assuming that your salary would decrease or increase to a similar extent.' The answers to this question, which was posed only in 1974 and 1981, show that no major changes have occurred between the years except in one respect: an increasing percentage of the few women who still have a short part-time working week are dissatisfied and want to work more. This points towards a continued increase in the average working week for part-time employees (Table 6.8).

Satisfaction with working hours is, on average, somewhat lower among full-time employees than among part-time employees. While part-time employees most often desire longer working hours, many full-time employees want shorter working hours (Table 6.8). Especially women with full-time jobs desire shorter working hours. As expected,

Table 6.8 Satisfaction with working hours, by sex and form of working hours in 1974 and 1981. Percentages

Ordinary working hours[a]	Men				Women				All	
	Short		Long		Short		Long			
	1974	1981	1974	1981	1974	1981	1974	1981	1974	1981
Part-time employees										
Currently satisfied	(95)	91	69	87	84	75	88	87	85	86
Shorter hours desired	(0)	3	9	3	1	1	4	4	4	3
Longer hours desired	(5)	6	22	10	15	24	8	9	11	11
	100	100	100	100	100	100	100	100	100	100
Full-time employees										
Currently satisfied	86	87	77	79	72	72	69	62	81	81
Shorter hours desired	12	10	23	19	27	27	31	36	17	17
Longer hours desired	2	3	0	2	1	1	0	2	2	2
	100	100	100	100	100	100	100	100	100	100

[a] Short: for part-time employees 1–19 hours, for full-time employees 35–40 hours.

Long: for part-time employees 20–34 hours, for full-time employees more than 40 hours.

dissatisfaction with long working hours is especially great among women with full-time jobs and children at home. Of these women, 35 per cent wanted shorter working hours. Among men with children and full-time jobs the equivalent figure was 12 per cent. The figures, which apply to 1981, were essentially the same in 1974.

These data show that many have the working hours they desire, but also that a fairly large minority wants to change their work load. Of all employees 14 per cent wanted shorter working hours in 1974 (15 per cent in 1981), while two per cent wanted longer working hours (five per cent in

1981). Therefore, between 16 per cent and 20 per cent wanted to change their working hours.

How do these findings relate to actual behaviour? Do individuals change their working hours in the manner one would expect based on the data above? Our material shows that some increase occured among the percentage of employees who changed their form of working hours. Above all it was full-time employees who switched to part-time employment. Between 1968 and 1974, 8 per cent of them swtiched to part-time work. Between 1974 and 1981 17 per cent switched to part-time work. This is mainly a result of the increased number of part-time pensioners. There is also a tendency among people with shorter part-time working hours to increase their hours. 66 per cent of them increased their working hours between 1968 and 1974. Between 1974 and 1981, 80 per cent switched to longer working hours. Among people with long part-time working hours, about 30 per cent changed to full-time and about five per cent switched to short part-time working hours. This pattern was stable. The net effect for employees as a whole is a slight movement toward shorter working hours. This is also the change which the employed as a whole desired.

From a broader perspective these changes in ordinary working hours are not, however, especially widespread. The figures measure changes over six and seven years respectively. The figure for one year is much less. During 1967, 2 per cent of all employees had been employed on both a full-time and part-time basis, a figure which increased to 4 per cent in 1980. The latter figure corresponds to approximately 150,000 people. But one should also remember that changes regarding working hours have occurred within each category of employment. On average about 50 per cent had exactly the same working hours in 1974 as in 1981. Those who increased their working hours, 21 per cent of all employees on both occastions, averaged 9.4 hours more per week. The remaining 29 per cent decreased their working hours by 9.5 hours per week. Partly, however, these high numbers are an overestimation caused by measurement errors and in many cases the changes are small, but to some extent they certainly reflect actual use of the possibilities provided by the law on working hours for individual adjustment of working hours.

Employees' actual working hours

The working hours which are actually performed are not the same as ordinary working hours. In addition to ordinary working hours there is overtime work, small second jobs, and preparatory work. On the minu;

side there is absence from work. We shall conclude this chapter by describing the changes in the different components of actual working hours.

The variations in overtime work are limited by the law on working hours. The general rule is that 50 hours per month, but no more than 150 hours per calendar year, is allowed. However, deviations from this rule are allowed if they are contained in a collective bargaining agreement or are approved by the National Board of Industrial Safety.

Second jobs, on the other hand, are often not regulated by legislation. In most cases it is up to the individual to determine whether or not he will take on such jobs and, of course, not everyone has the same opportunities to do so.

It has been assumed that because of 'the employment security laws' (see Chapter 7) and difficulties in recruiting desirable employees employers have become more interested in regulating the variations in their labour needs through the use of overtime work and second jobs. On the other hand one can presume that high marginal income taxes have reduced the inducements for these types of jobs.

Compensation for preparatory work is generally considered to be included within the normal salary. Such work is not dependent on the demand for labour either. Rather it is an attribute of certain types of occupations such as teaching. This also applies to overtime work.

As a whole, overtime work, extra work, and preparatory work make up between 5 and 8 per cent of employees total volume of work. No regular measurement of these types of work is included in the continuous labour market statistics. Therefore, it is not known how much they vary during economic cycles. However, our data indicate a certain stability through the years. Overtime work and extra work increased only marginally during the boom year of 1974 (table 6.9). This change was insignificant. This indicates that the extent of this type of work is only slightly affected by the demand for labour. Nor does the presumed impairment of the incentives for additional work seem to have led to a significant decrease of overtime or extra work in 1981.

It seems more likely that it is the family situation and the type of work which control the variations. Above all men, especially those with full-time employment, are the ones who have extra work and overtime work. Also, throughout the survey such work is most common in class I and least common in class III. This applied to an even greater extent to preparatory work. On this point, class explained about 20 per cent of the variation during the two later years.

Absence from work, the negative factor in this context, increased over the years. The percentage of employees who were absent from work at least one day during the week prior to the interview was 9.6 per cent in

Table 6.9 Overtime, extra work, and preparatory work, by sex and form of working hours in 1968, 1974, and 1981

	Percentage of employees in each category			Average hours/week for those with >0 hours		
	1968	1974	1981	1968	1974	1981
Overtime						
Men, full-time	19	20	17	5.2	6.6	6.2
part-time	16	10	9	(4.7)	(7.2)	(8.4)
Women, full-time	10	12	10	3.8	4.9	5.5
part-time	6	10	8	5.0	5.2	5.0
All[a]	15	16	13	5.0	6.2	6.0
Extra work						
Men, full-time	7	6	7	10.3	11.9	9.8
part-time	16	17	8	(11.4)	(12.8)	(14.6)
Women, full-time	3	2	4	(7.0)	(11.0)	6.0
part-time	3	4	5	(7.2)	(7.4)	8.0
All	5	5	5	9.7	11.2	9.1
Preparatory work						
Men, full-time	7	7	7	4.9	4.9	5.5
part-time	21	22	7	(9.1)	(8.6)	(4.8)
Women, full-time	4	6	7	7.6	5.0	4.8
part-time	5	7	6	(5.8)	5.8	4.8
All	6	7	7	5.8	5.4	5.2

[a] All = all employed, as the basis for calculation of the percentages.

1968, 10.2 per cent in 1974 and 14.4 per cent in 1981. Many different factors have affected this trend. New reforms and legislation are probably among the most important.

In the first place, the Law on Vacations was amended in 1978. In general, the amendment meant that vacations were lengthened from four to five weeks. This was mainly of importance in the private sector. Many groups in the public sector already had agreements which included longer vacations. The new law also involved improvements for part-time and short-term employees since vacations were assured even during the first year of employment.

Secondly, the Law on Parental Time Off was amended. The important amendments were passed in 1977 and 1979. The right to paid time off was regulated in the first law. Principally, this means that in connection with the birth of a child, parents have the right to a total of 180 days off. Above this, a total of 90 days off can be granted until the child has reached the age of 8 years old. For temporary care of sick children, a maximum of 60 days per child a year can be granted. The latter law also provides the right to unpaid time off until the child is 1.5 years old. In addition employees have the right to a six-hour working day until the child is eight years old or has finished his first year in school.

Thirdly, employees have a right to time off for their own education. The law, which came into effect in 1975, gives employees who want to educate themselves the right to the necessary unlimited time off from their employment. In the 1974 law regarding employees in the workplace with union positions, the right to the necessary time off for carrying out their union functions was established. Furthermore, a 1973 law established the right of immigrants to time off for language education.

As a fourth factor, the part-time pension reform of 1975 should be mentioned. If the employer has given his approval, this provides employees from 60–64 years old the right to a part-time pension if they decrease their working week at least 5 hours but continue to work at least 17 hours.

All these reforms plus the increase in part-time employment have affected the level of absenteeism. In the 1981 survey, the people who were absent from work at least one day during the previous week, were asked about the reason for their absence. The answers to these questions give us an idea about the average working week during the spring of 1981 with regard to absence from work (Table 6.10).

From the table we can see that a relatively large percentage of the absences occurred on paid holidays. In this case, this is a result of the many interviews which were done the week after Easter week. It also explains the relatively large percentage who took out vacation days. An additional large percentage of absences were due to 'a workfree day because of shiftwork'. Many of the days off for part-time employees fall into this category. If we only look at Tuesdays and Wednesdays, which were not holidays, we can conclude that these workfree days constituted about 36 per cent of all absences. Absences due to sickness made up 28 per cent and those due to time off constituted 24 per cent.

Since part-time employees have more workfree days than full-time employees, the absence total is higher among part-time employees. However, this only applies to short-term absences. Regarding long-term absences (absent for the entire week) there were no major differences between full-time and part-time employees. In addition we found that men working full-time were absent less than men working part-time and women in general (Table 6.11). To get a better picture of absenteeism we took a closer look at the reasons for absences among men and women in different classes. We found fairly large differences between the classes as well as between men and women. The higher rate of short absences

Table 6.10 Reasons for absence from work among employees during the week before the interview in 1981. Percentages

	Mon	Tue	Wed	Thu	Fri	Sat	Sun
Not absent	71.6	76.9	76.7	65.1	57.5	10.8	7.3
Workfree holiday	5.9	0.0	0.0	11.3	10.5	76.7	81.0
Workfree day due to shiftwork	7.2	6.8	6.3	6.5	8.0	4.5	4.5
Earned compensatory leave	0.5	0.6	0.7	0.9	5.5	0.2	0.1
Vacation day	4.4	4.6	4.5	5.7	1.7	1.3	—
Sickness with pay	4.3	5.1	5.1	5.1	5.1	2.7	2.5
Sickness without pay	0.2	0.1	0.2	0.2	0.3	0.1	0.1
Laid off	0.4	0.4	0.6	0.7	0.2	0.2	—
Absent for child care	2.2	2.2	2.2	2.0	2.2	1.1	1.1
Absent for studies	1.0	0.9	0.9	0.8	0.9	0.5	0.4
Absent for other reasons	1.2	1.3	1.4	1.4	1.6	0.8	0.6
Other absences	1.3	1.3	1.5	1.6	2.1	0.7	0.7

Table 6.11 Absenteeism, by sex and working hours in 1968, 1974, and 1981. Percentages

	Absent				
	All week			Tuesday	
	1968	1974	1981	1974	1981
Men, full-time	8.4	8.7	11.3	12.4	15.6
part-time	6.5	11.8	18.7	37.8	38.3
Women, full-time	11.0	12.1	17.1	18.9	23.3
part-time	12.3	11.4	17.2	31.0	36.1
All[a]	9.6	10.1	14.4	18.1	23.3

[a] All = all employed, as the basis for calculation.

among women is because they are sick more often. Women in class III have an especially high rate of absences owing to sickness. Moreover, the predominant portion of time off for child care was taken by women. Also, time off for studies is more usual among women (Table 6.12).

We shall now summarize the net effect of all the changes in the components of actual working hours that we have decribed by examining how the net working hours have changed. The net working hours are the sum of time in the workplace, minus times for breaks, plus overtime, preparatory work, and extra work. The trends in net working hours for men and women in both part-time and full-time employment appears in

Table 6.12 Reasons for absence, by sex and class on Tuesday of the measurement week in 1981. Percentages

Class	Men			Women		
	I	II	III	I	II	III
Not absent	83.6	84.8	81.3	71.7	76.6	64.7
Absent for child care	0.0	0.5	0.4	7.3	4.4	3.8
Absent for studies	0.4	0.4	0.5	2.9	0.9	1.8
Sick	1.6	3.8	5.8	3.2	3.8	7.6
Other reasons	14.4	10.5	12.0	14.8	14.4	22.1

Table 6.13 Average net working hours in 1968, 1974, and 1981, by sex and form of working hours

	1968	1974	1981
Men, full-time	42.4	38.3	36.6
part-time	22.9	23.6	23.9
Women, full-time	38.8	36.1	34.2
part-time	19.8	20.8	21.9
All of those with full-time employment	41.4	37.6	35.8
All of those with part-time employment	20.2	21.2	22.2
All[a]	37.8	34.2	32.2

[a] All = all employed, as the basis of calculation

Table 6.13. The average net working hours for part-time employees of both sexes increased. As expected, the average net working hours for full-time employees decreased. But the decrease is larger than one would have expected against the background of the changes in the average ordinary working hours. The actual net working hours for full-time employees was always less than the average ordinary working hours, but the deviation increased. If the figures in Table 6.13 are compared with those in Table 6.7 one finds that the deviation was 1.3 hours in 1968, 2.7 hours in 1974 and 4.3 hours in 1981. The reason for this has not yet been investigated. (This problem is also discussed in Chapter 14 in connection with an analysis of the trend in gross working hours.)

A concise picture of the development of net working hours is given in Figure 6.1. It clearly shows a shift in the distribution of net working hours that resulted in a substantial decrease in the most usual working hours between 1968 and 1974 while no such change appeared in 1981. We can also see how the 'part-time humps' for shorter and longer part-time

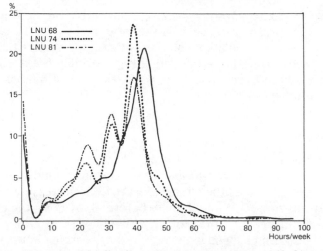

Fig. 6.1. Distribution of net working hours 1968–81

employment increased with the years. Finally, we should note that the percentage of people with extremely long working hours, 45 hours or more, decreased considerably. In absolute numbers they decreased from about 670,000 in 1968 to about 300,000 in 1981.

In concluding we shall examine which people have extremely long net working hours, defined here as 45 hours or more during the measurement week, as well as the changes which may have occurred. For this purpose, we shall use the regression approach described earlier (Chapter 2).

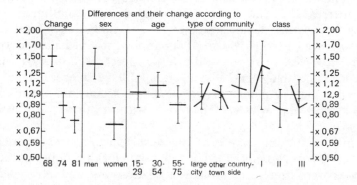
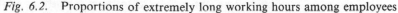

Fig. 6.2. Proportions of extremely long working hours among employees

Against the background of our earlier description of part-time work, extra work, overtime, preparatory work, and absenteeism, it is hardly surprising that we found long, net working hours to be concentrated among men and, to some extent, among people in class I (Figure 6.2). Furthermore, the regression analysis shows that middle-aged in class I are heavily overrepresented among those with extremely long net working hours. Middle-aged women in class II have the lowest rate of long working hours. Extremely long working hours are more than four times as usual in the former category as in the latter category. The changes in differences between population categories that have occurred during the years are, above all, that extremely long working hours have been increasingly concentrated in class I and have increased in large cities and decreased in other cities.

Summary

In this chapter we have described how working life changed in certain important respects between 1968 and 1981. The most important change is that women have entered the labour market to an increasing extent and established a stronger foothold than before. However, their working conditions still differ from those of men. We have shown the substantial differences between men and women regarding working hours and types of occupation. Part-time employment is much more common among women than men, but we have also been able to show that the increased level of employment among married women has resulted in equivalent increases in the percentage employed full-time and the percentage employed part-time. We have also shown that sexual segregation in the Swedish labour market is substantial even though it has decreased to some extent. There are two conflicting tendencies in this regard. On the one hand, the increased employment of women is connected with the expansion of occupations that were already dominated by women. On the other hand, women have entered into occupations dominated by men to an increased extent. That more women have definitely entered working life was also demonstrated by the fact that an increasing number had experienced unemployment. This applied in particular to younger women. However, there was still a larger percentage of men who had experienced unemployment. Men in class III have an especially high risk of unemployment. Among younger people, it seems that unemployment is now something which even those with a higher education do experience.

Another important feature of the developments between 1968 and 1981 was that working hours changed. The working hours of full-time employees were decreased through legislation and additional decreases also seem to have occurred. The extremely long working hours which were fairly common in 1968 were reduced substantially. Among the increasing number of part-time employees, the trend is in the opposite direction — they seem to be increasing their working hours. Regarding desired changes in working hours, full-time employees say that they want shorter hours and part-time employees tend to want longer hours. These are also the direction in which most individual changes in working hours occurred.

7

Working Conditions

RUNE ÅBERG

Introduction

Towards the end of the 1960s conditions in working life, and especially issues regarding the work environment, began to take a central position in public debate. A series of work environment studies, initiated by the labour union organizations, and the results of the first Level of Living Survey formed an important basis of information in this debate.

Intensive work on reforms to improve working conditions followed in the early 1970s. Various new laws were passed including the Employment Protection Act, which made it more difficult to lay people off, and regulated the order of such lay-offs in cases where these could not be avoided, the Joint Regulation of Working Life Act giving the unions a legal right to obtain information and negotiate on all matters concerning their working conditions, the Trade Union Representatives Act, which gave union representitives a legal right to be absent from work without reduction in pay for various union activities, and the Work Environment Act. This last act came into effect in 1978, but parts of it were already applicable by 1974. This law, lays down certain general aims while leaving methods of attaining them flexible, and has the National Board of Industrial Safety and the Occupation Inspection Board as its supervisory authorities. In places of work, the task is carried out by safety committees and safety representatives. Their job is to supervise the work environment and participate in the planning of new work premises and purchases of new machinery. In addition to the rulings of the work environment laws, there may also be agreements between the parties in the labour markets. Since 1971 the economic resources for measures to improve the work environment have come from a payroll tax that is 0.1 per cent of the salaries paid. The money is used, among other things, to cover the government's costs for the organization mentioned above and by the Worker's Safety Fund which is responsible for research, certain types of education and information within the field. Since 1975 employers have also been able to obtain guaranteed loans for improving the work environment.

One important aspect of the new Work Environment Act is that the concept of the work environment was given a very broad definition. One basic idea is that work, to the greatest possible extent, should be risk-free both physically and mentally, yet it should also allow for personal commitment, pleasure in one's work, and personal development. Stress and isolation are to be counteracted and one should strive to organize work so that employees themselves can influence their own working arrangements. Even the other laws mentioned, employment security, and opportunities to influence working life, are meant to contribute to the achievement of this public goal.

However, it was not only in public debate and in union and political reform work that issues regarding working life played a central role during the 1970s. Research in the field also became more lively. One of the important issues involved changes in the nature of work, and what this meant regarding mental demands and possibilities of utilizing skills. H. Braverman's *Labour and Monopoly Capital* (1974), came to have a great deal of influence. His thesis about the 'degradation' of work came to be accepted by many people. The thesis, in outline form, states that the capitalisitic order of produciton necessitates a continual labour-organizational trend in a 'Tayloristic' spirit with increased division of labour and increased control as important features as well as a technological trend in which the most profitable techniques, such as computers and automation, are used. This is assumed to lead to monotony and the removal of intellectual content from many types of manual tasks; in other words, they are degraded. Intellectual functions are thereby concentrated in a smaller number of jobs which leads to polarization between the many unqualified, monotonous, and heavily controlled jobs and the few stimulating and creative jobs.

Braverman's degradation thesis ran counter to the dominant idea in the 1960s according to which technological development would do away with unqualified, routine jobs or at least reduce their number substantially. Instead, new technology was not only to lead to an increased demand for skills in the labour force but also to greater freedom, since the new technology would not tie the individual down so much, for example to an assembly line, but would give the worker more supervisory functions. Of course, the new technology was to result in fewer industrial jobs but then the service sector would increase instead — a field with relatively more stimulating jobs. R. Blauner's *Alienation and Freedom* (1964) is usually mentioned as the work which has been the most important in the spreading of this idea.

One idea which implies a trend different from Braverman's can also be found in neo-classical economic theory and the expected effects of an increase in the general level of education according to this theory. If the public's level of education is increased so that the supply of well-educated people exceeds the demand, there is a downward pressure on salaries related to jobs with higher skill levels. A relatively low supply of workers with lower eduations leads to the opposite result among jobs with lower levels of skill. Their relative salaries then increase. In relation to their marginal productivity, many of these jobs will become too expensive and will therefore disappear. In accordance with the same type of reasoning it is assumed that the number of highly qualified jobs will increase. The net effect of a general increase in the level of education is therefore assumed to be an 'upgrading' and not a 'degrading'.

But it is not only an increase in the level of education which can lead to an upgrading in this indirect manner. There are also other factors which can raise the relative salary level of those with less skilled jobs. A solidaristic wage policy, pursued in Sweden during the fifties and sixties is one such example. It has often been claimed that the simpler jobs have become too expensive for employers and have therefore decreased so much that difficulties have arisen in the employment of young people and others without special skills. Thus there are different opinions about both the nature of jobs and the factors which cause change.

As we now proceed to examine how working conditions changed between 1968 and 1981[1] we shall not test any of the theories mentioned nor make any more thorough analyses of the effects of the political reforms that have been passed. But we shall try to describe the trends in terms which are relevant to a continued discussion of these issues. We have therefore allowed our descriptions to be influenced by both the general intentions behind the work environment reforms and the debate about job qualification requirements.

Both in concrete reforms and in public consciousness, the work environment has long been connected with the physical work environment and the physical stress to which the individual has been subjected. This is the first field we shall cover in our analysis. Other fields which are normally included within the broader work environment concept are mental stress from work, job qualification requirements, and job autonomy. We also have certain data regarding these factors which will be presented in the sections to follow.

Before the results are presented we shall briefly review some methodological problems. The first involves various ways of interpreting general trends. For example, if the percentage of people with monotonous jobs changes, this could be a result of change, in the job itself (the position). A particular job can change in character. This 'positional effect' is measured through changes *within* individual occupations, in our example via the percentage of monotonous jobs per occupational group. Each of the 15 occupational groups contains several independent occupations, which is why the positional effect observed by us is an approximation. However, the number of monotonous jobs can also increase or decrease because certain types of jobs disappear and other types are created. By studying the change in the percentage of jobs between occupations it is possible to measure these 'structural effects'.

Secondly, a change in the number of monotonous jobs can also be dependent on the interviewees (the individuals). In this case two problems can arise. In the first place, certain jobs can be overrepresented in our sample because of absences and part-time employment. If a job is so monotonous that the employee takes a leave of absence and is replaced by two part-time employees, the chances suddenly become three times greater that someone with that job will show up in our sample.[2] In the second place the answers in this area are partly based on the individual's subjective evaluation of his job situation. A change in personnel in a certain type of job can thus lead to registration of a change in the degree of monotony which is not really related to the job itself. Thus, a change in the aspiration level can also lead to the same effect.

This measurement problem has been the subject of a number of methodological studies which have come to the obvious conclusion that fact questions (for example, 'Must one be able to lift 60 kilos to be able to do your job?') are less sensitive to variations in individual evaluations and aspiration levels than subjective questions such as: 'Do you have problems with . . .?' We did not use qustions of the latter kind in our survey. However, even questions which do not involve a directly subjective evaluation can include subjective features. For example, 'is your job monotonous?'. There are no simple solutions to these problems. One must simply accept the fact that there is an interplay between the jobs and individuals being measured and interpret the results accordingly. This is of great importance in studying changes over time. One cannot be certain of the extent to which the changes are a result of changes in the subjective evaluations or changes in the character of the job.

The work environment debate in the 1970s is generally considered to have raised the aspiration levels of the population (Björkman and Lundkvist 1981; Wikman 1982). If this is true then the observed improvements can also, in general, be interpreted as actual improvements. On the other hand changes for the worse are more difficult to interpret. They could result from an actual deterioration, but they could also be a result of increased aspirations.

A third methodological problem involves the interpretation of data about the chances/risks of different population groups ending up in certain types of jobs, such as monotonous jobs. In this case the analysis will be made in accordance with the regression model presented in Chapter 2. However, only sex, age, and community type will be used as independent variables here. It would have been desirable to use occupation in the regression analysis, but this would have required a much more differentiated classification of occupations than our three-part class code. Therefore, we have a measurement of the net effect of all the processes which lead to differences in working conditions among different groups, defined by sex, age and community. Thus, for example, the differences between men and women could be a result of factors which lead them into different occupations as well as of different working conditions between men and women within the same occupations. Trends in the differences between different groups are also difficult to interpret; for example, if women end up in monotonous jobs to an increasing degree, this could be because typical women's jobs have become more monotonous or because monotonous jobs are increasingly being given to women.

The physical working conditions of employees

The changes in the physical working conditons of employees involved both improvement and deterioration. The extremely heavy jobs seem to have decreased in number. There were also fewer places of work subject to dampness and draughts, fewer extremely dirty jobs, and fewer jobs which involved working outside in very cold weather. On the other hand there was an increase in jobs which expose employees to vibration, monotonous movements, and improper working positions. The number of jobs which involve exposure to poisonous substances and high noise levels also increased.

These results are hardly surprising given the changes in the occupational distribution during the period. The decreases in farm-related jobs, industrial jobs, and construction jobs have meant that many heavy, outdoor jobs have disappeared. The increase in office jobs has meant that the number of indoor jobs has increased, and these do not usually involve problems related to dampness, draughts, or cold weather.

However, there are also tendencies in the material which are not as easily explainable in terms of structural changes. These relate to increases in jobs which involve exposure to noise, poisonous substances, improper working positions, monotonous movements, and vibration. To examine these changes more closely, we must look at the individual occupations. We therefore chose some indicators of working conditions to see how these changed within each occupational group.

According to Table 7.1 among metal workers a significant decrease in the percentage with heavy and physically demanding jobs can be found. Changes for each social class as well as for the population as a whole are also significant. This indicates that structural changes are important in this case.[3]

Table 7.1 Physical working conditions in 1968 and 1981 by occupational group. Percentages

	Heavy and physically demanding		Vibration		Poisons, acids or explosive substances		Very dirty		Noise		Deafening noise	
	1968	1981	1968	1981	1968	1981	1968	1981	1968	1981	1968	1981
Prof., exec. in private employment	1.5	1.3	0.8	3.3	7.5	13.2	0.8	1.3	12.6	13.0	3.5	2.2
Professionals in public employment	5.4	4.0	2.8	2.9	11.2	18.7	0.9	0.5	11.1	20.8	1.0	0.0
Class I, all	4.6	3.6	2.0	3.6	8.5	16.1	1.6	1.4	12.4	17.8	2.5	1.5
Farmers and farming wives	58.7	48.2	27.2	49.9	16.9	44.5	30.9	46.8	33.6	73.1	2.7	12.0
Small proprietors, wives	25.8	22.5	11.8	20.1	20.9	26.0	21.0	23.4	27.5	39.3	5.1	5.8
Foremen	24.2	16.8	5.9	10.4	33.6	33.4	11.6	9.7	57.7	51.3	13.2	17.7
Private technical, clerical	2.2	3.4	1.5	3.2	8.8	10.8	2.6	2.4	19.5	17.5	2.5	2.8
Public salaried	7.2	7.1	2.5	3.4	15.4	17.6	2.2	2.3	20.1	33.9	2.2	4.4
Class II, all	17.0	12.1	7.2	9.9	16.3	19.9	10.4	9.7	26.6	33.5	4.1	5.6
Agricultural workers	51.1	48.8	23.7	43.9	16.7	35.7	31.1	36.1	35.0	59.3	13.8	25.9
Metalworkers	28.9	20.9	13.8	22.8	30.8	39.1	44.9	44.0	74.4	77.8	34.6	40.6
Other manufacturing workers	22.4	21.9	8.5	14.7	20.7	31.4	22.9	22.0	66.8	68.9	26.4	33.9
Construction workers	60.9	54.3	24.4	45.1	29.0	47.2	45.9	45.9	64.1	74.0	12.2	22.9

Manufacturing workers, all	33.4	27.7	14.0	24.1	26.3	37.8	36.2	36.1	69.0	73.7	26.2	34.6
Workers in commerce	17.6	18.2	2.6	7.7	13.0	11.9	13.8	6.8	21.8	33.8	3.3	3.1
Other service workers	16.0	17.6	11.3	19.6	17.5	23.8	12.3	18.8	25.1	32.8	3.3	5.0
Service workers, all	16.8	17.9	7.1	12.8	15.4	17.0	13.0	11.9	23.5	33.4	3.3	3.9
Workers in local government	28.8	25.5	5.5	5.8	10.6	22.1	6.9	5.9	20.5	31.2	4.8	3.8
Workers in state government	24.1	20.7	18.0	17.3	19.9	22.5	19.9	12.4	34.7	43.9	6.1	7.2
Workers in public employment, all	27.2	24.4	9.7	8.6	13.7	22.2	11.3	7.5	25.3	34.2	5.2	4.6
Class III, all	30.0	25.3	12.4	16.8	20.2	27.5	25.1	20.4	45.9	50.0	15.2	16.8
All in the labour force 15–75	23.3	17.9	9.7	12.8	17.9	23.3	17.8	14.3	36.2	40.2	10.1	10.8
Proportion explained variation	0.17	0.12	0.07	0.15	0.04	0.06	0.15	0.19	0.19	0.17	0.13	0.17

On the other hand, jobs which expose employees to vibration have become more common in many occupational groups. This has especially occurred among farmers and industrial workers. It is also within these occupational fields that the exposure to poisonous substances and deafening noise levels has increased. Lesser noise disturbances can increasingly be found in the work environments of salaried employees, in hotels and restaurants and among municipal workers. However, the work environment indicators mentioned are such that they may have been affected by increased aspiration levels and improved information. For example, the knowledge that certain substances are poisonous may have increased. Therefore, the extent of a change in the actual exposure to such substances is uncertain.

Since the heavy jobs are mainly concentrated in industry, farming, and forestry, it is hardly surprising that middle-aged men from the countryside dominate these jobs. Women are highly underrepresented in heavy jobs but significant changes have occurred in that heavy work among women has become more common. Young people are also increasingly found in heavy jobs.

Job autonomy

The importance of controlling one's own working conditions without detailed external controls is often pointed out as an important aspect of job satisfaction and enjoyment. As we mentioned earlier, one of the intentions behind the work environment law was to increase the individual's influence over his own work.

To some extent we can shed some light on this issue with the help of the Level of Living Surveys. Unfortunately not all the same questions were posed in 1968 and 1974 which means that some changes may have been missed. This applies to 'the possibility of establishing ones own pace of work' and 'flexible working hours'. It is worth noting the high percentage, 73.6 per cent in 1981, who were able to set their own working pace. Flexible working hours, however, appear to a much lesser extent, 37.4 per cent. Given the decrease of those who state that they must stick to specific working hours, it is probable that flexible working hours were previously less common. The only indicator which points to more external control is the increased use of time clocks, but this probably relates to the increased use of flexible working hours. In addition, our data show that more people are able to make and receive phone calls, run errands, and receive visitors during working hours. On the whole this indicates an increased degree of autonomy on the job.

Looking at the various occupations we find that the changes in each occupational category have been in the same dirction as the general trend (Table 7.2). Also, the changes were generally greater within those groups

Table 7.2 Autonomy in the job by occupation, 1968 and 1981. Percentages

	Time clock		Punctuality demanded		Able to receive telephone calls on the job		Able to run errands	
	1968	1981	1968	1981	1968	1981	1968	1981
Prof., exec. in private employment	21.9	50.1	64.3	44.4	97.5	100.0	80.5	89.9
Professionals in public employment	0.9	-6.6	69.7	69.4	85.9	87.7	53.4	57.9
Class I, all	.10.0	30.0	66.4	59.4	90.3	91.9	63.4	68.3
Foremen	35.3	58.0	72.9	80.8	90.3	95.4	53.0	73.5
Private technical, clerical	31.5	47.7	68.1	52.2	93.1	96.0	41.9	57.0
Public salaried	3.8	19.4	83.9	77.6	84.6	89.8	24.6	32.7
Class II, all	21.3	33.5	73.7	67.2	88.3	92.1	37.2	45.5
Agricultural workers	12.9	10.5	52.2	60.8	47.7	48.8	48.3	59.9
Metal workers	76.6	33.5	88.8	81.0	65.3	86.7	14.3	25.3
Other manufacturing workers	59.8	54.3	80.3	77.2	66.4	82.3	16.2	26.1
Construction workers	17.1	7.9	76.4	64.7	54.3	58.8	38.3	64.3
Manufacturing workers, all	56.4	51.6	82.6	76.4	63.3	79.6	20.5	33.2
Workers in commerce	25.1	47.5	71.2	81.3	80.6	88.0	23.3	23.1
Other service workers	7.3	10.3	54.0	57.3	73.4	57.9	41.7	54.1
Service workers, all	15.8	32.2	62.2	71.5	76.8	75.6	32.9	35.8
Workers in local government	2.0	1.9	71.1	81.0	68.5	86.5	28.4	28.6
Workers in state government	10.3	16.6	92.4	79.1	62.3	78.3	17.1	32.1
Workers in public employment, all	4.8	5.3	78.3	80.5	66.4	84.6	24.6	29.4
Class III, all	32.8	32.5	75.2	76.4	66.0	79.6	25.7	32.8
Employees 15–75 years old	27.6	32.6	74.1	71.4	74.8	85.3	31.9	40.8
Proportion explained variation	0.31	0.30	0.06	0.07	0.10	0.10	0.10	0.13

in which the level of autonomy was previously low. It is therefore probable that these changes are the result of concrete changes in the workplace, rather than structural effects.

Men's and women's jobs seem to differ regarding autonomy in that women have jobs which are more difficult to leave during working hours. However, it is easier to reach women by telephone. Men seem to have jobs which given them greater freedom to leave during working hours. They also have time clocks in their places of work to a greater extent than women. In general, however, the differences between men and women have decreased.

Mental stress in the workplace

On the whole, two trends appear in our data regarding work-related mental demands. One of them involves speed and monotony. The number of jobs requiring speed has decreased while monotonous jobs have remained at about the same level throughout the period. Nor has there been any change in the number of jobs which are both monotonous and require speed. Thus, in these respects, working conditions have remained the same or improved. The second trend is in the opposite direction. More people say that they have mentally demanding jobs and more people feel mentally exhausted after work.

One obvious interpretation of this is that more people have jobs which, for example, require mental work and responsiblity and that the work assignments have become more varied without increasing the working pace.

This conclusion conflicts with Braverman's theory. However, it must be remembered that the answers in this case not only reflect changes in work assignments but also changes in individual's situations outside their jobs and in their consciousness. For example, women have come to constitute an increasingly larger percentage of the gainfully employed. They often feel mentally exhausted after work, and possibly consider their jobs to be more mentally demanding, because they have children and households to care for. It could also be that the debate on the work environment has caused more people to think about the psychological side of their own work environment. Individual criteria as to what constitutes mental stress may have been affected thereby.

However, this does not seem to have been of much importance. The results do not change much if sex and age are held constant. Doing that, one finds that it is farmers, who to an increasing extent run larger farms with more complex production programmes, who more often have jobs which are mentally demanding. This also applies to workers in industry, service fields, and local administration. Throughout the material the

Table 7.3 Mental working conditions of employees 1968-1981. Percentages

Mental working conditions	1968	1974	1981
Speed required	62.9	61.7	58.6
Monotonous	18.7	17.9	18.4
Speed required and monotonous	11.3	10.3	10.0
Mentally strenuous	30.2	36.5	41.7
Mentally exhausting	12.2	14.0	17.0

mental demands were highest among higher level salaried employees.

Otherwise there were very few significant changes *within* the occupational groups regarding work-related mental pressure and mental exhaustion after work. Nevertheless, signficant changes occurred among the gainfully employed as a whole. This is partly because most of the insignificant changes within the groups took place in the same direction as the general trend and partly because the occupational groups with higher percentages of jobs that involve mental pressure increased in size. Thus the trend towards increased work-related mental pressure seems to be a result of several factors — structural changes, positional changes and, perhaps, changes in values and personnel. It is difficult to exclude any of these factors on the basis of our data.

As to the decrease in jobs which require speed it is probable that most of the changes can be ascribed to changes in the jobs. The jobs requiring speed have become less common as the result of a higher degree of automation, but this could also be the result of a slowdown in the economy with a related excess capacity within many industries.

Jobs that require speed and are monotonous at the same time are most common among women and young people. But here the regression analyses shows that the differences between men and women are not as great among younger people, while women are substantially overrepresented among older people. The greatest change was found among young people, who to an increasingly greater extent had obtained monotonous jobs that required speed.

Middle-aged people and those from the large cities were particularly overrepresented among those with mentally stressful jobs. The differences between men and women have levelled off completely.

On the other hand, the substantial differences between the sexes regarding mental exhaustion after work have remained. Women are exhausted more often than men. This also applies to middle-aged people and people in large cities. No changes in this regard occurred between the surveys.

Qualification levels among employees

How changes in qualification levels should be measured has been a matter of dispute for a long time. One strategy is to classify each individual occupation, regardless of the employee's personal opinion of his job. We followed this method in our material by coding each occupation according to the so-called socio-economic code. This code has educational requirements for the specific occupation as one principle of classification. The occupations which require less than two years of vocational education, regardless of whether they are workers or salaried employees, constitute occupations with a low level of qualification according to our code.

The other strategy is to use answers to questions about an individual's working conditions. To determine which people in our opinion have jobs with a low level of qualification, we combined educational requirements with information about the character of the job. Jobs which are monotonous and do not require two years of vocational education were classified as having especially low qualification requirements. To represent the other end of the scale we constructed an index of the following questions: 'Is your job monotonous?' and 'Is your job mentally strenuous?' The jobs that were mentally strenuous but not monotonous were classified as having a high qualification level. In this section we added an additional variable that relates to employees who 'have subordinates'. We considered this to be an indicator of high qualification requirements because supervisory positions generally require a certain amount of independent action.[4]

The results unambiguously indicate an increase on the average, of employees' qualification requirements. This is apparent with regard to each of the indicators. The degree of qualification according to the socio-economic code only, indicates changes that are a consequence of structural changes which result from the disappearance of certain occupations and the appearance of others. The particular occupations were classified according to the same pattern for each of the three survey years. The percentage of unqualified jobs, according to this code, decreased from 49.4 per cent to 41.8 per cent between 1968 and 1981. The qualification measurement based on survey questions is assumed, in addition, to indicate changes in the nature of the jobs in particular occupations. Both types of measurements, however, show changes of about the same size, which indicates that the increase in qualifications is mainly of a structural nature, although it is often concentrated within individual occupational groups.

If we examine the individual occupations (Table 7.4) we find that the educational requirements have been raised, in particular, in manual jobs.

Table 7.4 Qualifications of employees 1968 and 1981. Percentages

	1968	1981
Has subordinates	21.4	26.0
Unqualified (SEC) and monotonous	19.9	12.5
Mentally strenuous but not monotonous	26.4	36.1

This also applies to jobs which are mentally strenuous but not monotonous as well as supervisory positions. The level of qualification has therefore increased in areas in which it was previously low. It is therefore reasonable to believe that the increase in mental stress, which was shown in the last section, is connected with this factor. More jobs probably require more competence and responsibility, and these increase the amount of mental stress. Of course, this does not hinder a reduction or removal of the intellectual content of many jobs, but the net effect of all the changes seems to be an increase in the levels of qualification.

Regarding unqualified and monotonous jobs, the regression analysis shows an overrepresentation among the youngest and oldest age groups, among women, and among employees in rural areas. The differences between men and women are strongly correlated with age in that the difference increases with increasing age. It was mainly among men in the countryside that unqualified and monotonous jobs were found, while among women it was in the large cities. No significant trend toward decreased sex differences was observed. The only change seems to have been that unqualified and monotonous jobs were increasingly found among young people.

The category of mentally strenuous but not monotonous jobs was meant to measure the opposite pole on the qualification scale. Qualified jobs, measured in this manner, were distributed among the different population groups in a manner which was the opposite of the situation with unqualified jobs. However, some variations were found. One was that the differences between men and women levelled off. The other was that the age differences remained stable over time.

Summary

Working conditions changed in various respects during the period studied. The changes, which have not been dramatic at all, were partly expected because of the shifts which occurred in the occupational structure. Many heavy and dirty jobs disappeared because of the decline in the industrial and farming sectors. The service sector's expansion led to an increase in less physically strenuous, indoor jobs.

However, changes also occurred within various occupational fields. The industrial work environment seems to have changed toward less physically strenuous work and less speed, while at the same time more people seem to have become subjected to poisonous substances, deafening noises, and vibration in their jobs. Even office environments seem to have become noisier.

In general, job autonomy increased. A majority of all employees, 74 per cent, can now determine their own working pace. Opportunities to leave during working hours, make phone class and receiving visitors during working hours increased in most occupational fields.

One important conclusion is that the number of monotonous jobs with low educational requirements has decreased. More and more jobs require mental exertion without being monotonous. We interpreted this as an increase in the level of qualification. We have not touched upon the causes of this situation. Our data can be used to support various theories, but 'Braverman's dequalification theory', on the other hand, is not supported by our data.

The changes we observed are the net effects of both structural changes and changes in individual jobs. They could be the result of more spontaneous trends related to economic and technological developments. However, they can also have been affected by specific political measures — for example, indirectly by educational policies and wage policies and directly by measures meant to improve the work environment.

Very minor changes occurred regarding the distribution of various categories of people in relation to different types of jobs, but a certain levelling off between the working conditions of men and women was detected. In the job types in which men were greatly overrepresented (jobs involving heavy work, supervisory positions, and jobs with a high degree of autonomy) the number of women increased, but differences between the sexes still exist.

Young people have always been overrepresented in unqualified jobs. This tendency seems to have been strengthened during the period.

The regional differences were stable over time. Heavy jobs and unqualified jobs were concentrated among people in the countryside while supervisory positions, office jobs, and qualified jobs were dominated by people from the cities, especially the large cities.

Notes

1. To save space 1974 has been left out occasionally. However, this has not resulted in any great loss of information since the figures for 1974 have fallen between those for 1968 and 1981 in almost all cases.
2. In a separate analysis we took changes in absenteeism and part-time work into account by using a weight system. The results, however, turned out to be essentially the same, which is why the unweighted figures are shown here.
3. However, this is not a reliable method for establishing the existence of a structural effect. Small insignificant changes for separate occupational groups can conceal positional effects which, when summed up, are sufficient to constitute a significant effect. Our conclusion is therefore also based on our knowledge of the structural effect's direction and the systematics of the insignificant changes within occuapational groups.
4. Naturally, whether these indicators in reality measure qualification or not is a decisive question. To test this to some extent we used the ULF survey data from 1979. This includes information about the opportunity to learn new things on the job and whether the only important aspect of the job is the salary. There was a high correlation between these questions and our indicators. Of those with unqualified and monotonous jobs, 63 per cent worked only for the money and 24 per cent could learn new things on the job. Among other employees the equivalent figures were 18 per cent and 62 per cent respectively. Of those with mentally strenuous, but not monotonous jobs, 10 per cent worked only for the money and 72 per cent could learn new things. Among the others the figures were 32 per cent and 50 per cent. The latter figures are almost identical with those obtained if supervisory and non-supervisory personnel are compared. We took this as an indication that the measurement has an acceptable level of validity.

8

Economic Resources

RUNE ÅBERG, JAN SELÉN, and HENRIK THAM

Introduction

In this chapter, we will look at the development of economic resources in the Swedish population, focusing upon changes in the distribution of income from 1967 to 1980. Incomes and their distribution can be studied today against a background of extensive research in the field. The first Swedish income distribution study (Benzel 1952) covered the years 1935, 1940, 1945, and 1948. Thereafter, a detailed analysis of Swedish incomes and purchasing power in 1966 and 1967 was conducted within the framework of the Low Income Commission (SOU 1970:34 and SOU 1971:39). The subsequent years, up to 1976, were studied by Esberger and Malmqvist (1972) and by Spånt (1976 and 1979). In the latter study, estimations were made of the long-term development of income distribution for adult men from 1920 onwards, as well as of the distribution of household incomes from 1935. Other studies in the field include Jakobsson and Norman (1974) and Lindbeck (1981). Also significant for our knowledge of income distribution are the regular descriptions of income distribution in the annual studies on household incomes published by SCB since 1973.

The results of these earlier studies point to a substantial equalization in income during the 1930s and 1940s, and a relatively stable distribution until the late 1960s, followed by another equalization. From the comparative studies that are now available, it would seem that Sweden and the Netherlands had a more equitable income distribution than most other OECD countries at the beginning of the period studied in this chapter (Sawyer 1976).

There may be many reasons for a particular income distribution, or for how it develops. Taxes and transfers of resources that transform an 'initial' into a 'final' income distribution come to mind first. How this is achieved is dependent upon the design of the tax system and government allocations of resources, in addition to an individual's opportunity and propensity to make use of the available means for turning gross into taxable income.

Much of the modification in income distribution, however, is due to other factors possibly influenced by political measures to varying degrees. One gets an idea of the complexity of the causal mechanisms underlying an adjusted income distribution by looking closely at its components, or sources. Capital incomes, consisting of interest, dividends, profits from sales/capital gains, are spread among a small fraction of the population and therefore do not influence the total income distribution very much. Some people's incomes are derived from business operations — their own enterprises or agricultural activities. The number of people generating their incomes in these ways and the profitability of their activities influence the distribution as well. The third and most important source of income is employment. Finally, we have different types of transfers of which pensions are the most significant. Employment income, or earned income, and pensions together constitute 95 per cent of recorded incomes, which is why the distribution is very sensitive to shifts in these types of income.

The distribution of earned incomes is influenced by many factors. One is wage relations. If the differences in wages have decreased, other things being equal, the income distribution is becoming more equitable. If the differences increase, the distribution is becoming more inequitable. The second component determining the distribution of earned income is the distribution of working time. For the gross income, cutting the work volume in half has the same effect as halving wages, for example. The third component is the employment structure. The income distribution changes towards more equalization if there is a growth in the number of jobs paying close to average wage. An increase in the proportion of jobs in extreme income brackets makes the distribution more inequitable. Finally, the level of employment (or unemployment rate) should be mentioned. This can be highly significant for income distribution before taxes and transfers in cases where the distribution is computed for the total adult population. Each rise in the employment rate implies, other things being equal, an equalization, since the extreme category of zero-income earners decreases. If the distribution is computed for employed people, the income distribution effects of the employment changes are dependent upon where in the employment structure they occur.

The factors mentioned here undoubtedly have independent effects on income distribution, but the assumption of holding everything else constant is unrealistic. Changes in one of the components often lead to changes in other components. Changes in the level of unemployment are linked to changes in working hours. Wages influence the labour supply and vice versa. Wage relations influence structural transformations, and so on. Many circumstances, sometimes directly or indirectly influenced by political or union measures, may influence each component. The income distribution we find is the net effect of several different, sometimes opposing factors. It is therefore a complicated task to conduct a detailed causal analysis in this field.

In the discussion of the determination of income distribution, most attention is usually focused on the more general factors. One of these is political power relations. With political power centred in the working class, the design of taxes, transfers, industrial policies, employment policies, and the like, are assumed to benefit the weak and to equalize incomes more than would happen if they were left to spontaneous market mechanisms.

Other commentators maintain that growth is the key factor. The greater the economic growth, the fewer the distributional conflicts and the easier it becomes to redistribute resources and make incomes distribution more equitable by political means. But economic growth also implies structural transformation with expansion of jobs in the high- and middle-income brackets. This is especially true in the transition from an industrial to a post-industrial society. As a rule, an expansion of higher education with a relative increase in the well-educated labour force will result, leading to decreased relative wages for the highly educated. The equalization in this field is seen as something automatically following economic and technical progress.

As mentioned above, wage relations are an important determining factor in income distribution. Most advanced discussion has been in the area of wage determination. According to neo-classical economics, it is supply-and-demand relations on sub-labour markets that determine wage differentials. These relations in their turn are set by a series of factors such as the supply of educated people and changes in the marginal productivity of various firms. But there are other explanations in which the strength of the trade unions and negotiating procedures used to establish wages are the key items. Strong trade unions and a high percentage of organized workers as well as centralized, co-ordinated negotiations, are felt to lead to diminished market influence over wages, and to smaller wage differentials. Naturally, union wage ideology plays an independent role in this context.

In Sweden, the Social Democrats have had a decisive influence on the state apparatus throughout the post-war period. Economic growth was high until the late 1970s. Union organizations have been strong. Wage negotiations were centralized in the middle of the 1950s, and that system prevailed to the end of the 1960s. Thus, many potential influences have encouraged income equalization.

In the following, we will describe the development of incomes and their distribution. This description starts with individual incomes which constitute the corner stone in income formation. We view individuals as actors in the market, and as such, they have varying chances to earn money. The distribution of individual incomes, mainly using total income, therefore reflects dissimiliarities in market conditions.

But individual incomes do not reflect much about consumption or purchasing power. It is on the household level that the net effect of taxes and transfers can be meaningfully illustrated. Many transfers are directed to households rather than individuals. Even taxes are influenced in part by family situations. Moreover, the household and not the individual is the relevant consumption unit. The distribution of the household's economic resources and consumption surplus therefore constitutes the second element in our description.

One question which can be raised is whether declared income is a good measure of economic resources. Many people enjoy material advantages or earn money that never appears on their tax returns. Examples are the exchange of services, black market jobs, or other untaxed employment benefits. These amounts have perhaps also increased with time. In order to avoid these problems as far as possible, we take an individuals assets to indicate the distribution of economic resources. We have chosen to construct a measure of economic resources based on some material possessions and some types of consumption rather than merely on taxed wealth.

Distribution of individual incomes

Distribution of size of income

In describing individual incomes, we use information from the tax authorities. Total income is the overall concept. It includes income from employment, capital, property, temporary employment, agricultural property, and business enterprises. Deductions are made for expenditure in the generation of these incomes. The total now also includes taxable social benefits such as sickness compensation, parents' allowances, medical allowances, and unemployment insurance.[1]

One concept of income sometimes used here and most often used in prior income-distribution studies is total net income. In this concept, total tax exemptions are subtracted from the total income. Such exemptions derive primarily from interest outlays, often for loans against property. Another income measure is taxed income. Further exemption is allowed here for insurance policies, periodic maintenance payments, employment deductions, and basic exemptions. Taxed income forms the basis of the final tax determination. With data on final debited tax, it is possible to compute income after tax — in simple terms, total income minus final tax.

From Table 8.1 we can see that the average total income, computed for all those with such income and in 1980 money values, increased from 48,300 SEK in 1967 to 56,400 SEK in 1980. The average income after tax increased from 34,200 SEK to 38,000 SEK in the same period. For the entire period, there was a real income average increase for income-earners both before and after tax.

The substantial changes during this period however are in the distribution of these incomes. In Table 8.1, trends in the average incomes among the different decile groups are shown. We can see that real incomes for the top 10 per cent earners have dropped during the period. There have been income increases for the remaining groups, the greatest ones in the lowest income brackets. The income distribution has thus become more equitable.

Table 8.1 Average total income and average proportion of debited tax in various decile groups 1967, 1973, and 1980

Decile group	Average income 1000s SEK			Per cent debited tax		
	1967	1973	1980	1967	1973	1980
1 and 2	6.7	9.1	16.1	4.7	3.1	10.5
3	19.6	22.5	30.9	12.5	10.1	21.9
4	28.6	32.2	40.2	19.0	16.0	26.4
5	38.9	43.3	49.2	23.4	18.1	28.7
6	48.3	53.8	58.1	27.0	27.2	29.9
7	57.1	62.6	65.6	28.6	33.9	31.5
8	66.2	71.1	73.5	29.9	37.6	33.7
9	78.6	83.4	85.0	31.4	41.7	36.0
10	133.0	130.2	128.1	37.0	46.6	41.5
Total	48.3	51.7	56.4	21.9	23.5	27.1
N =	4687	5181	5801			

Because of progressive tax system, income distribution after tax is always more equitable than before tax. The proportion of total income in the various decile groups that goes in taxes is given in Table 8.1. That the proportion increases with rising income is almost a truism; that the tax input in the four highest decile groups has decreased since 1973 while increasing for other groups is perhaps more noteworthy. The redistributive effects of taxes have thus declined. There are several possible reasons for this. One is that low incomes rose more than high ones. Another is that the tax increments, especially the non-progressive municipal taxes, were paid in full by low-income earners while high-income earners were able to lower their taxes by raising their tax relief.

In our study of income distribution, there are compelling reasons for including a discussion of tax relief. They result from the incurring of debts. For the individual tax-payer, this means not only expenditure on interest and mortgages but reduced taxes as well. Moreover, regardless of whether the debt is in real assets or is consumed, an inflation-gain results from the reduction of the debt value at the same rate that the general price level rises. If debts are placed in index-linked real assets, there is a tax and inflation-linked accumulation of wealth. Accordingly, tax relief can be seen as an indicator of adjustment both to an inflationary economy and to a high tax burden. The chance to exploit this adjustment mechanism is strongly related to income. Compared to a low-income earner, a high-income earner can borrow money more easily and can probably also more easily afford the expense of a mortgage and interest payments. Moreover, tax gains from family maintenance exemptions are greater for high-income earners, which is why real costs for loans are lower. Therefore, high rates of taxation in combination with inflation and tax relief on interest payments presumably cause the transfer of economic resources to high-income earners. In all likelihood, the sums involved here are tremendous. Even if great uncertainty surrounds the amount, there is little doubt that redistribution by these means has increased. In 1967, 18 per cent of all income-earners claimed tax relief. Thirteen years later, this figure had increased to 40 per cent. The sum of all tax relief, at 1980 price levels, increased from 3.5 to 22.8 1000s million SEK (Table 8.2)

As expected, high-income earners who make use of tax relief far outnumber those low-income earners who do. Relief also represents a greater share of their incomes. This tendency has become stronger since the end of the 1960s. But a slightly smaller percentage of the total tax relief was claimed by the highest decile group in 1980 than in 1967. This is due to the fact that the average income for high-income earners dropped in relation to that of other groups. There is little doubt that inflation causes transfers of large sums each year and that these transfers usually end up in the possession of the highest earners. But, as the Real Taxation Commission stressed, there are also many low-income earners who make gains. Our data indicate that income equalization may eventually weaken the association between income and inflation gains.

Using the theories of income given above we can now summarize the distribution of income. The distribution measure used is the maximal

Table 8.2 Distribution of tax relief among various decile groups 1967, 1973, and 1980

Decile groups by total income	Proportion with tax relief Percentages			Tax relief in per cent of total income			Proportion of the total tax relief		
	1967	1973	1980	1967	1973	1980	1967	1973	1980
1- 2	2	5	11	0.5	0.5	1.5	1	1	5
3	4	15	22	0.2	0.9	2.5	1	1	2
4	8	17	27	0.6	1.0	2.5	2	2	4
5	13	28	32	0.7	1.4	2.9	3	4	4
6	18	33	45	0.8	2.2	3.5	5	7	5
7	27	43	52	1.3	2.8	5.2	10	10	9
8	29	50	62	1.3	3.2	5.8	11	13	11
9	33	52	64	1.4	3.9	7.7	15	19	17
10	47	66	74	2.6	5.6	11.8	51	43	43
Total	18	31	40	1.0	2.2	4.5	99	100	100
N =	4687	5181	5801				3.5[a]	8.8	22.8

[a] Total tax relief, 1000m. SEK

Table 8.3 Income inequality for individual incomes 1967, 1973, and 1980 (maximal equalization percentage)

	1967	1973	1980
Total income			
everyone over 20	36.7	31.8	23.1
everyone with income	29.2	27.5	22.9
Total net income			
everyone over 20	36.7	31.5	22.4
everyone with income	29.0	27.3	22.2
Income after tax			
everyone with income	25.7	23.5	19.5

equalization percentage. This is a measure for the percentage of the total income needed to transfer from people with incomes above the median to those below it to achieve equalized incomes for everyone. We chose this distribution measure from those available because it is easy to understand intuitively and because it has been used in earlier Swedish studies of income distribution. Table 8.3 shows that, according to all concepts of income, there was a dramatic equalization of individual incomes in the 1970s. This is even more so if the distribution is gauged with all adults as the base. The development is all the more vivid going back further in time. In Figure 8.1 the developments since the beginning of the 1950s are shown. Our calculations of the maximal equalization percentage for total net income is compared here with corresponding data from Spånt who consistently used this concept of income (The reason for the slightly lower inequality in our data is that we included previously non-taxable social benefits.)

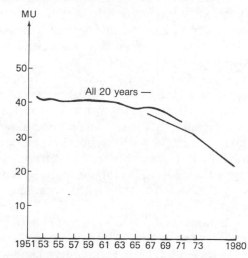

Fig. 8.1.   Development of income equalization 1951–80. The maximum equalization coefficient

The sharp drop in income inequality shown in the figure is partly due to the fact that the proportion of income-earners has increased. Between 1967 and 1980, the proportion of income-earners among 20 to 74 year olds rose from 84 to 97 per cent! But it is also shown that even if only income earners are included in the calculations, an equalization has still occurred.

According to our definition, income from business enterprises and capital must be added to earned income. These types of income make up a small and diminishing proportion of the combined incomes. The proportion of enterprise incomes has decreased from 8 to 4 per cent, and incomes from capital have remained around 2 per cent. People with total incomes above the median income have a greater share of these two income types. In 1967, 79 per cent of enterprise incomes and 74 per cent of capital incomes went to the highest earning half of the population. The figures for 1980 show that the picture has partly shifted. The corresponding figures were 53 and 64 per cent. The distribution of business and capital incomes therefore is such that income distribution is somewhat more equitable. But since these factors constitute such a small part of the incomes, even large changes in these types of income have only a small effect on the total income distribution.

It is mostly changes in earned incomes and pensions that decide income distribution. Therefore we shall now study these more closely.

Horizontal distribution of employment income

Up to this point, we have described the distribution of individual incomes in the total population without considering the differences between individual categories. Benzel labelled this type of distribution 'vertical'. The distribution among population groups was 'horizontal'. Knowledge about changes in the horizontal income distribution is important for understanding changes in the vertical distribution. Dissimilarities among groups are also significant in discussing distribution policies. Therefore, we will study changes in the horizontal distribution for the two most important types of income — earned incomes and pensions, in this section. Of special interest is the distribution among occupational groups. The reason for this is that income, and thus pensions, are largely determined by wage settlements in the labour market. Wages are perhaps determined more by the circumstances of the specific occupations than by those of individuals. Furthermore, income distribution is affected by structural transformations and by the resulting redistribution of the employment structure. Occupation is thus the basis for the horizontal division that is indispensable for understanding changes in the vertical distribution.

We will begin the description of income differentials among occupational groups by trying to identify the part of these differentials that can be attributed to wage differences. Working hours must be held constant. We have chosen to do this by comparing earned incomes for full-time, year-round employees. With earned incomes, we mean income from employment, including taxable social benefits.[2]

From Table 8.4 we can see that the only groups with decreasing real wages since 1967 are the higher salaried employees in both the public and private sectors. All others have seen significant real wage gains. In relation to the average wage, the higher salaried employees have lost much more than the other. Other groups who lost in relative wages are foremen and construction workers in the private sector. The lower public salaried employees and state employees are also losers. Those salaried employees who have gained in relation to other groups are technical and clerical personnel. For workers, it is within the service branches that relative wages have risen the most. In short, people who had the highest wages at the outset of our study have lost, and those with the lowest wages have gained.

However, this cannot solely be a change in wages. The average income within the broad occupational categories involved here could also rise as a result of the elimination of low-paying jobs within the occupational

Table 8.4 Earned Incomes for full-time year-round workers 1967, 1973, and 1980. (1000s SEK computed in 1980 money values)

	Earned incomes			Per cent of average wage			Coefficients of variation		
	1967	1973	1980	1967	1973	1980	1967	1973	1980
Prof., exec. in private empl.	153.0	146.3	137.2	238	199	179	50	36	43
Professionals in public empl.	141.9	132.0	115.2	220	179	150	40	37	36
Class I, all	146.9	136.5	123.7	228	185	161	46	38	42
Small proprietors	52.8	56.9	69.1	82	77	90	52	66	45
Foremen	75.3	84.7	84.5	117	115	110	28	22	27
Private technical, clerical	63.3	72.5	79.9	98	99	104	46	39	33
Public salaried	67.8	73.8	74.4	105	100	97	36	27	25
Class II, all	65.9	74.2	76.9	102	101	100	40	33	31
Agricultural workers	35.6	55.4	55.5	55	75	72	58	30	53
Metal workers	56.1	64.6	65.5	87	88	85	20	25	21
Other manufacturing workers	52.8	61.5	64.1	82	84	84	31	25	23
Construction workers	64.8	69.5	73.4	101	94	96	32	21	23
Manufacturing workers, all	56.7	64.5	66.7	88	88	87	32	25	23
Workers in commerce	45.2	53.1	57.9	70	72	75	32	29	25
Other service workers	45.2	53.2	65.9	70	72	86	55	47	26
Service workers, all	45.2	53.2	61.9	70	72	81	46	40	27
Workers in local government	54.1	62.0	66.1	84	84	85	35	27	23
Workers in state government	62.1	71.5	71.2	96	97	93	25	19	21
Workers in public employment, all	57.9	65.5	67.2	90	89	88	31	25	23
Class III, all	53.1	62.0	65.2	82	84	85	38	29	25
Population 15–75 years old	64.4	73.6	76.7	100	100	100	57	45	42

category or the emergence of better paying ones. In Table 8.4, the coefficient of variation within each occupational category has decreased. There have been large decreases especially for occupations with sharp increases in real wages. This may be a sign of a structural effect, but it may also be due to the fact that low-paying occupations within the category gained more substantial wage increases than the others. In any case, the diminishing coefficients of variation indicate that it is not only among occupational groups, but also within them, that an equalization has taken place.

One way to reduce the influence of structural changes is to study developments in wages for individuals who were in the same occupational group on all three occasions when measurements were taken. Unfortunately, again one is not only measuring wage effects. The career opportunities embodied in each occupational category are also reflected in the figures. In spite of this, the pattern is the same. Higher salaried employees, especially those in the public sector, lost in relative wages. They also suffered absolute decreases between 1973 and 1980. The lower salaried employees in private service, on the other hand, improved their relative position throughout the period (Table 8.5).

Without doubt, these figures reflect a wage equalization. But the degree to which the increasingly equitable distribution of individual incomes can also be attributed to changes in working time or to structural transformations is unclear. As for the effects of structural changes, we know from Chapter 6 that it is mainly the management categories in business, and public employees in all social classes that have increased their relative proportion of employed people. A relative growth has thus occurred in groups that are highest and lowest on the relative wage scale. In other words, the shift between the crude occupational categories we have used has worked against increased equality in individual incomes. We do not know what has taken place within the occupational groups. Nor does it appear feasible that the great increase in part-time work and other changes in working times would have equalized earned incomes for employees. In Chapter 6, it was maintained that the net effect of all changes in working hours was more likely to lead to a more inequitable distribution of working hours. Nor were we able to find that part-time work increased more in the high-paying occupations than in others. In conclusion, the equalization of earned incomes during this period appears to be mainly due to decreased wage differentials.

Income differentials between the sexes have begun playing an important role in political discussion and the public debate. Men's incomes have always been higher than women's. Three factors explain this — men work longer hours and more often have better paying jobs, and women receive less pay than men for the same types of work.

Union wage policy goals have long aimed at eliminating different forms of wage discrimination. The principle of equal pay for equal work has been the ideal. There is a lot of evidence indicating that this goal has been partially achieved. Available wage statistics show that for most occupations, wage differentials between men and women have decreased (Yearbook of Labour Market Statistics 1982).

Table 8.5 Earned incomes for full-time year-round workers in same occupational groups 1967, 1973, and 1980 (in 1,000s SEK computed to 1980 money values)

	Earned incomes			Per cent of average wage			Coefficients of variation		
	1967	1973	1980	1967	1973	1980	1967	1973	1980
All employees	74.6	87.8	89.6	100	100	100	49	41	37
Prof., exec. in private empl.	135.4	161.3	153.7	182	184	172	36	32	34
Prof. in public employment	140.7	141.2	131.7	189	161	147	32	34	32
Foremen	78.4	92.8	93.2	105	106	104	16	19	20
Private technical and clerical	65.0	82.9	90.7	87	94	101	31	27	24
Public salaried	68.5	79.3	84.4	92	90	94	30	19	17
Metal workers	59.4	71.7	70.1	78	82	78	25	16	15
Other manufacturing workers	55.9	67.3	68.8	75	77	77	25	20	20
Construction workers	63.8	73.9	79.7	86	84	89	37	15	18
Workers in local government	59.1	74.0	76.1	79	84	85	26	19	10
Workers in state government	63.9	74.7	78.0	86	85	87	18	13	9

When comparing the earned incomes in our data for full-time year-round working males with corresponding incomes for women, we find that the sex differences are still relatively large (Table 8.6). For all non-seasonal workers in 1980, the earned incomes of women was 80 per cent of that of men. About the same income relation between the sexes applies within the individual occupational groups. In the light of these wage statistics, it is less likely that this is due to wage discrimination than to the fact that overtime and second jobs, are more common among men, and that women within each occupational category have lower paying jobs.

Table 8.6 Earned incomes for full-time year-round working women as proportion of men's incomes in various occuptional groups 1967, 1973, and 1980

	1967	1973	1980
Prof,. exec. in private employment	0.60	0.72	0.80
Professionals in public employment	0.91	0.81	0.81
Class I, all	0.81	0.75	0.76
Foremen	0.78	0.96	0.71
Private technical, clerical	0.63	0.69	0.79
Public salaried	0.74	0.82	0.84
Class II, all	0.71	0.76	0.81
Metal workers	0.77	0.74	0.84
Other manufacturing workers	0.71	0.78	0.82
Construction workers	—	—	—
Manufacturing workers, all	0.69	0.75	0.81
Workers in commerce	0.52	0.47	0.80
Other service workers	0.52	0.47	0.80
Service workers, all	0.64	0.64	0.80
Workers in local government	0.66	0.80	0.82
Workers in state government	0.81	0.93	1.00
Workers in public employment, all	0.70	0.80	0.85
Class III, all	0.67	0.73	0.83
Population 15–75 years old	0.68	0.73	0.79

It is worth noting that income differentials between men and women were greater previously. Among full-time year-round workers in 1967, women had about 30 per cent lower earned incomes. The equalization of recent years can in part be explained by reductions in differences in extra and overtime work, but also by the fact that the lowest paying jobs, where women are overrepresented, have made greater strides forward in wages than in other jobs.

Pensioner's incomes

In Sweden, many people receive pensions of various kinds. Some recipients include children, widows, people who for whatever reason are given early retirement, or those who have accepted a partial pension. But the largest group, which is continuously expanding, is old-age pensioners. Their economic situation is the subject of this section. Since our material for the then relevant years is limited to people up to 74 years old, this section deals with the 'young' old-age pensioners.

On average, the finances of old-age pensioners have improved considerably. The total incomes for year-round pensioners rose from 23,100 SEK (1980 year price level) in 1967 to 40,000 SEK in 1980. This is an increase of 74 per cent. Pensions, which constitute the greatest part of pensioner's incomes (about 85 per cent), rose by 79 per cent.[3] In comparison, earned incomes for full-time year-round employed persons increased by 19 per cent.

The increase in the average pension income is ascribed to new pension programmes as well as to modifications in the way in which people qualify for pensions. The most momentous change during the period was when the ATP (general supplementary pensions scheme), under which the first payments were made in 1963, began to expand. From pensions being sent to some tens of thousands of pensioners initially, by 1980 about 770,000 were receiving ATP. This figure represents 65 per cent of all old-age pensioners. In Swedish crowns (SEK), the payments grew from about 60 million to 9000 million between 1965 and 1980 (SOU 1977:46).

Since ATP is a system where the amount of the pension is determined by the volume of work performed and the size of income during working life, the total payment for pensions increases in line with the increase in the number of ATP-pensioners, with the increase in the number of qualifying years for each pensioner, and with the increase in income total serving as the basis for the pension calculations. The two last factors make the pension paid per ATP-pensioner larger, and the first makes the ATP-pensioners more numerous. All these factors have contributed to the fact that the average amount of pension has increased. The most important explanation for this increase is that there are more ATP-pensioners at the same time that the payments per pensioner have risen as a result of the higher average number of pension-based years. These conditions will continue to contribute to an increase in the amount paid out in pensions until everybody is covered by the system.

But the ATP-system is not the sole contributor to the increase in payments for pensions. Most wage-earners today have contracted for their pensions in the collective agreement with their employers. Within the state and municipal sectors, as well as for salaried employees and industrial workers, agreements have been entered meaning that income at the time of retirement and the number of years in service will determine the size of the pension. Standing agreements for salaried employees in the private sector were reached in the early 1960s. When the ATP system was introduced in 1957, it was primarily public salaried employees, in banking and insurance, as well as in many industrial companies, who had contracts for pension benefits. For the working class, this was extremely rare.

However, there are still pensioners who have no supplementary pension at all. Above all, this is true for self-employed people and farmers, who fall outside the supplementary pension scheme, but there are many older and disabled people who have also been unable to fulfil the conditions of the scheme. For them, there is the old-age pension, and in some cases private pension insurance. People receiving only old-age pensions likewise have received higher pensions over the years, as these are linked to the basic scale and in that way inflation-proof (as is ATP). In 1969, a pension supplement was initiated for old-age pensioners with low or no ATP pensions.[4]

The circumstances described here have not only influenced the size of pensions, but the distribution of pension incomes as well. The effects on distributions, however, are such that some of them change with time. In a transitional period, such as the period observed here, one could expect rather sizeable dissimilarities in pension incomes stemming from differences in the period during which pensioners accumulated pension points. When the system has been in operation so long that everyone has been able to obtain full pensions, this differentiation factor will disappear. But at present, it plays an important role and leads to age-based pension differentials.

Another significant factor leading to dissimilarities in pensions is the length of working life up to pension age. Women in particular receive lower pensions as a rule because they have often been housewives, and thus economically active for fewer years than men. Many women do not reach the maximum 30-year gainful employment rule. For today's pensioners, this often leads to substantial differences in pension incomes between the sexes, but the increasing employment of women will probably reduce this gap in the long run. Women still have low-paying jobs more often and more often work part-time than men. These differences may be long-lasting. On the other hand, the wage equalizations, as well as the rule on the fifteen best years as the basis for pension calculations, hint that sex differentials in pension incomes between the sexes may finally come to an end.

A third significant factor in this context is occupation. Formerly it was the case that most salaried employees had good pensions. More highly paid salaried employees and self-employed people had private pension insurance. This is reflected in our material where we find considerable class differences in the 1967 pensions. These class disparities had been reduced by 1980, but were still large. Naturally, they will last as long as wage differentials and career opportunities are not the same among the classes. There is, however, good reason to believe that the equalization among classes will continue, as wages are converging, and since both ATP and pension benefits established in collective agreements raise working-class members above very low pension levels.

Table 8.7 shows developments in incomes for old-age pensioners under 75 years old, by sex and class. Incomes increased dramatically in absolute numbers for all classes, but the increase in pension incomes was not as large for women as for men. The pension gap among classes is broad among women, and did not change appreciably in this period. But it changed for men. The increase in pension incomes in absolute numbers was especially large for men in class 1. Their pension incomes rose by about 48,000 SEK from 1967 to 1980, while the increase for men in social group II and III was about 18,000 SEK. For men, there was thus an equalization of pension incomes between classes II and III, while the gap between them and class I remained.

Table 8.7 Pensions and total income, by social class and sex for year-round pensioners between retirement age and 74 years

	Average SEK, 1980 price level				In per cent of average pensions and income for all			
	1967		1980		1967		1980	
	Pens.	Total income	Pens.	Total income	Pens.	Total income	Pens.	Total income
Class I								
Men	50.2	81.7	98.1	12.4	264	333	288	308
Women	28.0	30.1	41.7	48.7	147	130	122	121
All	41.7	62.0	68.4	84.2	219	268	201	209
Class II								
Men	25.0	43.0	43.1	53.5	131	186	126	133
Women	19.8	25.8	28.6	35.8	104	111	84	89
All	22.1	33.4	35.4	44.0	116	144	104	109
Class III								
Men	18.1	21.1	35.7	38.8	95	91	105	97
Women	14.5	12.1	22.1	25.0	76	52	65	62
All	16.1	16.1	28.3	31.5	84	69	83	78
All	19.0	23.1	34.0	40.1	100	100	100	100
N =	479	479	763	763				

For pensioners in class III, pensions are the overwhelmingly dominant source of income. In the other two classes, however, other forms of income made up much of the pensioners' incomes. People with the highest pensions also had most extra income. This is still true, but not to the same degree as before. Pension incomes rose at a much faster rate than the extra incomes, so that pensions are the increasingly dominant income for all pensioners.

Household incomes

Household classification

We shall now study purchasing power by describing disposable income, consumption surplus after deductions of costs for certain basic needs, and, to some degree, factor income. As has been emphasized, such descriptions must concern the household rather than the individual.

A basic problem when the family or household is chosen as the unit for analysis is how a household is to be defined. Our solution is the following: a household contains, in addition to children, either single, or married, or cohabiting persons, as given in the interviews. Below, cohabiting persons are included in the category of married people.[5] One requirement for being a part of a household is that the interviewee is not permanently residing in a public institution, such as an old people's home, a nursing home, or the like. A lodger is counted as a separate household.

For more correct inferences about households in the population, some specific measures are required because of the lack of data for children and parents. Interviewees who live with their parents and are under 18 years old, or 18 years or more but cannot support themselves are excluded as are the corresponding households. Others who live with their parents are counted as separate households. Children of interviewees living at home are included as part of their parents' household if they are under 18 years, or are older but cannot support themselves. Other children living at home are not counted. Older children are counted as self-supporting if they are economically active earners.

The other important problem concerns the classification of households. Here we proceed from the social and occupational classification earlier applied to individuals. For the sake of clarity and for statistical reasons, it is however necessary to reduce the number of classes. For married people, the household is classified according to the occupation of the spouse deemed the head of household.[6]

Secondly, household containing only non-earners are treated separately; thus, students and the old are shown apart, the latter by class. Unfortunately, class I here contains too few households for presentation. We also include households where at least one spouse is a farmer, independently. The remaining groups are workers, lower salaried employees, small proprietors, and class I.

When the household consists of a married couple in different occupational groups, the enumeration above is useful to determine the head of household. With the exception of farmers, as noted, the head of household is the spouse belonging to the group later in the enumeration.

Consequently, in a household with one worker and one lower salaried employee, the latter will be selected as head of household; a household with two pensioners, one of whom belongs to class II and the other to class I, will be assigned to pensioners I.

The household classification and resulting distributions in 1968 and 1981 are given in Table 8.8.

There the proportion of non-earning households increased over time, as did the proportions for lower salaried employees and class I. The corresponding decrease in worker households could, in part, be linked to the rising incidence of women working outside the home, since the occupational class of the household, with the exception of single housewives (who are placed in the corresponding class of pensioners), is never determined by a housewife in the classification.

Table 8.8 Distribution of households among occupational groups in 1968 and 1981. Percentages

	1967	1980
Students	2.7	2.9
Pensioners III	10.4	12.2
Pensioners II	4.0	5.9
Pensioners I	0.7	1.3
Workers	41.2	34.2
Lower-salaried II	23.1	25.0
Small proprietors	6.6	6.5
Class I	6.2	8.2
Farmers	5.0	3.8
10 000s inhabitants	332	365

Note that occupational groups, here as in other analyses of individual incomes, are determined by the circumstances at the time of the interview, while income data, as seen below, refer to the year before. This error probably leads to slightly underestimated disparities in income between the groups.

Disposable household incomes

As a measure of a household's economic resources, disposable income is used, that is, factor income minus direct taxes plus transfer payments. The exact definition is given in the appendix to this chapter. No computations are made for 1973 because income information for cohabiting non-married people was lacking for that year.

Average disposable incomes for households classified by occupation, number of adults, and number of economically active earners, are presented in Table 8.9. Let us first look at the occupational groups in total, that is, the two columns on the left. We can see that the incomes increase over time for all groups except class I. All changes except those for students and class I are significant. The average increase for all households is about 23 per cent. As to the relations between the groups, the lead by class I diminished between 1967 and 1980, while the incomes of pensioner households improved by comparison. The relative income for other occupational groups is fairly unchanged. Differences within the household groups decreased over time according to the coefficients of variation, which for 1980 are between 5 and 30 per cent lower than in 1967 (not shown in table).

An equalization both among and within the household groups has occurred. We must have strong reservations, however, about comparisons including either farmers or small proprietors. For wage-earners, disposable income is a relatively accurate measure of economic situation (see for example SOU 1970:34, 104), but this is hardly true for farmers and small proprietors. For example, it has been shown that the relatively low disposable incomes of farmers do not correspond to a lower consumption level in housing standards or car ownership (Johansson and Hedström 1979).

Furthermore, time comparisons are more uncertain for farmers and proprietors than for the other groups. Changes in tax legislation presumably had an effect on the choice between investments and income-consumption for business owners. For many farmers, a change took place in accounting systems for taxation in the 1970s. This change may have caused a decrease in declared incomes.

Compared with earnings for individuals in Table 8.3, there is a similar pattern for disposable incomes in Table 8.9. The differences among the household groups, however, are smaller than the differences in individuals' earnings. Such a result could be explained both by the redistributive effects of the tax and transfer payment systems, and by the occupational and income differences between the spouses.

Inequalities in disposable income among occupational groups is in part due to the dissimilar composition of households. When households are classified according to the number of adults and the number of economically active earners, it is unmarried people who have the lowest disposable incomes, while married people with two earned incomes have the highest (Table 8.9). The ratio between the average incomes for married persons with two earners and one earner respectively, lie between 1.1 and 1.3. That the ratios are below two is a consequence of the income differences between spouses. When we look at households with the same

Table 8.9 Disposable income for households, by occupation, civil status, number of economically active earners, and year. 1000s SEK, 1980 prices

	1967	1980	1967			1980		
	all	all	unmarried	married		unmarried	married	
				0/1	2 earners		0/1	2 earners
Averages								
Students	26	30	23	(50)	—	29	(48)	—
Pensioners III	23	39	19	31	—	31	53	—
Pensioners II	29	47	24	44	—	36	58	—
Pensioners I	(53)	67	(43)	(72)	—	(39)	(90)	—
Workers	47	58	31	54	67	40	65	83
Lower-salaried II	62	76	39	70	80	48	76	94
Small proprietors	53	63	31	56	65	34	59	77
Class I	106	101	(60)	109	123	62	92	119
Farmers	35	43	19	39	(60)	25	(45)	55
All	50	62						
Percent of average wage								
Students	52	49	46	(99)	—	47	(78)	—
Pensioners III	46	63	38	63	—	50	85	—
Pensioners II	58	75	48	87	—	59	94	—
Pensioners I		108						
Workers	93	93	62	107	134	65	105	134
Lower-salaried II	124	122	78	140	159	77	122	152
Small proprietors	106	102	62	113	129	55	95	125
Class I	212	164	120	218	246	101	149	193
Farmers	70	69	37	77	(119)	41	(73)	88
All	100	100						

household composition, the differences among occupations are less.

For class I, disposable income decreases over time for married households with one earner. For married households with two earners, family income is unchanged or decreases slightly. The trends are similar for class I as a whole. The reason why household incomes in class I have not dropped more despite the sharply diminished earnings of individuals may be due to the fact that the supply labour has increased more here than in other groups. The fact that the proportion of housewives in this group especially has sunk is an indication of this.

If we instead look at disposable income per consumption unit, there is no tendency towards a decrease over time for class I (not in the table). This indicates a decrease in the average size of families in this group.

Household consumption surplus

The consumption surplus indicates how much money households have available after deducting from disposable income those expenditures required to maintain a certain basic standard. The cost of the basic standard is calculated similarly to the subsistence level norms and housing costs according to a convention. The amount remaining after the deductions is divided by the number of consumption units within the family so as to improve the comparability among households of different sizes.

The subsistence level has been computed as the basic amount for respective years (a price index according to the National Insurance Act), multiplied by 0.95 for single people, 1.65 for married households, and with 0.4 times this basic amount added for each child — roughly similar to public assistance guidelines. The given coefficients also denote the consumption units for the different individuals.

Housing costs are set at the minimum of the actual housing costs, and housing costs according to a norm based on the number of family members living at home. The norms assume that everyone has his or her own room, with kitchen and living room excluded. Thus, the requirement for good space standard as given in the chapter on housing conditions (Figure 10.1) are fulfilled.

Information has been obtained about the costs for various dwelling sizes from housing and rental studies (SCB 1970 and SCB 1982). The standard rent is then computed as the rent for an average two-room apartment, plus an average room-rent sum multiplied by the number of family members except one. The rental differences among dwellings of different sizes makes this procedure reasonable. The standard rent was the same for the whole country in 1980, but was set higher in 1967 for Greater Stockholm than elsewhere. Rental information from the level-of-living survey is adjusted back one year to 1967 and 1980 by means of consumer price indices for dwellings.

The findings of the calculations on consumption surplus[7] are given in Table 8.10. There is a clear overall rise in the consumption surplus over time. All changes for occupational groups in total, with the exception of class I and students, are significant. In relative terms, the increase is substantial. In absolute terms, it is less than the increase in disposable income. The differences between the occupational groups decrease from 1967 to 1980, but are still large. According to the estimates in the table, the 1967 surplus in class I was more than three times that for working-class households, In 1980, the difference had shrunk so that the consumption surplus in class I was only twice as large. The level for pensioners rose drastically, but the surplus in 1980 for these groups was barely higher than the level for corresponding classes of households with economically active earners in 1967.

Comparisons of civil status show that married households with one income earner have less consumption surplus than unmarried ones and married ones with two income earners. The differences among the latter groups are small and cannot be established statistically. The information in the table indicates that the change over time was less advantageous for married households with one income earner than for the others. For married households in class I with one income, the decrease is estimated at 25 per cent while the consumption surplus for class I in its entirety is unchanged or only slightly increased. To summarize then, the base for the material standard unquestionably improved and became more equitable in the seventies. However, it must be asked whether other changes which do not show up here could have counteracted this improvement. Reduced home production within the household or increased dependence on the money economy or goods market would be examples of such factors. Another is child care costs which have not been taken into consideration in our calculations. Available information shows that child care purchased outside the home has become more common as well as more expensive (SOU 1983:14). It seems that this expenditure varies to a crucial extent depending upon where one lives and what form of child care is chosen.

Effects of tax and transfer systems

An interesting question is whether there has been any change in the total redistributive effects of the personal income taxation and transfer systems. Does the equalization of the households' disposable income established above also apply to different income classes? And is such an equalization a product of both an initial income equalization and the direct effects of the tax and transfer systems? Of interest here is also how income and consumption surplus varies between high and low income households.

Table 8.10 Consumption surplus per consumption unit for households, by occupation, civil status, number of earners, and year. Averages in 1000s SEK, 1980 prices

| | 1967 | 1980 | 1967 | | | 1980 | | |
	all	all	unmarried	married 0/1	2 earners	unmarried	married 0/1	2 earners
Students	5	8	5	(5)	—	8	(8)	—
Pensioners III	−1	9	−1	0	—	8	11	—
Pensioners II	4	13	3	6	—	13	13	—
Pensioners I	(18)	23	(17)	(20)	—	(13)	(30)	—
Workers	9	16	11	6	11	17	11	18
Lower-salaried II	5	22	17	13	16	22	15	23
Small proprietors	9	12	10	7	11	11	5	14
Class I	30	32	(32)	27	34	35	20	33
Farmers	0	4	0	0	(8)	3	(3)	4
All	10	17						

The analysis requires a specification of what is counted as transfers or taxes and allowances, and what is counted as factor income. We have done this in the usual way by assigning all supplements to and deductions from salaries, wages, and property and entrepreneurial income, that is, factor income, to transfers. Computed in this manner, transfer payments as a proportion of disposable income, in total, more than doubled in the period studied, from 15 per cent to 34 per cent.

For the purposes of analysis, the decile distributions for 1967 and 1980 are given. The procedure is that households are sorted by factor income and divided into ten groups of equal size. These decile groups are of equal size with regard to the totalled household weights. In this manner, we get around the fact that the Level of Living Survey is a sample of individuals and increases comparability between the years. The results of the computations are given in Table 8.11. Here the differences between the decile groups are reduced when moving from average factor incomes to average disposable incomes. The differences between the average consumption surpluses in their turn are even smaller if one looks at the absolute but not the relative differences.

The distribution of factor income became more unequal over time; the maximum equalization percentage increased from 27 to 32 per cent. The distribution of disposable income, however, became more equal with a decrease from 23 to 20 per cent. A more equal distribution over time is also evident for consumption surplus.

From the last columns in the table, it is clear that the size of the households and the number of earners within the household, with some exceptions, increase with decile group. In a comparison of household sizes between the years, we see that the high- and low-income households increase in size over time, while the middle groups decrease. The number of economically active earners per household increases over time, with the exception of the first deciles for which the number was very low in 1980. We decided to sort by factor income with the clear result that non-earners tend to land in the first decile groups to a higher degree in 1980. It is quite true that the factor incomes in the first deciles are higher in 1967 than in 1980, whereas the proportion of pensioner households rises here from about 40 per cent to about 75 per cent during the period.

According to the table, the factor incomes have increased for high-income households. This does not correspond with the trends in total incomes for full-time employed high-income earners seen in Table 8.1. The explanation for this assuredly lies in the increase in the percentage of economically active earners in the population.

The differences between factor income and disposable income for the various decile groups are shown clearly in Figure 8.2. We see that the differences are greater in 1980 for the first and the last decile groups.[8]

Table 8.11 Factor income, disposable income, consumption surplus per consumption unit, size of households and number of earners for decile groups, by factor income 1967 and 1980. Averages, 1000s SEK or numbers, 1980 prices

	Decile group	Factor income	Disp. income	Cons. surplus	Household size	Number earners
1967	1	6	17	−4	1.40	.44
	2	20	20	0	1.26	.47
	3	31	29	4	1.66	.76
	4	42	36	9	1.74	.94
	5	52	42	11	2.02	.99
	6	62	49	12	2.43	1.12
	7	73	56	13	2.68	1.27
	8	86	66	15	2.84	1.46
	9	104	76	19	2.86	1.58
	10	172	109	36	2.84	1.57
1980	1	0	33	7	1.46	.19
	2	5	39	8	1.55	.24
	3	20	38	9	1.55	.66
	4	42	46	13	1.83	1.02
	5	58	50	17	1.78	1.11
	6	70	58	19	2.12	1.17
	7	85	66	19	2.48	1.39
	8	105	79	19	2.98	1.71
	9	129	91	24	2.97	1.85
	10	194	118	35	3.11	1.88

The redistribution among the groups increases both absolutely and relatively. One measure for the relative redistribution is the totalled absolute differences between factor income and disposable income as a proportion of the total factor income. This measure varies with the area between the curves and is 26 per cent for 1967 and 38 per cent for 1980.

The changes between the years can be summarized as follows: the differences in factor income between households have increased with increased differences in the percentage of earners. The distribution of disposable income has become more equal and the differences in consumption surplus per consumption unit less equal. Thus, the tax and transfer systems seem to have a more redistributive effect in 1980 than was the case in 1967. The most likely explanation for this is the effects of the increased number and the improved conditions of pensioners. Even excluding pensioner households, however, we find such a redistributive effect over time with the maximum equalization percentage unchanged for factor incomes and decreased for disposable incomes.

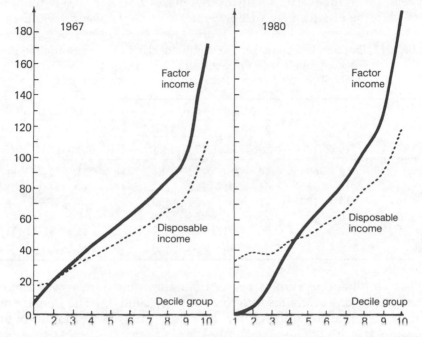

Fig. 8.2 Factor income and disposable income for households in 1967 and 1980. Adjusted curves from the averages for decile groups, which are defined according to factor income. 1000s SEK, 1980 prices.

Families with Children

In the Swedish debate on distribution policies, the differences between families with children and others is an oft-recurring theme. A contribution is made here with an account of the distribution of economic resources between 1967 and 1980 for households with different numbers of children at home under the age of 20. The results of the comparisons between groups are, as regards the consumption surplus, dependent upon norms for basic consumption. It is possible that this favours households with several children to some degree, since all children are given equal weight.

In Table 8.12 the distribution as well as the average disposable income and the consumption surplus for different household groups are given. Pensioners are omitted in order to make the comparisons more relevant. The proportion of households with one child decreases over time, while the proportion of two-children families increases. Disposable income is higher for households with children than for those without, and increases with an increase in the number of children, with the exception of large families. The incomes for the various families-with-children groups increase over time. The relative differences, however, seem to have shifted to the disadvantage of households with three or more children.

Table 8.12 Disposable income and consumption surplus per consumption unit for households with different numbers of children 1967 and 1980. 1000s SEK, 1980 prices. Pensioner households excluded

No. of children	Proportion		Disposable income				Consumption Surplus			
			average		per cent		average		per cent	
	1967	1980	1967	1980	1967	1980	1967	1980	1967	1980
0	58	60	44	54	82	81	14	21	124	111
1	19	16	65	81	120	122	11	19	88	101
2	15	18	70	89	130	135	7	14	58	78
3	6	5	73	86	135	131	5	8	41	46
4+	2	1	70	(91)	129	(137)	2	(6)	17	(31)
All			54	66	100	100	12	19	100	100

The consumption surplus per consumption unit is relatively small, particularly for households with three or more children. The findings do not indicate that the situation for these households in relation to other households with children improved during the 1970s. Despite an increase, they were still low in 1980, and households with three or more children do not seem to have a greater consumption surplus than two-children families in 1967. In comparisons between households with and without children, it is important to keep in mind that child care costs are not included. If they were, the consumption surplus would contract for families with children, and probably more so in 1980 than in 1967.

Consumption and wealth

One purpose for studying different income measures is to get an idea of the material standards of living enjoyed by individuals and households. By adjusting incomes from employment, capital, and enterprises, with various types of transfers of resources, the measure for disposable income is attained, thus providing a more accurate picture of how the individual or the household lives in material terms. However, the picture is still incomplete. The economic situation is also influenced by gifts and inheritances, capital gains, home production, non-taxable employment perguisites, and capital growth of various kinds.

One method of circumventing these difficulties occasioned by different concepts of income, may be to turn directly to the consumption and wealth of the individual or the household. How is the material well-being distributed when actual consumption is studied? Such data are not available in the official statistics in the same way as the different measure of income. The Level of Living Survey, however, makes such a study possible.

Consumption

In order to attain a more comprehensive picture of the economic standard of living, it would be appropriate to use an index of consumption and assets. One possible measure in this context is access to a cash margin. Other typical economic assets are owning a house and possessing a car, boat, or summer cottage. A holiday trip during the past year must also be a sign that assets are not completely lacking. These indicators were built to an index that gives *one* possible measure of the individual's economic resources. The index is constructed in the simplest manner, so that one point is received for every economic asset. The individual thus could have from 0 to 6 points on the index.

By necessity this is a rather arbitrary index. Owning a single-family or detached house, even if mortgaged, involves a much higher value than having taken a holiday trip, although the two are given equal weights. The arbitrariness, which is unavoidable in all index construction, can be controlled to some extent by examining whether alternative indices yield about the same results for trends and distribution among groups.

Using the individual variables in the index warrants a few comments. As in other contexts, whether one claims to be able to borrow the money within one week is also counted as access to a cash margin. Owning a house is measured by ownership of a detached house or of a flat in a housing association or co-operative. Caravans are counted as summer cottages. No valuation was made of the cars or boats, since such information was lacking in the 1968 study. Nor has any gradation been made of holiday trips, although an affirmative answer naturally conceals consumption of a rather varying range.

People who stated that their parents pay for their housing are not included in this account of the distribution of economic assets. Thus, most of the young people, primarily students, who live in their parents' home drop out of the analysis. The reason for this is that these people are difficult to classify by economic assets. Without owning either car, boat, summer house, or house, they may have full access to such a standard of living. Married people on the other hand, are counted here as owners of a house, a car, and so on, even when these items formally are in their spouse's name.

Table 8.13 Proportion of adult population 15–75 years with different numbers
of economic assets 1968, 1974 and 1981. Percentages. (Total index
based on 'owns car', 'owns boat', 'owns summer house', 'took
vacation trip last year', 'has cash margin', and 'owns dwelling')

Number of economic assets	1968	(cf)[a]	1974	(cf)	1981	(cf)
6	2	(2)	3	(3)	4	(4)
5	7	(9)	11	(14)	15	(19)
4	19	(28)	24	(38)	28	(47)
3	29	(57)	28	(66)	25	(72)
2	25	(82)	20	(86)	17	(89)
1	13	(95)	10	(96)	8	(97)
People with only one asset						
car	1.6		1.2		1.1	
boat	0.2		0		0	
summer house/caravan	0.1		0.1		0	
vacation trip	2.6		2.3		2.1	
cash margin	6.9		5.3		3.9	
dwelling	1.8		0.7		0.6	
0		5 (100)		4 (100)		3 (100)

[a] cf = cumulative frequency

Fluctuations in the proportions of the adult population that have
different numbers of the economic assets are shown in Table 8.13. The
cumulative frequencies reveal that the proportion with at least a given
number of assets increased throughout the period. For example, almost
half had at least four assets during 1981, compared with slightly over
one-quarter in 1968. The averages for the number of economic assets on
the three measurement dates were 2.7, 3.0, and 3.3.

For those people claiming only one economic asset, the asset in
question is shown in the table. The remaining groups naturally are all
composed of different combinations. Among those people with two
assets, the largest group consists of individuals with cash margins and
holiday travel. Two of the combinations of three assets account for more
than half of that group, namely those with cash margins and cars, with a
third asset of either holiday trips or house ownership. The combination
of the four assets of cash margin, car, holiday trip, and house ownership,
is the most common for 1974 and 1981, with 15 and 18 per cent of the
population.

The distribution of economic assets among social and occupational
groups is presented in Table 8.14. As expected, members of class I have
more economic assets than those in class II, who in their turn have more
than class III. The number of economic assets has risen during the period

Table 8.14 Average economic assets and proportion with at least four assets among social and occupational groups 1968 and 1981

	Average economic assets		Proportion with at least four economic assets (%)	
	1968	1981	1968 -	1981
Economically active I	3.7	4.0	55	69
Housewives I	3.9	4.1	64	73
Students I	2.2	2.6	13	22
Pensioners I	3.0	3.5	29	51
Class I, all	3.5	3.8	50	62
Economically active II	3.2	3.7	37	61
Housewives II	3.2	3.5	39	54
Students II	2.3	2.4	21	17
Pensioners II	2.1	2.8	12	34
Class II, all	3.1	3.6	35	57
Economically active III	2.6	3.2	27	45
Housewives III	2.5	3.0	22	37
Students III	1.6	2.6	4	22
Pensioners III	1.5	2.2	5	15
Handicapped	0.9	1.2	2	5
Class III, all	2.4	3.0	22	38
Population 15–75 years	2.7	3.3	29	47
Proportion explained variance	0.27	0.18	0.15 -	0.12 -

for all classes. The increase has been faster in the two lower classes. This is manifest in the figures for the average number of assets as well as the proportion with at least four assets. The same results are attained if the cut-off point is set at a minimum of three or five assets.

The findings indicate that an equalization has occurred between the classes for economic assets. In particular, class II has greatly narrowed the gap with class I. In 1981, however, relatively strong differences between the classes were still observed.

One can with some justification object that the picture given here of the distribution among classes would be different if the index were defined otherwise. An index based on assets such as TVs, showers, and modern stoves, for example, would hardly show the distinctions between classes today. If, on the other hand, measures such as trips outside Scandinavia, summer cottages worth more than 100,000 SEK, and more highly valued personal property were included, greater differences among social and occupational groups could be established. That this is in part true is seen in Tables 8.15 and 8.16. With extreme distributions where very few or almost everyone has some assets, however, the explained variance is small.

Table 8.15 Mean value for cars, boats, and summer cottages among owners in different social classes, 1981 (1000s SEK)[a]

| | Mean values for | | |
	Car	Boat	Summer cottage[b]
Class I	20	24	165
Class II	19	20	129
Class III	14	14	82
All	17	18	115

[a] Total population, including residents in parents' home.
[b] Caravans are excluded here.

Cars, boats, and summer cottages are used in our index with no regard to their actual worth. In Table 8.15, sizeable differences are found among the classes when the values are noted among those owning a specific property. For example, summer cottages in class I are worth twice as much as those in class III.

Table 8.16 shows that the relative differences between the classes are greater for holiday trips outside Scandinavia than for holiday trips in general. For the former, however, the differences among classes are relatively less in 1981 than in 1968. The main trends therefore seem to be the same if the index in part is defined differently.

Table 8.16 Proportion in different social classes who took any holiday trip, middle european trip, or southern european trip previous year. 1981. Percentages[a]

	Any holiday trip	Central European trip	Southern European trip
Class I	82	24	17
Class II	70	12	12
Class III	60	7	9
All	66	11	11

[a] Total population, including residents in parents' homes

For one central measure in the index on economic assets, namely home ownership, the developments are different than for the other measures. The proportion of people living in dwellings owned by housing associations or co-operatives does not vary among the classes, whereas substantial changes have taken place since 1968 as to members of which classes own houses. The proportion of households in the different social and occupational groups that live in single-family houses is given in Table 10.7. Table 10.7 clearly shows that home ownership is disproportionately high in classes I and II. The lower public salaried employees in particular rapidly increased their home ownership from 1968 to 1981. The 1968 differences among the classes were thus reinforced.

Wealth

Two other measures of economic assets will be mentioned before various findings are compared and summarized. Recorded wealth is a reasonable measure that should be included when accouting for distribution of economic resources. Unfortunately, it is inappropriate for analysis. The quality of these data is defective, since wealth not subject to taxation is not always very carefully scrutinized by the tax authorities. Nor does merely computing wealth as assets minus liabilities accurately depict the individual's or household's material standards. Heavy debts are often associated with great wealth and may indicate a fairly high level of consumption.

These problems, however, can be partially avoided; first, by restricting the analysis to taxable wealth, and second, by also studying tax relief. A study of the changes in the ownership of wealth during the relevant period demands that consideration is given to the various limits to taxable wealth, and also to changes in money value. The comparison therefore will refer to proportions in different groups with a capital worth of 300,000 SEK or more (in 1980 prices) for the years 1966 and 1980. The classification of households is the same as was used in the section on their purchasing power.

From Table 8.17, it is clear that no increase occurred in the proportion with capital wealth of at least 300,000 SEK. However, the differences between the groups are considerable and do not follow class divisions precisely. A clear boundary separates employees from proprietors. In an account by class, farmers would bring up the proportion with capital wealth in class II, since most of them belong to that class.

This shows that a simple comparison among classes is not totally accurate. Not only does the proportion of proprietors vary but also that of one- and several-person households, which in turn influences the wealth profile. To control for effects of these circumstances, a tabulation of wealth for married households among employees in the different classes will be given here separately.

Table 8.17 Proportion of households with wealth of at least 300,000 SEK 1966 and 1980, by different employment groups. Percentages (1980 money values)

	Proportion with wealth	
	1966	1980
Students	3	0
Pensioners III	2	2
Pensioners I and II	17	14
Workers	1	2
Lower-salaried II	3	4
Small proprietors	14	8
Class I	16	9
Farmers	23	19
All households	5.3	4.9

Table 8.18 Proportion married households with wealth of at least 300,000 SEK 1966 and 1980, as well as tax relief 1967 and 1980, by social class. Only employees (1980 money value)

	Proportion with wealth (%)		Proportion with tax relief (%)		Per cent of average tax relief	
	1966	1980	1967	1980	1967	1980
Class I	12	10	62	90	221	194
Class II	3	6	41	81	98	99
Class III	1	4	33	73	66	63
All	2.6	5.4	38	79	100	100
Average tax relief (SEK)					4100	14 800

In Table 8.18 an increase is shown in the capital worth among employees who are members of married households. Among the households with only one adult, however, the capital worth decreased. A trend towards equalization between the classes is clear. This is the same as the one observed in the index on economic assets.

Slightly different results were obtained, however, when wealth and consumption were studied by means of tax relief (see discussion on individual incomes in this chapter). More households make use of tax relief, and a marjority of the economically active households claimed relief in 1980. The picture given by the distribution of tax relief, however, is in part due to the type of comparison being made.

Table 8.19 Households' tax relief 1967 and 1980, by occupational groups. (1980 money values)

	Proportion of the total tax relief (%)			Proportion in tax relief (%)		Per cent of average tax relief	
	1967 (a)	1980 (b)	1980 (c)	1967 (d)	1980 (e)	1967 (f)	1980 (g)
Students	0	0	0	5	25	34	19
Pensioners III	1	1	1	10	23	27	21
Pensioners I and II	2	2	1	18	33	54	49
Workers	23	18	23	23	58	62	51
Lower-salaried II	26	29	28	32	69	92	94
Small proprietors II	12	14	15	42	75	112	160
Class I	32	31	25	55	81	242	260
Farmers	3	5	7	10	34	169	199
All households	100	100	100	25	57	100	100
Average tax relief (SEK)						4100	13 900

In column (c) the proportions are calculated on 1967 group sizes.

It is clear from Table 8.19 that the working class decreased their proportion of the total claiming tax relief between 1967 and 1980, in favour of small proprietors and lower salaried employees (columns a and b). This change is nevertheless due to the fact that working-class households decreased in number, while the higher classes increased. When consideration is given to changes in class size, it is clear that the working class has the same proportion of the total tax relief in 1980 as in 1967. On the other hand, class I has declined in comparison with class II (column c).

Shifts in the proportion of total tax relief among the classes can be partly achieved by changes in the proportion with tax relief in the classes, and partly by increases or decreases in the size of tax relief. It can be seen in the table that the proportion with tax relief increased the most among the working class (along with farmers) (columns d and e). On the other hand, the size of increases in tax relief among those claiming relief was relatively higher in the upper classes (columns f and g). However, when only married households among employed persons are studied the difference between the size of tax relief decreases over time (Table 8.18). The findings of the investigation of tax relief are to be expected, judging from the trends among home-owners during 1970s. But a different picture emerges from the one seen in the analysis of taxable wealth, and the index on economic assets. The picture of a dramatic equalization of the material standards between the classes from 1967 to 1980 is no longer as clear cut.

Conclusion

The findings of the study of the development of economic resources can be summarized as follows:

1. Incomes and consumption in Sweden rose between 1967 and 1980.
2. A clear equalization of incomes can be observed for this period.
3. The income equalization is an effect of political measures.
4. Equalization is less pronounced for consumption and wealth than for incomes.

The manifest equalization of incomes seen for the period 1967 to 1980 appears to be primarily politically determined. One cause of the equalization is the increase in employment that reduced the number of zero-income earners substantially. Another is union wage policies that have led to a decrease in wage differentials. A third reason is the prevailing distribution policy, under which the system of transfers of resources has contributed to income equalization. The greatest share has been increases in pensions.

The rise in income applies to all groups except professionals in public employment, who have experienced a slight drop in individual incomes (but not in household incomes). The development in incomes alone, however, does not provide a complete picture of the economic situation of different groups. A comparison in consumption using an index on economic assets shows an increase in economic resources for all groups, that is, even for the higher public salaried employees.

If wealth and consumption are measured by home-ownership and tax relief, glaring disparities emerge between the classes. These differences did not decrease between 1967 and 1980. Class II is closer to class I, while class III is still lagging seriously behind. So class I, despite a long-term income equalization, has succeeded in holding on to its solid lead in economic resources. This is probably mostly due to the use of tax relief and the high rate of inflation during the 1970s.

The development in incomes from 1967 to 1980 has resulted in less inequality between groups. Does this point towards a continued equalization? Judging from recent years, it does not. In the introductory discussion, it was described how periods of income equalization alternate with periods of relatively stable distribution. The period covered by the Level of Living Surveys has perhaps now reached its end. As shown earlier, the changes in wage levels is highly significant for incomes. The most recent income distribution study shows that the equalization of earned income and disposable income has not continued into the 1980s (SCB 1983b, Table 8 and 1983c, Table 2). Much of the evidence indicates that a new period is unfolding with unchanged distribution, or even broadening income gaps.

Notes

1. This does not apply to 1967 and 1973. For the sake of comparison, therefore, these benefits were calculated at their value before tax and added to the totalled income for these years.
2. For data technical reasons, it was impossible to exclude income from occasional economic activity such as selling one's house. So that the comparisons would not be misleading, this type of income was also included in 1973 and 1980. Since this type of income is so small, our view is that the error is negligible.
3. Some uncertainty is inherent in the data on pensions, since it was based in 1967 on interviews, while in 1980 it was taken from tax documents. The data in both cases cover all pensions and annuities.
4. A more detailed description of the pension system construction and operations is given in SOU 1977:46 'Pension Questions, etc.' (in Swedish, but with an English summary).
5. The Level of Living Survey is a sample of individuals. A household of married people then has about twice as great a chance of being selected as does a single person household. For this reason, households of married persons are weighted as half as heavy as other households in the calculations.
6. A detailed description and testing of the procedure used is found in Erikson (1981).
7. Here reservations about farming households are even stronger than previously, since the estimates of the actual housing costs for these are extremely doubtful, as was pointed out in the chapter on housing conditions.
8. When average disposable incomes as calculated for decile groups defined by disposable income and not factor incomes, appreciable differences are obtained for the two first decile groups. The averages are then 12,000 and 20,000 in 1967, and 19,000 and 24,000 in 1980 for these groups. The worst-off households in 1980 thus have better resources than their 1967 counterparts.

Appendix: definition of disposable income

The variable is based on total income without tax relief which should be neutral in relation to the different forms of residence. In 1980, several social benefits were liable to taxation. This was not the case in 1967. Therefore, for 1967 the interview data must be used along with register data, probably slightly reducing the quality of the variable, see

Söderström (SOU 1971:39).

Disposable income in 1980 was equal in total income as declared on the tax returns of the interviewee (ip) and of the spouse (m) + student loans for ip and m + child allowances (computed according to norms from the number of children) + maintenance payments for single people with children (computed as 0.41 times the basic amount for each child) + housing allowances + pensioner's amount for non-taxed pensioners + incomes according to employers' and authorities' data for the remaining non-taxed people – final tax charged including fees for social benefits for entrepreneurs.

Disposable income 1967 = totalled income according to tax returns for ip and m + seamen's incomes for ip and m + labour-market allowances for ip and m + retraining subsidies for ip and m + student loans for ip and m + child allowances (computed according to norms) + maintenance advances (norm computed) + family residence allowances + incomes according to interview data for non-taxed people – final tax charged including fees for social benefits for entrepreneurs.

For cohabiting unmarried couples in 1967, interview data were used for m. Repayment of student loans was not included since these data were lacking for 1967. Periodic support payments were not subtracted from the income as these data were lacking.

9

Educational Resources

JANNE JONSSON

Education — intrinsic value and resource value

Education, and the knowledge gained thereby, can be considered to have an intrinsic value and a resource value. The intrinsic value of an education can be said to involve a person's abilities to liberate his thinking capacity and live a richer inner life. This is reflected in, for example, the search for knowledge for its own sake and in the classic scholarly ideal: a society on a high level of morality and culture.

Resource for the individual

For the individual, education is a resource for controlling and consciously directing his living conditions (S. Johansson 1970a, 25). Education provides a basis for understanding the society we live in and its decision processes. Knowledge of legal rights, and how to make use of them (for example, appealing against an authority's decision), is strongly correlated with education, which thereby constitutes an important resource for counteracting powerlessness.

However, education is a resource for the individual in different ways and within different fields. It is not only a resource in the political arena, but also in the marketplace, private life and leisure. But the most obvious value of education is as a resource on the labour market. The type and level of a person's education determines to a great extent the occupational position which he will attain, which then affects, for example, his working environment, income, power, and social status.

The education of a job applicant can be said to be decisive for employers in two ways: a person with a certain education has a certain specified field of knowledge and a person with a high level of education presumably has certain desirable personal qualifications (for example, personal drive, talent, discipline, and the capacity to learn). In this way the educational system functions as a screening mechanism (Stiglitz 1975).

The competency provided by a formal education is most important as a means of selection when a person is applying for his first job. An occupationally experienced employee has naturally increased his knowledge and skills which, in turn, increases his/her competitive strength.

On the labour market, education can be described as a relative resource which is dependent on, for example, the demand for labour and the supply of people with a particular education (see for example, SOU 1971:61, 124).

Resource for groups of individuals

Different groups in society have different and often opposing interests, and in conflicts between these groups education can be an important resource. Conflicting groups can be expected to be organized within sections of the occupational structure,[1] as those with similar positions in the division of labour share common interests. Educational issues have often been given a central political role by the working class, and have even 'been considered to be the most important strategic instrument for dismantling the class boundaries'.[2] Alongside the national school system, the working class has, through its unions and broad educational associations, carried out its own educational programmes. The purpose has been partly to increase the level of education and political consciousness and partly to prepare itself for taking over the leadership of the country.

Resource for society

Education is also a resource for society. A higher level of education among the population benefits society as a whole. We mentioned earlier the idea of a morally and culturally advanced society, but beyond this the participation of citizens in the society's decision-making processes is of great importance for democracy to develop. It is therefore natural to assert that an increased level of general education leads to increased welfare in society, not only because all these who get a higher education thereby get increased resources, but also because an increased average level of education contributes to the welfare of all citizens.

At the end of the 1950s and especially in the early 1960s the belief in education — and research — grew, both as the most important single factor behind individual economic success and behind the growth of the gross national product. Even if many people had too much faith in its economic effects, education has probably contributed to the growth of the welfare society. It is undeniable that the belief in education, along with economic growth, led to a substantially increased investment in education. The results have been, for example, longer compulsory schooling and an increased variety of specializations in education, more extensive courses in working life and increased availability of adult studies and study circles.[3] This has caused many people to predict the growth of what is called 'the learning society' in which increased leisure for the population is used to a great extent for studying. In this society education would constitute an important and recurring feature for citizens of all ages.

Equality in educational opportunities

Education consequently constitutes a central resource for the individual. The demand for equal educational opportunities therefore stands out as one of the most important goals in regard to equality. In Swedish educational policy, the goal of equality means that the distribution of education between citizens shall be determined by talent and interest. Educational opportunities shall not, in other words, be related to other factors such as sex, class origin, or type of childhood community.

The goal of equality is, however, neither uncontroversial nor easy to fulfil. It has its basis in the liberal demands raised during the 1800s as a reaction against inherited privileges — the idea of equality of opportunity is thereby closely connected to the idea of social mobility. But the obvious inequalities which are inherent in different social environments mean that the entire idea of equality of opportunity is only a chimera. It has been compared with 'the impertinent courtesy of an invitation offered to unwelcome guests, in the certainty that circumstances will prevent them from accepting it' (Tawney 1964, 110).

If one concentrates on the idea that everyone shall have the opportunity to compete on equal terms for higher positions in an unequal society, there is furthermore a risk that the inequality will be regarded as 'just' and that the existing differences in rewards between different occupations will thereby be consolidated.

The meritocracy — a new type of elite rule

There have also been warnings about other consequences which fulfilment of the equality goal could cause in an otherwise unequal society. The 1946 School Commission expressed, for example, the apprehension that all intellectually gifted children would choose a theoretical education, and that the working classes would thereby lose their potential leaders (SOU 1948:27, 9). In line with this idea representatives for both workers and farmers described inequality in educational opportunities, somewhat paradoxically, as a 'useful inequality' which strengthened democracy, even though it could affect individuals quite negatively.[4]

These ideas can also be found in Michael Young's classic social satire *The Rise of the Meritocracy 1870–2033* (1958) in which the author cautions against an excessively effective recruitment of intellectually gifted people from each of the social classes. The result could be a new type of class society, a meritocracy, in which the gifted and well-educated constitute a privileged elite that will come to enjoy all of society's rewards: high incomes, power, and status. The new power structure would also appear to be 'just' since only personal qualifications would be used to determine whether or not an individual will reach a high position in society. Fears have been expressed that today's modern societies now contain certain meritocratic tendencies.

The important questions

Regarding education as a resource, we shall concentrate on its importance in the labour market by examining the correlation between educational levels and occupational positions. To what extent does education determine class position? Have the opportunities for 'working your way up' decreased? Is education as a resource declining or increasing in value?

Of the various educational policy goals, the goal of equality seems to be the most central. Is it still true that men have greater opportunities than women to obtain a higher education? Has the difference between urban and rural areas disappeared? Do class boundaries still exist in spite of all the educational reforms that have been carried out?

Finally, the answers to the questions above raise broader and more speculative questions: Where are we heading? Is the learning society close at hand? Do the trends indicate a more equal distribution of educational opportunities? Are we getting closer to a new type of class society — the meritocracy?

Data

Our data regarding the adult population is drawn from three different surveys. The first is the Labour Market Survey which was carried out in 1967 and included a section on education. A proportion of these interviewees were then selected for the first Level of Living Survey in 1968. Therefore no questions about education were posed there. However, almost identical questions about education were posed in the 1974 and in the 1981 Level of Living Survey to essentially the same sample.[5]

After a series of follow-up interviews and the application of other methodological controls, the reliability of the answers to the questions about education was found to be satisfactory. The measurement errors which were observed had hardly any effect on the main results of the surveys. Minor changes and small differences in the material should not, however, be used as the basis of any conclusions.

How was education measured?

In the following review of the results we will use both years of education and educational level as units of measurement. Years of education is useful for describing more general trends, and is measured here as the combined total of years completed with full-time studies in school and in vocational education. During the last decades, the question of quality in education has often been debated. Since we essentially lack any measures of knowledge and ability, we assume that a year of education is of equal value regardless of when it took place.[6]

The level of education is an adequate measure with regard to the hierarchical structure of working life, and appears to reflect the differences in opportunities on the labour market. Since the education system has undergone major changes during the 1900s, a short background to our division into levels of education will be given.

Educational reforms

Some form of obligatory education has existed in Sweden since 1686, but the memorable year for public education was 1842 when the community school system was introduced. This involved five to six years of compulsary education for all children. However, in practice, it was not until forty years later that compulsory education, with a more regulated attendance, was established. For a long time the community schools were schools for the poor and provided no opportunities for further studies. The children of the wealthy received private educations and were sent to secondary school. Thereafter, in more rare cases, they went to university to obtain an academic degree.

At the beginning of this century a 'middle class reform' was put into effect and lower secondary schools were introduced as a link between community schools and the higher school system. The differentiation (selection for a higher education) occurred after the third year in community school — from 1928 it was after the fourth year. Liberal and socialist circles criticized this system of parallel schools which, in practice, meant that the higher classes in community schools were for children of workers and farmers and higher education was for the children of the bourgeoisie. Nevertheless this system remained in effect until the 1950s. In the meantime compulsory education was lengthened from six to seven years, and in practice even to eight years throughout most of the country.

An Act of Parliament in 1950 produced the most dramatic educational reform since the introduction of community schools, namely the comprehensive elementary school system. After a decade of experiment and adjustment, this system established nine years of compulsory education for all children. Since there are very few private schools in Sweden, almost all children now go through comprehensive elementary schools.

With the introduction of the comprehensive elementary schools, the lower secondary schools disappeared. The fact that they were essentially incorporated into the compulsory education system is an indication of the greatly increased educational level in the population. The lower secondary school diploma, as well as the upper secondary school diploma, is no longer granted, which means that within the Swedish education system degrees are only granted at the university level.

Vocational education was independent of the public education system for a long time. The apprentice system and independent vocational schools were dominant until after World War II. During the 1950s and especially the 1960s, several major reforms were introduced regarding vocational education, which then expanded substantially. Regarding the older types of vocational education one should note the difference between vocational schools which were based on a completed community school education (lower vocational school) and those which required a lower secondary school diploma. The former were mainly manufacturing and mechanics schools for boys (the normal educational background for skilled workers) and domestic science schools for girls. The latter included various technical, commercial, and economic branches of education as well as, for example, nursing schools.

From the broad variety of vocational schools organized in different ways, the new 'gymnasium', a secondary school, was created, and placed under the management of local government. The older upper secondary schools were also made a part of this system, which meant that two levels of education became organizationally unified, but in reality remained separate. The 'lower' level of secondary school consists of two years of secondary education, while the 'higher' level consists of three to four years of secondary education. The higher levels of secondary education have undergone great changes in content. Above all the choice of courses leading to different vocations has been successively increased.

One goal of the latest reforms has been to provide all citizens with the opportunity of further education. Even students with two years of secondary schooling, in theory, have a reasonable chance of continuing their studies. For those who have already left school the expansion of the adult education system provides an opportunity for higher education.

Education at the university level has changed in character. The number of degree programmes made up essentially of required courses and directed towards certain occupations, has increased substantially. After a reform in 1977, various kinds of further vocational education were given academic status. This mainly involved the two-year nursing and teacher training courses of that time. However, to make it possible to compare the data from the latest survey wth the previous ones, these courses are classified as further vocational courses in 1981 as well.

Educational level

As indicated above, the foundation of the Swedish education system has changed during the past three decades. In very rough terms we can distinguish two separate educational hierarchies, one which existed up to the 1960s and thereafter the current hierarchy:

1. Community school
2. Lower vocational school
3. Lower secondary school   3. Elementary school
4. Vocational secondary school   4. Two-year secondary school
5. Upper secondary school   5. Three-year secondary school
6. Vocational upper sec. school   6. Further voc. school
7. University degree   7. University degree

To be able to use the level of education as a measurement that applies to the entire population, we combined the educational hierarchies in a manner that is shown by the numbering of the various educational levels.[7]

The average years of education per educational level remained fairly constant during the period. The spread of years of education was relatively large for each level (Table 9.1).

Table. 9.1 Average years of education per educational level in the adult population (15–75 years old) in 1967, 1974, and 1981. Variation intervals in the years of education on each educational level as well as the percentage of people outside this interval. Non-students

Level of education	Years of education			Variation intervals	Percentage outside this interval		
	1967	1974	1981		1967	1974	1981
1. Community school	6.6	6.7	6.6	6–8	6	6	4
2. Lower voc school	9.0	9.2	9.2	7–11	8	8	8
3. Lower sec/elem school	9.8	9.6	9.4	8–11	10	7	6
4. Voc low sec/2-y secondary	11.9	11.9	11.8	10–14	12	12	10
5. Upper sec/3-y secondary	12.9	12.9	12.6	11–14	14	11	10
6. Post upper sec	14.8	14.6	14.4	12–16	16	11	11
7. University degree	17.4	17.4	17.5	14–20	10	10	13

More people are studying for longer periods

The educational reforms have led to a substantial lengthening of the average amount of time spent in education by the adult population, which is shown by Figure 9.1. However, this is not a question of an 'education explosion' which can be attributed to a particular reform or decade. Rather, there has been a fairly even growth in the average years of education throughout this century.

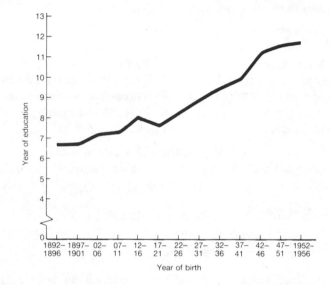

Fig. 9.1   Average length of education in different groups of cohorts. Non-students[a]

[a]   In the age-groups 1942–46 and 1947–51 together, 6.2 per cent were still studying at the time of the interview in 1981. The corresponding proportion for the youngest age-group is 8.1 per cent.

The shift towards an increasing number of people at the higher educational levels is also demonstrated clearly by Figure 9.2. One can see that the share of people at the three highest levels more than doubled between 1967 and 1981.

The change in the composition of education is emphasized if the age groups are compared. When the oldest group in the 1967 survey (born 1892–1910) went to school, an upper secondary school diploma was an exclusive privilege reserved for 2–3 per cent of the population while 80 per cent had no education beyond the compulsory six-year community schools. With regard to those educated during the 1960s and 1970s, it was very common that they continued their education after completion of

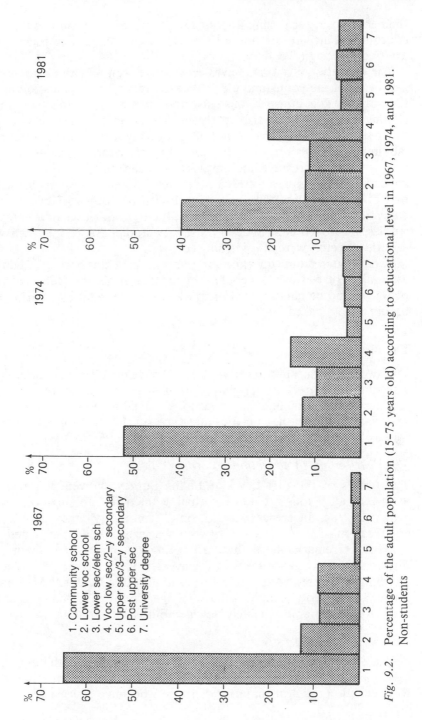

Fig. 9.2. Percentage of the adult population (15–75 years old) according to educational level in 1967, 1974, and 1981. Non-students

1. Community school
2. Lower voc school
3. Lower sec/elem sch
4. Voc low sec/2–y secondary
5. Upper sec/3–y secondary
6. Post upper sec
7. University degree

their compulsory schooling – about 75 per cent of this group had a higher education. Furthermore, more than 20 per cent continued their studies after completing secondary school.

The educational reforms have, as we have seen, created a substantial gap between the young and old. What the minister of education at that time called 'This injustice, this class boundary between the generations' (Palme 1967, 116) was also foreseen. The critics claimed that, among other things, older people would have a difficult time competing in the labour market against younger, well-educated people. To prevent this, and to try to create some fairness between the generations, adult education programmes were considerably expanded during the second half of the 1960s and throughout the 1970s. Reforms to facilitate adult education (improved student financing, the right to leaves of absence for studies, improved admission to university studies for people with work experience, etc.) were also introduced.

Even though adult education programmes have not been utilized to an especially great extent by people over the age of 50, the fears that older people would be handicapped in competition in the labour market have hardly been realized.[8]

The distribution of education

The sweeping education reforms of the 1950s and 1960s had equality, to a substantial degree, as their major point of reference.[9] In the following section we shall examine the extent to which education is still related to sex, class origin (father's class), and type of childhood community, as well as how these relationships developed from 1968 to 1981.

The distribution of education according to sex

The results of the first Level of Living Survey showed that men, on average, had a longer education than women (L. Johansson, 1971a). However, the difference was so small among younger people that equalization of the difference between the sexes could be expected.

What is remarkable is that, according to our measurements, the differences between the sexes in the average years of education have if anything, increased both relatively and in absolute figures.[10] Men have a longer average education in each of the age groups and, on average, men went to school approximately seven months longer than women (see Figure 9.3).

The differences in average years of education can, for the most part, be explained by the sex distribution of the different educational levels. Men constitute a clear majority of those who have at least received an

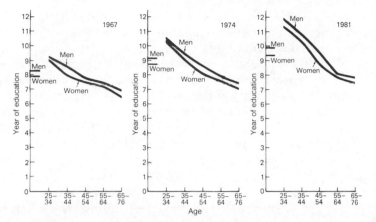

Fig. 9.3. Average years of education for men and women, respectively, in the adult population (15–75 years old) according to age (five age groups) in 1967, 1974, and 1981. Non-students[a]

[a] The lines on the vertical axis show the average length of education for those adults (25–75 years of age) men and women respectively, who were not studying at the time of the interview.

upper secondary school diploma or completed three years at secondary school. Not even 30 per cent of the people with academic degrees in 1981 were women.

Accordingly, on the whole, men dominate the higher educational levels and the changes between 1967 and 1981 were insignificant. In a regression analysis — in which age, class origin, and type of childhood community have been held constant — this conclusion is corroborated.[11] The importance of a person's sex in educational attainment was substantial and unchanged for the population as a whole between 1967 and 1981. The differences were, however, smaller for people in the younger age groups, which indicates a trend toward equalization. Such an interpretation is also supported by other more recent statistics (Educational Statistics Yearbook 1981; SCB 1985) which show that the percentage of women in further education by now is higher than the percentage of men. An equalization between the sexes has also occurred regarding what could be called the prestigious academic subjects (for example, medicine, law, and business economics). However, these are still dominated by men which indicates that sex differences in the youngest age group are somewhat underestimated.

The differences between the sexes were lower among the interviewees from higher class origins. Among people who grew up in large cities, sex was less of a determinating factor for getting a university degree. Instead, sex differences seemed to be especially large for people who had grown up in small cities and towns.

In the first Level of Living Survey not only was it shown that education had a high correlation with income, but also that the income of women was substantially lower than that of men, even for those with the same level of education (L. Johansson 1971a). Since then many efforts have been made to improve the situation of people with low incomes, and women constitute a majority of this group. We can also conclude that the sex differences in income[12] in relation to educational level have decreased considerably. However, men working full time in 1980 earned 10,000 to 20,000 SEK (13–26 per cent of the average income) more per year than their female counterparts at each education level.[13] The difference is smaller in the younger age groups, but this result is difficult to interpret. It could be a sign of further income equalization, but it could also indicate that the income differentiating mechanisms do not take effect until later in the occupational career.

Inheritance of educational opportunities?

Lineage is the classic determination of inherited inequality. In feudal societies it was the parents' position, and not an individual's abilities or achievements, which was decisive for their children's opportunities in life. In a book published in 1883, the liberal teacher and educational politician Fridtjuv Berg attacked the system of education. He asserted that, among other things, 'in reality schools are organized in accordance with the circumstances of the parents, and that society thereby offers the children of the so-called better classes a richer education, while the children of people of small means are given a poor education.' (Berg 1911, 71, author's translation).

What, then, has happened in the past century? Does our society and its education system still contain mechanisms that result, in practice, in the inheritance of educational opportunities between generations?

One can assume that parents often have a strong desire that their children will rise socially and perhaps end up in the highest class. Furthermore, one can assume that parents in class I, in addition to the motivation, have the resources for realizing their desire, including economic and social resources and a tradition of higher education. One way to transmit their class position to the next generation is by giving their children a higher education.

An analysis of average years of education also shows that there is a strong correlation with class origins. In 1981 people from class I homes had, on the average, over 4.5 years more education than the equivalent group with fathers in class III, 13.6 years compared to 8.9 years. However, the differences decreased slightly between 1967 and 1981.

The importance of class origin in relation to educational opportunities is clearly shown in Table 9.2. Only a small percentage of the people from class I homes were at the lower educational levels and over 25 per cent had academic degrees. Of people from the working class, almost 50 per cent had only compulsary education and not more than 8 per cent had even an upper secondary school diploma or a three-year secondary education.

Table 9.2 Percentage of people with class origins in classes I, II, and III respectively, on each educational level in 1981. Non-students

Level of education	Class of father		
	I	II	III
1. Community school	8.2	32.5	48.6
2. Lower voc school	2.7	12.3	13.7
3. Lower sec/elem school	9.4	11.3	11.4
4. Voc low sec/2-y secondary	23.0	23.8	18.1
5. Upper sec/3-y secondary	11.9	6.2	2.7
6. Post upper sec	19.2	7.2	3.4
7. University degree	25.6	6.8	2.1
Total	100.0	100.0	100.0

Nevertheless, a regression analysis shows that the effect of class origin on the level of education has decreased during the period of the surveys. Class origin tends also to be less important for younger age groups. At most of the educational levels class origin plays a greater role for women than for men, just as it is more important for people who have grown up in the countryside.

Even if a relatively large percentage of people from class I homes have an academic degree, they do not constitute a majority of people at this level (Table 9.3). Instead, people with middle-class backgrounds constitute 51 per cent of the academically educated, and more than 20 per cent come from working class homes. People with father in class II dominate the three highest educational levels, while the majority of people in the three lowest levels come from working class backgrounds.

There is indeed a high correlation between higher education and class origin, but the highest educational levels are clearly far from being an exclusive privilege for a small group of upper class children.

The prevailing dependence of education on class origin can seem surprising. In addition to the introduction of free, comprehensive schools, various other social reforms have been introduced such as free school lunches and free textbooks at the elementary and secondary levels as well as substantially improved access to study loans at the university level. That these and other attempts to diminish the biased class recruitment to higher education have not been more successful, can

Table 9.3 Percentage of people per educational level in 1981 according to class
origin. Non-students

Level of education	Class of father			Total
	I	II	III	
1. Community school	1.2	32.5	66.3	100.0
2. Lower voc school	1.2	39.0	59.8	100.0
3. Lower sec/elem school	4.7	40.1	55.1	99.9
4. Voc low sec/2-y secondary	6.3	45.9	47.7	99.9
5. Upper sec/3-y secondary	14.7	53.4	31.9	100.0
6. Post upper sec	18.8	49.7	31.5	100.0
7. University degree	27.4	50.9	21.7	100.0

presumably to a certain extent be explained by more subtle, culturally
influenced differences between the social classes (Bernstein 1975,
Bourdieu 1973). The tradition of education can be assumed to be an
especially important factor. An examination of the relative influence of
the parents' education and class origin on the interviewee's education
showed these background factors to be approximately of the same
importance (Jonsson 1985). Similar findings are reported from English as
well as from American data (Kerckhoff 1974). The effect of the
stratification system itself on educational attainment is also likely to
persist. Educational choices can, for example, be dependent on whether
they are considered to mean social demotion or promotion for the child,
and also on relative costs and benefits related to higher education
(Boudon 1974). The importance of estimating and explaining the effects
of class origin and cultural origin on education has recently been
highlighted in Sweden, while official data indicate an increased class-
recruitment to higher education in the last few years (SCB 1985).

*The importance of the childhood community in relation to educational
opportunities.*

The oldest people in our survey grew up at a time when Sweden was still
an agrarian society. The main responsibility for education at that time
was with the parents — community schools had been in existence for less
than a generation. It was natural for the sons and daughters of farmers,
smallholders, and agricultural workers to start supporting themselves
and their families as soon as possible. The years of education of these
groups still appear to be short, even if the high average age and
disproportionate sex distribution are taken into account.

Those who have grown up in the countryside have an appreciably
shorter education, on average, than those who have grown up in cities.

Table 9.4 shows that, in somewhat simplified terms, the average length of education increases with the degree of urbanization of the childhood community.

Table 9.4 Average years of education in the adult population (25–75 years) in 1981 according to age and childhood community. Non-students

Type of childhood community	Age					
	25–34	35–44	45–54	55–64	65–76	All
Rural	11.0	9.4	8.4	7.2	6.8	8.4
Villages, small towns	11.8	10.6	9.2	8.2	7.8	9.8
Other towns	12.1	12.0	11.3	8.8	8.8	11.0
Large cities	12.2	12.0	10.8	9.8	9.8	11.2

The regression analysis also indicates that the importance of the type of childhood community to the opportunities for higher education is unchanged and substantial. The likelihood of a person from the countryside being found in the three highest educational levels was consistently low. These levels are dominated by people who grew up in large cities. On the other hand, people from the countryside are increasing their representation in all the other levels. As we pointed out earlier, the importance of class origin to education is greatest for people who have grown up in the countryside.

Education and occupational position

We have described education as a decisive factor with regard to the individual's future occupational position and claimed that educational level was the measurement which best reflected the labour market's structure. The relationship is obvious for some groups — one does not become a doctor or a lawyer without an academic degree — but not as obvious for others; for private executives in class I and for most class II occupations, the same formal requirements regarding education do not exist.

The results in Figure 9.4 indicate that if we know a person's educational level, we can fairly accurately predict his position in the occupational hierarchy. The likelihood of a person with an education on one of the three lower levels belonging to class I, or of someone with an academic education having an occupation in class III, is very small indeed — in 1981 it was about 2 per cent in each case. The trend also seems to indicate that increasing numbers of people with a middle level

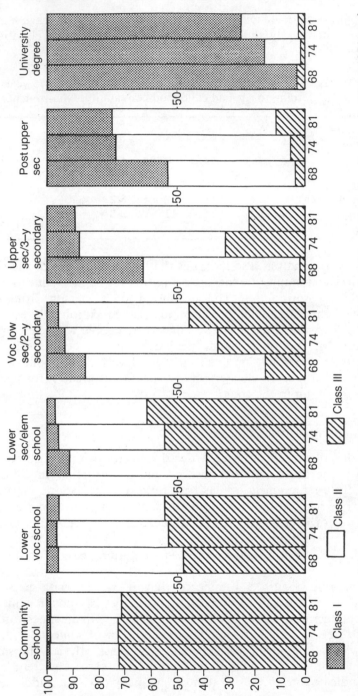

Fig. 9.4. Percentage of the adult population (15–75 years old) at each educational level, according to class, in 1968,[a] 1974, and 1981. Non-students

[a] Educational level applies to 1967, but class membership applies to 1968.

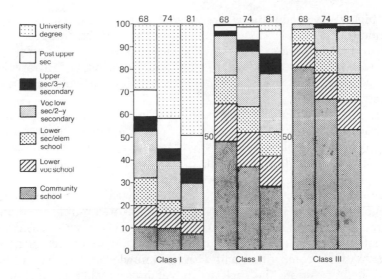

Fig. 9.5. Percentage of the adult population (15–75 years old) in classes I, II and III respectively, according to educational level, in 1968,[a] 1974, and 1981. Non-students

[a] Educational level applies to 1967, but class membership applies to 1968.

education (3 and 4) ended up in class III, and that a greater share of the people in the three highest educational levels had occupations in class II.

In 1968 an academic degree practically guaranteed an individual a high occupational position. In 1981 three-quarters of the academically educated still went into class I occupations, but the decrease is striking. While the likelihood of a person with an academic degree ending up *outside* class I increased, the share of the academically educated *in* class I also increased (Figure 9.5). An academic education thus seems to have gone from being a sufficient but not necessary condition for getting an occupational position in class I to being something which is increasingly required without being sufficient in itself. The possibility of 'working your way up' has presumably decreased to an equivalent degree.

Class I is becoming, in educational terms, increasingly homogeneous because of its increasing percentage of people with academic degrees. This can, to some extent, counteract the heterogeneous aspects which class I displays with regard to class origin (see Chapter 3). At the same time, class III and even class II are becoming, in educational terms, increasingly heterogeneous since more and more people with middle level and higher level educations are unable to compete successfully for occupations in class I. These people should be an increasing resource for the working class if they also share the values of the working class. It can also result in the stratification, or even division, of a previously homogeneous class, which could make it more difficult to carry out collective action.

If it is assumed that an academic education leads to a common cultural identification and sharing of values between individuals, the trend would lead to more similar frames of reference and a greater sense of community within the upper class. This would probably increase the socio-political strength of class I.

Another tendency, however, is that the Swedish school system has changed, in Turner's terms, from one of 'sponsored mobility' to one of 'contest mobility' (Turner 1960). Before the reforms the selection of students who were to go on to higher education was made at an early stage. Without competition and with the knowledge that they all would reach high positions in society, university students could, in their seclusion, assimilate the culture, customs, and habits which distinguished society's élite. With selection later in the system and increasing competition both to get in and within academic education, this homogeneity has presumably decreased. Increased specialization at the academic level has probably had the same effect.

Education — a relative resource

The trend from 1967 to 1981 of a marked increase in the percentage of highly educated people entailed a decrease in the likelihood of obtaining a job in class I on the basis of a given educational level, while the equivalent likelihood of getting a job in class III has increased. This supports the idea of education as a relative resource, or a 'positional good' (Hirsch 1976).

In order to examine more closely how the value of education as a resource in the labour market has changed, we studied the percentages of people at each educational level who had occupations in class III in 1968 and 1981 respectively (Table 9.5). The comparison is made between student groups from the last years of the community schools (born 1937–1940) and student groups who were almost exclusively covered by the comprehensive elementary school reform (born 1954–1957).[14]

The general increase in education is displayed by the two columns on the right: the percentage with only a compulsory education was reduced by half between 1967 and 1981 and the percentage with further education tripled.

All the people in the 1968 group with education at the three highest levels ended up in class I or II. In 1981 there was still a high correlation between university degrees and occupational positions in class I and II,[15] but every third person at both of the other levels had an occupational position in class III at the time of the interview. A larger percentage of those who had had two years of secondary education had class III occupations in 1981 than the people with vocational secondary school had in 1968. People with only an elementary school education in 1981 seemed also to have a more difficult time in competing for higher positions that those who only had a community school education in 1968.

The base in Table 9.5 is relatively small, which means that one should refrain from interpreting the details. However, taken together with the results presented earlier, the trend seems clear: *as the general level of education has increased, the value of each education level has decreased on the labour market.* The increasing number of people with a higher education do not have the same relative advantages today as their predecessors had as a result of their education. In turn, the decreasing number with only compulsory education are having a more difficult time competing in the labour market than the equivalent group previously had. At the same time, with this 'educational inflation', the necessity of higher education has increased in the labour market.

Education has been mentioned as a screening mechanism. As a result of the inflation in education, the educational level has become less informative as a selection criterion for higher occupational positions. The consequence could be that employers will intensify the selection process for such occupations, for example, by requiring higher school marks or an even higher education. This is, however, hardly sufficient in all cases, which means that employers may start using selection criteria other than education to a greater degree. Personal contacts, references, and work experience as well as personal qualities can in this manner become increasingly important as assets in the labour market. However, with the growing specialization in education, another dimension has been added to the selection process. Selection is probably becoming increasingly dependent on the individual's branch of study.

Where are we heading?

The learning society

We have described 'the learning society' as a society in which education constitutes an important and recurring element in people's lives. Our results also indicate that increasing numbers are obtaining an increasingly longer education, in more varied forms, and that they get education more frequently.

Table 9.5 Percentages of people born 1937–40 and 1954–57 who belonged to class III in 1968 and 1981 respectively, according to educational level. The percentages of people per educational level in the same age groups in 1967 and 1981. Non students

Educational level		Class III		Percentage per educational level	
1967	1981	1968	1981	1967	1981
1. Community school	Elementary school[a]	71.3	85.8	52.9	26.0
2. Lower vocational school	—	56.4	—	15.2	—
3. Lower secondary school	—	36.1	—	11.8	—
4. Vocational secondary school	Two-year secondary	22.4	67.9	13.4	46.4
5. Upper secondary school	Three-year secondary	(0.0)	36.2	(1.8)	11.8
6. Vocational upper sec. school	Further voc. school	(0.0)	32.5	(2.4)	10.0
7. University degree	University degree	(0.0)	4.3	(2.6)	5.8
		N = 382	N = 400	100.1	100.0

a The community school and the elementary school are compared as being the obligatory education for the two age-groups, respectively.

About 10 per cent of the adult population was engaged in studies in 1981, which is an increase of about 2 percentage points since 1967. The increase occurred in each age group. In 1981, more than 30 per cent stated that they often participate in courses/study circles in their spare time. This figure was 19 per cent in 1967. Official data (SCB 1983a, 121) show that the percentage of employees who had participated in a course during working hours increased from 27 per cent to 36 per cent between 1975 and 1979.

Other tendencies, such as increasing contacts between schools and working life and the use of education as an instrument of labour market policy, seem to support the idea that we live in a learning society.

Certain objections however can be raised to such an interpretation of the trends — over 60 per cent of the adult population is not involved in any type of educational programme. The percentage of people over 40 years old who are engaged in studies is still very small. It also seems that the educational opportunities available after a 'normal' education is finished (such as study circles and courses) are mainly used by people who already have higher education, which consequently reinforces the existing differences between people with higher and lower education.

The educationally equal society

Are we then moving towards a society in which everyone, regardless of sex, class origin, and childhood community, has equal educational opportunities?

The importance of the type of childhood community to higher education was constant between 1967 and 1981 — people who grew up in the countryside are still clearly underrepresented at the three highest educational levels.[16] Regarding the importance of sex, the results provide an ambiguous impression. In relation to the entire adult population in 1981, women still constituted a smaller percentage of those at the higher educational levels, and the differences in average educational length, if anything, had grown. However, sex was less important in the younger age groups and women made up a majority of those in 1981 who reported that they were studying during the week before the interview. Even if this indicates a possible future equalization, there are reasons to be careful regarding such a conclusion — for example, men still have a longer education and clearly dominate what we have called the prestige branches of education.

Even though its importance is obviously decreasing, class origin still seems to play the most decisive role with regard to the opportunities for higher studies. This is in spite of the educational policy reforms which have emphasized equality in recruitment as a goal.

Our results can be interpreted as indicating that an equal distribution of education is coming closer, but the impression is nevertheless that fulfilment of the goal of equality in educational opportunities is still remote.

The meritocratic society

The trend toward increasing numbers obtaining longer and higher educations should be seen against the background of an expanding, high technology society. Social scientists have stated that experts, technocrats and people dedicated to research will form a new power élite in a society characterized by the production of services rather than goods (see, for example, Bell 1973; Gouldner 1979). This post-industrial society, where the stratification is based on, above all, educational credentials and technical skill, would thus contain pronounced meritocratic features.

But when addressing the questions whether we are heading towards a meritocracy, the education–social class linkage is not a sufficient indicator. Instead, we argue that both the connection between class origin and education, and the dependence of power, status, and economic returns on occupational position, must be included in an elaborated definition of a meritocratic society. Hence, we will point out three criteria for our definition:

1. Total equality in educational opportunity; the individual's own qualifications are decisive for admission to higher studies.
2. A strong correlation between education and occupational position.
3. Substantial inequality in societal rewards between occupations which require a higher education and occupations in which a shorter education is sufficient, especially with regard to income, power, and status.

We have already shown that we are far from fulfilling the first criterion, society's goal of equality. Despite a tendency towards equalization, there is still likely to exist a significant 'pool of ability' within the underrepresented groups.

As the correlation (Pearson's r) between education and social class position (three classes) has decreased from 0.56 in 1968 to 0.49 in 1981, it seems as though we have not drawn closer to the meritocratic society according to the second criterion either. The meritocratic tendency of educational credentials becoming more necessary for reaching a high social position is here counterbalanced by a tendency for such merits to become less valid as a ticket of admission to higher social strata.

A fundamental analysis of other types of data than ours would be necessary in order to examine how the valuation of various occupations in terms of societal rewards has changed. However, we have studied one of the main types of rewards, namely income[17] and its distribution

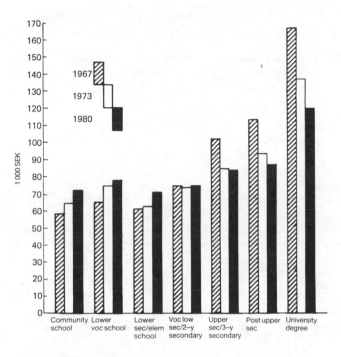

Fig. 9.6. Total income in constant prices (1980) for full time employees in Swedish crowns (1000 SEK) according to educational level in 1967, 1974, and 1981[a]

[a] Income relates to 1967, 1973, and 1980

among people at different educational levels. The high correlation between total income and educational level is shown in Figure 9.6. The income differences, on the other hand, declined substantially, especially because of a decreased average real income among the growing group with higher education.

The so-called human capital school looks at investments in and returns from, for example, education from a purely economic perspective. An increased supply of people with a certain kind of education (for example, academic) that is in demand should, according to this theory, lead to decreased differences in salaries (Becker 1975, 76). Our results seem to support this theory, but there are other possible explanations of this trend such as a change in union policy regarding wages.

The question of the relationship between education and the individual's access to power must essentially be left unanswered. However, an examination of the individual's powerlessness in terms of the absence of political participation and policital resources, according to educational level, is shown in Tables 9.8 and 9.9.

Table 9.6 Political Participation. Percentage of passives[18] in each survey year according to educational level. Non-students

Level of education	1968	1974	1981
1. Community school	39	35	30
2. Lower voc school	28	19	15
3. Lower sec/elem school	32	36	24
4. Voc low sec/2-y secondary	24	20	11
5. Upper sec/3-y secondary	26	22	15
6. Post upper sec	15	15	10
7. University degree	5	7	3
All	35	29	20

Table 9.7 Political Resources. Percentage of politically impoverished people[a] in each survey year according to educational level. Non-students

Level of education	1968	1974	1981
1. Community school	24	21	17
2. Lower voc school	13	9	7
3. Lower sec/elem school	11	14	9
4. Voc low sec/2-y secondary	9	7	4
5. Upper sec/3-y secondary	7	3	0
6. Post upper sec	2	3	1
7. University degree	0	1	1
All	19	14	9

[a] Political resources: a politically impoverished person is a person who cannot formulate an appeal against an authority's decision himself and does not know anyone who can do it for him. See S. Johansson 1976.

The lack of power is decreasing at all levels and nothing indicates that the substantial differences between people at different educational levels are increasing. The distribution of society's rewards between people with more or less education has thus not gone in a meritocratic direction with regard to income and power (as measured above).

On the whole, Sweden must be regarded as far from being a meritocratic society, in the sense that we have understood it here. We also conclude, tentatively, since our data are inadequate, that it is hardly on its way to becoming one.

In other studies, the effects of IQ (Intelligence Quotient) on education, class, and income, have been interpreted as signs of meritocracy. As indicated by those studies, both concerning the relationship between IQ and school leaving age (Halsey, Heath and Ridge 1980), and between IQ and adult economic success (Bowles and Gintis 1972), the fear of Young's meritocratic vision is vastly exaggerated.

Results and trends

The general impression given by the changes which occurred between 1967 and 1981 within the field of education is ambiguous. On the one hand, and possibly most obviously, the population's educational resources have increased dramatically. This applies to both education in school, which more and more people are taking advantage of to obtain higher levels of education, and study groups and courses during working hours. On the other hand, we found that we still have an unequal distribution of education between different population groups. Even if these differences have decreased in general terms, the importance of class origin is, nevertheless, still substantial. In addition, neither study circles nor job-related courses compensate those with less education; just the opposite, the differences between people with more education and with less education increase through the use of these forms of study. However, here there is also a trend toward equalization.

Education is a relative, positional resource in the labour market and the trend is inflationary; an academic degree, for example, is no longer sufficient to guarantee an occupation in class I and it is becoming increasingly rare for people with only compulsory educations to obtain occupations outside class III.

The inflation of education has also meant that it is becoming more necessary to have an academic education in order to obtain an occupation in class I. The chances of working one's way up to a high position are accordingly declining. In spite of this the income differences between those with more and those with less education have decreased substantially. The possible disappointment about the continued unequal distribution of educational resources among the population therefore should be weighed against the fact that equality in society is dependent on many factors other than educational policy alone.

Notes

1. These groups, defined according to occupational position, are partly reflected in the class-division in our investigation.
2. The quotation comes from Alva Myrdal's presentation of the Equality Group's report at the Social Democratic Party Congress in 1969 (Sveriges

Socialdemokratiska Arbetareparti 1970, 637, author's translation).

3. In Sweden 'study circles' have their origin in the popular movements of the early twentieth century as an alternative to the main school system. Even today, study circles are run by adult education associations connected with political parties (first and foremost the Social Democratical Party), trade unions, free churches, and the temperance movement. During this century, study circles have come to be more of a complement to the state schools (and are also granted financial support by the state), and have become a popular leisure activity. The courses are mainly held in the evenings, usually once a week, and although the choice of subjects is constantly changing, art, languages, and political studies are typical of the range of courses offered.

4. Isling (1980, 222-6) refers to, among others, Gunnar Hirdman, a leading personality in the field of adult education, and Nils Wohlin, in the agrarian party, who feared that young people from the farmer's class would be drawn into 'the very unproductive white-collar careers'.

5. That the questions in the education section of the first survey were answered one year earlier than the other sections should not cause any great difficulty in interpreting the results. However, a certain amount of caution may be called for in examining the relation between educational level and especially occupational position and income. Furthermore, the 1967 questions were answered in February, while the 1974 and 1981 surveys took place in May and June. This could possibly mean that the levels and years of education of the 1967 students are somewhat underestimated in comparison with those who were studying in 1974 and 1981.

6. Another problem is that previously it was fairly usual that students who failed their exams had to repeat one or more classes. In these cases the additional year of education is hardly an additional educational resource for the individual.

7. In absolute terms, the division is reasonable. However, it is problematic in certain cases, which is pointed out later, especially if one wants to distinguish a group with only compulsory education.

8. Extended education for younger generations, however, may have created, or reinforced, the generation gap in society. The distance between sexual maturity and social maturity (the point at which the individual can support himself and move away from his parents) has, for example, increased, which can lead to more conflicts between teenagers on the one hand and parents and teachers on the other.

9. In the government bill (Proposition 1950:70) regarding guidelines for the development of the Swedish educational system, the following statement was made on page 60: 'Education can never be allowed to become 'the prerogative of a certain class in a democratic society. It should be available in all its forms to every member of society according to their abilities, without regard to sex, community of residence, social position or economic conditions' (author's translation).

10. Similar results were presented by the SCB (1983a) with a measurement of 'actual educational time'. The SCB also used another measurement —

'formal education time' — and thereby found a more equal distribution between the sexes.

11. The results from the regression analyses (apart from the importance of sex, the effect of class origin, and the type of childhood community are also analyzed) will be presented here in summary form only. The regression approach is described in Chapter 2.

12. Total income: The sum of income from employment, capital, temporary income sources, farming, other real property, and a business.

13. Some possible reasons are that women go into a different part of the labour market from men (for example, more often into the public sector), and that women have a weaker connection with the labour market.

14. When the question on class membership was posed the community school group was 28–31 years old and the elementary school group was 24–27 years old. Furthermore, the former group had about two years more than the later group to be gainfully employed. These factors could mean that the community school group had some more time to advance within the occupational hierarchy.

15. Those with academic educations are actually going into class II to a greater extent.

16. To some extent this is probably a question of preference. Occupations that are connected with higher education are usually located in cities, and some people are emotionally and/or socially attached to their home district.

17. Total income: see note 12 for definition.

18. Political participation: a person is politically passive who is not a member of a political party, not a member of a union, has never participated in a demonstration, has never personally attempted to influence a responsible official in regard to a decision on a societal issue, has not spoken at a meeting, and has not written a letter to or an article in a newspaper (See S. Johansson 1976 and Chapter 11).

19. Political resources: a politically impoverished person is a person who cannot formulate an appeal against an authority's decision himself and does not know anyone who can do it for him. See S. Johansson 1976.

10

Housing Conditions

TOFTE FRYKMAN

Background and issues

Efforts to provide the population of Sweden with 'sound, spacious, well-planned, and practical dwellings of good quality at reasonable costs' (Proposition/Govt. Bill/1967:100, 172) were initiated with the housing policy outlined by the 1946–1948 Swedish Parliament. However, the housing shortage and overcrowding continued to be a problem of broad dimensions throughout the 1950s and 1960s; although rapid improvements have followed since then.

At the time of the first Level of Living Survey in 1968, Sweden was in the middle of implementing the 'one million programme' — a million new dwellings were projected for construction between 1965 and 1974. In 1966, the norms for overcrowding were made stricter, whereupon an additional 1,675,000 people were classified as living in overcrowded conditions according to the housing census of 1965. On the basis of the new norms, there was to be a maximum of two people per room, kitchen and living room excluded. Rents for newly built three-room flats (standard dwelling for a two-child family) were not to exceed 20 per cent of the average industrial wage (Proposition 1967:100, 172).

At the beginning of the seventies, housing policies were aimed more at modernizing the older housing stock than had previously been the case.[1] Guidelines for the late seventies were established in the 1974 Housing Decree (Proposition 1974:150). The parity-loan[2] system was replaced with interest subsidies. At the same time, there was a return to open subsidies to housing construction via the national budget. The loan system was reorganized and cash down payments for newly built single-family houses were literally cut in half. The goal was 'equal houses, equal costs'. The Minister of Housing said: 'As I have made clear before, I feel it is urgent that equivalent housing entail similar financial burdens regardless of the form of ownership or tenure. Apartments built in different periods should fetch prices that largely correspond to the differences in user-value' (Proposition 1974:150, 350). With the help of this policy, households would have a greater chance of choosing dwellings according to their need.

Increasing interest rates and inflation, combined with the effects of the tax system, however, resulted in conditions which conflicted with the hopes of redistributing housing resources. Parliament's attempts to counterbalance these were only moderately successful. As for the State's input in the housing area between 1976 and 1981, expenditure on rent allowances remained unchanged in real money value, whereas interest and tax subsidies were doubled (Proposition 1982/83:100, App. 3).

Without attempting a thorough analysis of housing policy, three characteristic goals for Swedish efforts can be discerned:

1. Housing unit space is to be distributed according to size of household. The larger the household, the larger the dwelling; in other words, distribution should follow need rather than economic resources. In addition, everyone should be able to live in a dwelling up to modern standards.
2. The form of ownership, or tenure, is to be neutral as to income and wealth. Supply as well as household needs are the deciding factors.
3. Housing costs are to consume only a 'reasonable' share of income.

The following discussion will illustrate how housing conditions have developed against the background of these goals. How have improvements in standard been distributed since the sixties? Have more people been able to choose size of dwelling, quality, and form of tenure according to need? Has the housing standard thereby become more or less equitably distributed? Has the share of income spent on housing shifted?[3]

Space does not allow us to enter into a thorough discussion and analysis. This discussion will thus remain descriptive.

Definitions

The distribution of housing standard among the population is determined primarily by the behaviour of households on the housing market. Household behaviour in turn is determined by preferences and resources, such as income, wealth, education, and composition. Housing and tax policies influence consumption and thereby distribution. Nearly all official measures are aimed either at the dwelling as a good, or at the household as the consumption unit. If the distribution is to be related to the policy in effect, the unit of account must be the household.

In the chapter on economic resources, the authors described the procedure for estimating the number of households as well as for grouping them into social classes.

Since it is the distribution of households on the housing market that is of interest, every person without command over a dwelling was excluded (as were people living in public institutions). The household distribution obtained is shown in Table 10.1. In contrast to the social classification of households used in the chapter on economic resources, pensioners I are included in social class I. There is no evidence in the present material that retired people alter their housing standard in relation to the economically active on the grounds of their pension. There are so few pensioner households I that a special accounting of this group is not possible.

Table 10.1 Distribution of households, by class, in the population 15–75 years, in 1968, 1974, and 1981. Percentages

Class	1968	1974	1981	Diff. 1968–81	Change in no. households
Workers	38.5	35.6	32.2	− 6.3	− 2
Lower salaried	24.2	27.2	26.2	+ 2.0	+ 27
Class I	7.9	9.4	10.2	+ 2.3	+ 52
Small proprietors	7.5	6.4	6.7	− 0.8	+ 4
Students I–III	1.5	1.3	1.9	+ 0.4	+ 52
Farmers I–III	5.7	4.2	3.7	− 2.0	− 27
Pensioners II	4.4	5.1	6.5	+ 2.1	+ 75
Pensioners III	10.3	10.8	12.6	+ 2.3	+ 44
Total	100.0	100.0	100.0		+ 17
Number of households 1000s	2 833	3 071	3 317		

In order to describe the size as well as composition of households, we have classified them according to type of family. First, we have grouped them according to whether or not there are children under 21 years living in the household. The age limit for children is set this high because actual parental responsibility for support seldom ceases earlier today. We want to reflect the actual household composition.

Second, households are classified according to the interviewees' information as to whether they are single of cohabiting/married. This means that single households without children are not necessarily one-person households. There may be other people in the household, such as children 21 years or older living at home, other relatives, or people sharing the household. This applies to all types of families.

As can be seen from Table 10.2, the number of households with children has remained largely unchanged since 1968. The family type that has increased is households without children.

Table 10.2   Households, by family type. Percentages. (Children under 21 years living at home)

Family type	1968	1974	1981	Change in no. households 1968-1981 %
Households without children	*58.5*	*60.9*	*64.0*	+28
Single	29.5	30.8	34.6	+38
Married	29.0	30.1	29.4	+18
Households with children	*41.5*	*39.1*	*36.0*	+2
Single with 1 child	2.3	2.9	3.0	(+56)
2+ children	1.2	2.0	2.2	(+206)
Married with 1 child	16.2	13.7	11.1	−20
2 children	14.7	14.5	14.4	+15
3+ children	7.1	6.0	5.3	−13
Total	*100.0*	*100.0*	*100.0*	
Number of households 1000s	2 833	3 071	3 317	+17

Married = married or cohabiting

Distribution of space and equipment standards

The standard of space is usually measured by a ratio or index (the method used relates the number of people in the household with the number of rooms in the dwelling, excluding kitchen and living room, and the resulting standard of space is called a room standard). The spatial measure used in the Level of Living Survey of 1968 was further developed by Eriksson and Lindquist (1981) and we have used this measure. The steps in the scale are given in Figure 10.1.

The room standard has improved substantially since 1968, as is clear from Table 10.3. Overcrowding decreased quite rapidly, especially up until the middle of the 1970s. Almost every fifth household was overcrowded in 1968, while less than every tenth was crowded in 1974, and just over 3 out of 100 in 1981.[4] The majority of all households now enjoy at least a good standard of space,[5] which exceeds by a large margin the norm defining overcrowding. Everyone in these households has at least one room at their command, besides the kitchen and living room. This represents an extraordinary improvement since 1968, when barely one-third of all households had so much room to move around in.

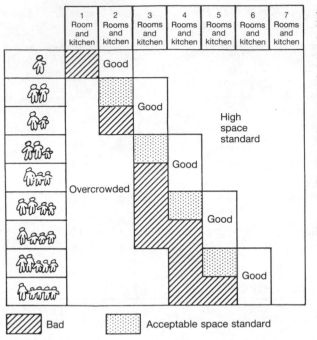

Fig. 10.1. Floor area index shows how different sizes of households and household compositions in different apartment sizes are classified. 'Children' are not necessarily children. This designation may also denote adults who are not married or cohabiting with any other person in the household. (Own reworking, from Erikson–Lindquist)

Table 10.3 Household space standards 1968, 1974, and 1981. Percentages.

	1968	1974	1981
Overcrowded	18	8	3
Unacceptable space standard	25	23	17
Total unacceptable standard	43	31	20
Acceptable space standard	21	21	16
Good space standard	22	27	34
High space standard	14	21	30
Total spacious dwellings	36	48	64
Total	100	100	100
Number of households 1000s	2833	3071	3317

Comparing the percentages in Table 10.3, overcrowding declined rapidly between 1968 and 1974. Also another 12 per cent of all households achieved good space standards. During the period 1974–1981, overcrowding did not drop as much as expected,[6] whereas another 16 per cent of all households did attain good space standards. The state of affairs at the end of the seventies was more that spacious standards were being pushed even higher than that bad ones were being eliminated.

Distribution of space standards

To answer the question as to whether the overall space standards have become more equitably allocated, we constructed a dissimilarity index. The index is designed so that the distribution of the space standard for each type of family in itself is compared with the average age distribution among all other types of families combined. With this, we basically measure what percentage of households in a certain type of family would need to change dwelling size in order to reach the standard of the average of all the others. The plus sign indicates overrepresentation in good and high standards and thus underrepresentation in the lower classes. Parentheses were placed around the sign in one case, reflecting overrepresentation in one of the higher as well as in one of the lower classes; the sign indicates the general direction.

When the index is computed, we do not distinguish between the two categories, acceptable and unacceptable space standards. The reason for this is that acceptable is valid only for households with two cohabiting adults (with and without children), and that unacceptable is mainly valid for single people and households with children (see Figure 10.1). So, we get four classes taking only the size of dwelling and number of residents into account — while missing some aspects of household composition. Thus, the index will underestimate the actual difference between the living arrangements of the different groups.

Table 10.4 Dissimilarity index for distribution of space standards, by family type

	Disparity with other groups' average	
	1968	1981
Single without children	+19	+12
Married without children	+16	+14
Single with 1 child	+10	+15
2+ children	−19	−17
Married with 1 child	−18	(−)9
2 children	−21	−17
3+ children	−28	−38

Married = married or cohabiting.

The index shows that in 1968 single people without children had the most space, on average, closely followed by married people without children. Even single people with one child lived better than the average.

In general, 10–20 per cent of these households would lower their space standard if they were to live like the average of other groups. The remaining family types, all households with children, had space standards implying that every fifth household would need to improve their standards to reach the average standard of other households. Relatively speaking, married households with three or more children had the worst standards, and thus the greatest need for policies aimed at raising them.

For those with the best space standard, the situation in 1981 is not particularly different from that in 1968. As for improvements, married households with one child are the group that has done the best. But there is a paradox: at the same time that there are more people with high space standards, there are also more who are overcrowded. Therefore, it is no longer true that this group as a whole clearly lives in worse conditions than others — as was the case in 1968.

Between 1968 and 1981, the gap between the space standards of various family types on the whole narrowed (lower index figure for 1981 than for 1968). The space standard thus has become more equitably distributed. The equalization has been to the advantage of families with children, especially those with one child. Two-children families have attained a relative improvement in their space standards. In contrast, households with three or more children were relatively worse off in 1981 than in 1968. They have not anything like the same improvement in standard as other households.

Has there been an equalization among the classes? We will try to answer this question using our dissimilarity index in Table 10.5.

Table 10.5 Dissimilarity index of distribution of space standards, by class

	Disparity with other groups' average	
	1968	1981
Workers	− 22	− 19
Lower salaried	(−)4	+ 2
Class I	+ 32	+ 27
Small proprietors	+ 17	+ 15
Farmers	+ 19	+ 18
Students	− 35	− 35
Pensioners II	+ 29	+ 21
Pensioners III	+ 11	+ 9

In 1968, class I had the best room standard, followed by the pensioners in class II. Workers and students had the least space. The gap between the classes was generally large.

There were no changes in 1981 in the internal ranking order for the groups. Nevertheless, the numbers had consistently dropped (except for students), which means that the space standard now is more equitably distributed. It is also worth noting that lower salaried employees lived in worse conditions than the average for other groups in 1968, but were better off than the average for the remaining groups in 1981.

The gap between the classes is still large. Working-class households, who were worst off in 1968, have barely been able to claim 'their share' of the rise in standard. The goal of using this 'added space' towards a social equalization for the benefit of the least fortunate has almost entirely failed. Our survey indicates that most of the increment in space has contributed to closing the gap between class I and II households.

Standard of distribution of equipment

In the present study, the equipment standard was measured with stricter criteria than in the Population and Housing Censuses. Modern living is measured by access to hot and cold water, sewers, toilet, shower/bath, central heating, as well as to a modern cooker and refrigerator. Dwellings are semi-modern if 1–3 of these items are absent. Other dwellings are classified as not modern. If one item is lacking, it is usually the bath or shower. If several are lacking, the most common are hot water, central heating, toilet, modern cooker or refrigerator. (See L. Johansson, 1971b, 24). In 1968, it was seen as sufficient if the person merely had access to the equipment (on the premises), whereas in 1981 the question referred to equipment in the dwelling itself.

Table 10.6 Distribution of housing equipment standards 1968 and 1981, by family types. Percentages

	Modern		Semi-modern		Not modern	
	1968	1981	1968	1981	1968	1981
All households	76	95	15	4	9	1
Households w/o children	68	93	20	6	12	1
Households w/ 1 child	86	98	9	2	5	(−)
w/ 2 children	88	98	8	2	4	(−)
w/ 3+ children	87	98	9	2	4	(−)
Overcrowded or with unacceptable space standards	71	90	19	8	10	2

As is seen in Table 10.6, the equipment standard improved quickly after 1968.

A small proportion of households lived in non-modern or semi-modern dwellings in 1981. The problem of inadequate furnishings which existed at the end of the 1960s has largely been remedied. The problem remaining in 1981 is attributable primarily to households without children, many of them in semi-modern dwellings. On the other hand, it is still the case that households with too small a dwelling also face deficient equipment standards more often than others.

Forms of tenure

Much of the rise in space standards is closely linked to moves from multi-family houses to detached houses. On the Swedish housing market, type of house is almost synonymous with form of ownership/occupancy, or tenure. Of those people living in single-family houses in 1981, 89 per cent owned their own home, a rise from 83 per cent in 1968. About 7 per cent of the single-family residents rent their homes. The form of tenure is also of interest in its significance for the distribution of wealth among households. Privately owned houses constitute the largest single item in the household's collective wealth. Living in single-family houses demands that an individual has a sufficiently high and predictably stable income. Personal savings or connections must be substantial enough to make the cash down payment necessary to break into this market. During the inflationary economy of the seventies, stable incomes and good bank connections probably sufficed.

Four forms of tenure are used in our study: owner occupancy; rental rights (personal contract with the property owner); co-operative rights (tenant-owned apartments); and others (sub-leases, no lease, wrecker leases, and the like). For reasons of space, only the first two types will be taken up in the discussion below. Farming households are also excluded since their form of tenure is so intimately bound to their source of income. They do not choose the type of tenure as do other households.

Class and form of tenure

In the Level of Living Survey of 1968, relatively small differences were established between the classes in ownership of single-family houses (L. Johansson, 1971b, 57). As seen in Table 10.7, working-class households owned their houses to about the same degree as all households in the survey (31 per cent). The proportion owning their homes was lowest among lower salaried employees (24 per cent) and highest among small proprietors (47 per cent) and members of class I (42 per cent).

Table 10.7 Households with different forms of tenure, by class. Percentages

	Share		Differences	Index
	1968	1981	68–81	81/68
Owns dwelling[a]	31	41	+ 10	133
Workers III	30	32	+ 2	108
Lower salaried II	24	45	+ 21	191
Class I	42	61	+ 19	147
Small proprietors	47	66	+ 19	141
Pensioners II	38	39	+ 1	103
Pensioners III	35	35	0	99
Rents dwelling	48	43	− 5	89
Workers	49	52	+ 3	107
Lower salaried	55	37	− 18	68
Class I	40	27	− 13	68
Small proprietors	36	24	− 12	66
Students	53	77	+ 24	144
Pensioners II	40	39	− 1	96
Pensioners III	48	49	+ 1	101
Co-operatively owned	13	14	+ 1	104

[a] Students excluded because too few observations.

In 1981, small house ownership was quite differently distributed among the classes. Compared with 1968, about twice as many lower salaried employees lived in their own homes, while single-family residence increases by 47 per cent in class I and by 41 per cent among small proprietors. This proportion increased by a mere 8 per cent among the working-class, and remained about the same among retired households.

Changes in the single-family house sector have had repercussions in the class composition of rented and co-operatively owned dwellings. The proportion who rent dwellings has increased among working-class households and students, while decreasing in all other classes in our material. The exception to this is pensioners III for whom a small increase was noted. The increase among students is due to the fact that in 1968 students lived without leases (other forms). For co-operatives (not reported), the proportion increased among pensioners, in particular among those in class III. The proportion who live in co-operative dwellings decreased in the remaining classes, except among salaried employees.

Owning single-family residences has become exceedingly class-bound since 1968. The altered net distribution is shown in Table 10.8.

Table 10.8 Number of owner-occupied households 1968 and 1981, by class. 1000s households

	Real number		Exp. no.	Difference 1968–1981		Total	
	1968 1.	1981 2.	1981 3.	4.	5.	number 6.	% 7.
Workers	324	342	317	−7	25	18	4
Lower salaried	161	389	204	43	185	228	47
Class I	93	207	141	48	66	114	23
Small proprietors	100	146	103	3	43	46	9
Pensioners II	47	85	82	35	3	38	8
Pensioners III	101	144	145	44	−1	43	9
Total	826	1313	992	166	321	487	100
Changes %	100	159	120	34	66	100	

Col 3. indicates computed number of households in 1981 if all classes had chosen owner-occupation to the same extent as in 1968

Col 4. (col 3. − col 1.), indicates computed change in number of owner-occupied households resulting from changed size of classes.

Col 5. (col 2. − col 3.), indicates computed number of households who chose owner-occupation because of changes in household 'preferences' and resources.

The change in small-house ownership is divided into two components. One reflects the amount caused by the change in the number of households in the classes (col. 4.). The other (col. 5) shows how much of the change is due to the fact that the households have higher resources, modified 'preferences' and possibilities for ownership. This is based on the notion that as many members of all classes wanted to own their own detached house in 1981 as did in 1968. If the 1968 'market situation' had applied in 1981, the number of households in small houses would have increased by 20 per cent (col. 3). One-third of the increase in single-family house living can be attributed to shifting social class composition (col. 4), while two-thirds is determined by the households' increased resources and altered preferences (col. 5). Of the total increase of 490,000 households in owned houses, 13 per cent belonged to class III (workers and pensioners). The remaining 87 per cent consisted of class I and II households. As many as 47 per cent were lower salaried employees and 23 per cent were members of class I (see Table 10.1 where their proportion of total households is given). There are many reasons for these developments, which probably should be the subject of future research.

Family type, class, and form of tenure

One reason that members of the different classes are increasingly living under different forms of tenure may be that class household compositions are not the same. If so, it may well also be the case that working-class households with children live in small houses as much as other households with children, with the large differences in social distribution still intact.

For 1968 it was more common for working-class households with children to live in their own homes than it was for lower salaried employees with children to do so. The most frequent pattern was ownership of single-family residences in class I and among small proprietors. In 1981, close to 8 out of 10 households in class I and among small proprietors lived in small houses. Among lower salaried employees, just over 6 out of 10 now live in small houses, while somewhat less than every second working-class household with children lives in a dwelling of their own.

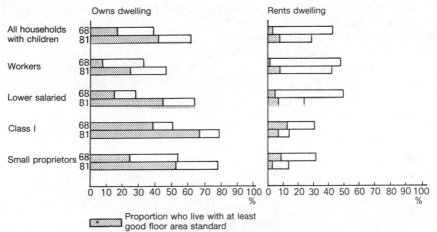

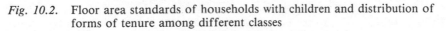

Fig. 10.2. Floor area standards of households with children and distribution of forms of tenure among different classes

Even for households with children, the inequities among classes have increased. As seen in Figure 10.2, this is highly significant for the distribution of space standards among households with children. In owner-occupied small houses, an average of 70 per cent of the households with children also enjoy good space standards or better, while only one-quarter of such households living in rented dwellings do so.

To sum up; at the same time as the total housing standard has risen, differences in standard remain and are even growing for households with children in the different classes and in different forms of tenure.

Notes

1. For a general account of the subject see R. Johansson, and B. Karlberg 1979 chap. 1, and Lundqvist 1981, 19.
2. The parity-loan system was designed to redistribute capital outlays over the lifetime of a building. It was introduced in 1968. The basic idea was that interest and mortgage payments should start at a low level and increase in parity with costs of buildings constructed later.
3. The section of this chapter dealing with this problem has been omitted from the English version. Very briefly, the results show that housing expenditure increased moderately in real terms and that the share of a household's income spent on housing has remained largely unchanged.
4. According to the Population and Housing Census 1980, 4.3 per cent of the households were overcrowded (among the total population).
5. Our survey shows 64 per cent, while Eriksson and Lindquist find 61.1 per cent in 1980 for the entire population. Their figure is based on their own work. J. Eriksson and M. Lindquist 1983, 7.
6. See Proposition 1974:150 quoting the Housing Minister: 'With the pace at which overcrowding is now being eliminated, we can expect our 1967 ambitions to be realized during the 1970s. Therefore, we should eventually be able to count on an even higher space standard' (p. 348).

11

Political Resources

RYSZARD SZULKIN

Introduction

In the public debate in Sweden it is often claimed that the political activity of citizens is low. The individual is involved in the pleasures of private consumption and lacks a broader interest in societal issues. The time of mass mobilization and mass participation has passed and has been replaced by a growing political apathy. According to this view usually based on spontaneous impressions, the citizens are the weakest link in Swedish democracy.

Providing a correct answer to this issue is not easy. In the Level of Living Survey we tried to measure certain aspects of political activity. The starting point for construction of the 'political component' within the Level of Living Survey was the classic model of democracy as defined by John Stuart Mill. According to Mill the normative goal of democracy is to promote citizen participation in politics. Mill's main ideas were summarized by Sten Johansson (1971, 30) in the following manner:

1. Only if everyone participates in the political process is there a guarantee that the interests of all citizens will be taken into account when political decisions are made.
2. Participation itself trains the participants so that they can habitually protect their interests.
3. Participation develops the personality so that the citizen feels himself to be part of a whole and accepts responsibility not only for himself but for the whole as well.

In other words, democracy's primary goal, realization of the people's will, can only be achieved if everyone participates in politics. Political activity is, furthermore, from the individual's point of view a rational attempt to influence public policy in accordance with his own or his group's interests. Political participation also has an educational function, it promotes a feeling of responsibility for society among the citizens and develops the individual's public spirit.[1]

The general statements which make up the normative model above do not, however, directly indicate any concrete empirical measures which can be used for gathering information on political participation. To be able to construct these measures one must consider which channels of influence on the political process are available to citizens in the representative democracy model. The following items were considered to be the most important ways of exercising democratic influence:

1. Through elections citizens determine which political party shall control the government and attempt to carry out its programme.
2. Through membership in political organizations and participation in political meetings citizens can try to influence the development of political alternatives.
3. Through expression of opinions in newspapers and in political meetings as well as participation in public demonstrations, citizens can mould public opinion and try to influence concrete political issues.
4. Through contacts with people in positions of responsibility citizens can attempt to influence their decisions on concrete political issues.
5. Through participation in trade unions citizens can defend their interests as employees.
6. Through defending themselves in writing against public authorities citizens can assert their personal interests.

In this chapter we shall — for the period covered by Level of Living Survey data — describe how these different channels of political influence have been used. We will give an account of the extent of political participation and its changes between 1968 and 1981 and analyse the relation between political activity and the individual's position in the social and demographic structure. However, it it unrealistic to believe that every citizen will participate in every form of political activity. Therefore, we shall also investigate whether the utilization of political rights has a cumulative character, that is, if people who participate in one form of activity also tend to participate in other forms.

We have chosen to anlayse the political conditions with a number of indicators related to political participation. Studies of the current political process can be based on other research strategies. The more structurally oriented school would, for example, concentrate on the structures — institutions — which exist in a society. The origins and functions of institutions and their changes over time as well as the interaction between different institutions and between people and institutions would be analysed. Other views — which partly coincide with the former — place the emphasis on the political decision-making process. The nature and consequences of this process are studied. Regardless of which strategy one favours, the study of how the democratic potential inherent in a liberal democracy is used by citizens should still be of interest.

Political participation

If the endeavours, hopes and experiences of ordinary people are to affect the ordering of society, then ordinary people must participate in politics. The extent to which this occurs will now be examined. First, a picture of participation from 1968 to 1981 in the various channels of political influence is provided; thereafter the level of activity, and its changes, in various population categories is analysed.

An overview

Taking part in elections is the most common political activity. By comparison with other countries, Swedish electoral participation is high (Korpi 1983, 56). Table 11.1 gives a summary of election participation percentages according to the Level of Living Survey[2] and according to election statistics. The table shows that our investigation systematically overestimates election participation. Normally the explanation put forward for the fact that survey investigations generally overestimate election participation (see Holmberg 1981, 23, 32) is partly that people who do not vote are overrepresented among those who fail to respond and partly that those who do not vote tend to 'remember' that they voted. Both the Level of Living Survey and the election statistics indicate, however, some increase in the tendency to vote in general elections during the period studied.

Table 11.1 Participation in elections according to Level of Living Survey and the election statistics. Percentages

	1968		1974	1981
	L[a]	N[b]	N	N
Level of Living Survey	89.8	91.1	95.6	94.3
Election statistics	82.8	89.3	90.8	90.7

[a] = Local elections
[b] = National elections

The Swedish political system is constructed in such a way that the parties have a decisive influence on the political process both on election day and otherwise (for a detailed account of the role of political parties in Swedish society see Birgersson and Westerståhl 1979, chapter 3). Although Table 11.2 shows an increase in membership of political parties and organizations during the period 1968–81,[3] the increase is marginal. The same is also true of participation in political meetings. The percentage of people holding elected positions in political organizations increased among both members and the population in general. One possible explanation for this result is that the number of positions within the political organizations increased during the period. Another possibility is that the existing responsibilities were spread out among more people. The increase could even be a result of both of these factors.

Table 11.2 Political membership, participation in political meetings and political positions. Percentages

	1968	1974	1981
Member of a political party or organization	12.6	13.7	14.0
Attended at least one political meeting during the past year	13.4	14.7	13.9
Holds a political position (percentage of membership)	16.7	19.1	21.9
Has held political position (percentage of membership)	19.8	19.3	17.1
Holds political position (percentage of total population)	2.1	2.6	3.1
Has held political position (percentage of total population)	2.5	2.6	2.4

The political decisions which are made at different levels of society as well as other questions of public interest must, in a democracy, be open to public debate and critical analysis. Participation by the population in various forms of activity aimed at influencing public opinion is reviewed in Table 11.3. The number of people who have at some time spoken at a meeting, written to a newspaper, or taken part in a public demonstration clearly increased during the period studied.

However, one should observe that Table 11.3 is based on the broadest possible interpretation of participation in the various forms of opinion shaping activities. We asked the persons interviewed if they had ever participated in these activities. This necessarily means that some people who had participated many years before and thereafter were passive are classified as active. Further, we did not attempt to distinguish between politically relevant public activities and other activities. Neither newspaper contributions, nor participation in debates and public demonstrations is necessarily of a political character.[4] The definite

Table 11.3 Participation in opinion shaping activities. Percentages

	1968	1974	1981
Spoken at an association or organization meeting	24.9	27.3	32.3
of which, made a speech	12.6	15.1	20.1
Written to a newspaper	9.9	11.4	15.9
of which, an article	5.6	6.0	8.5
Participated in a public demonstration	14.1	16.4	23.4

increase in participation in public activities noted above could, however, be interpreted as a definite increase in the propensity — and ability — of the public to put forward their views.

We have also tried to shed light upon the extent to which citizens attempt to influence the authorities' decisions directly. The number of respondents who contacted a responsible official to attempt to influence a decision increased during the period. The percentages for the respective years were 7, 10, and 12 per cent. There are certain difficulties, however, in analysing these results. As pointed out by S. Johansson (1971, 48) it is: 'somewhat problematical to know exactly which meaning the persons interviewed gave this question and if different persons from, e.g., different social groups gave it the same meaning'.

To summarize, it could be said that the use of formal outlets for action provided by a representative democracy increased during the period studied. The increase mainly involves various types of activity which require personal effort and are directed towards moulding public opinion. On the other hand, taking part in political organizations, which probably are of decisive influence on the development of the major political alternatives, has remained relatively constant.

Election participation in various population categories

Election participation has been the subject of many political science and sociological studies (see, for example, Holmberg 1981, Korpi 1983). Here it is enough to provide a short summary of the most important findings of these studies and present the election participation results in different classes according to our investigation.

The high level of election participation in Sweden is a result of stable development since the 'democratic breakthrough' in 1921 (Korpi 1983, chapter 4). There are very few people who systematically — in election after election — choose not to vote (Holmberg 1981, 32). This high level of participation means that the differences in participation between various social and demographic groups are small. Still, the higher classes display a somewhat greater tendency to vote (Korpi 1983, chapter 4 and Table 11.4).[5]

Table 11.4 Participation in elections, by class, according to Level of Living Survey. Percentages

	1968	1974	1981
Class I	95.9	98.3	96.7
Class II	94.8	96.7	96.7
Class III	87.9	94.2	92.1

Differences in election participation between men and women, on the other hand, disappeared. According to the electoral register for the 1979 election women even voted to a somewhat greater extent than men. Age and regional differences were insignificant in the 1979 election (Korpi 1983, chapter 4). This is also corroborated by our data.

Political organizations and political meetings

The social and demographic structure of the political organizations was analysed with the regression approach described in Chapter 2. The independent variables also used in this analysis are sex, age, community type, class, and survey year. The results are shown in Figure 11.1. As we can see, membership varies substantially with sex, age, community type, and class. Men, older people, people living in the countryside and people belonging to class I are clearly overrepresented among those belonging to political organizations. However, the differences tended to diminish over time except with regard to community type.

From this analysis it is also apparent that class differences are most accentuated among old people and among those who live in the countryside (this is not, however, shown in the figure).

Differences based on sex and class regarding the degree of political organization are shown in Table 11.5. As indicated, the degree of political organization among men from class I and II has decreased while it has increased slightly among men from class III. However, these changes are statistically insignificant. Among women the degree of organization has increased in each of the classes. The change is significant, however, only for women from class III. In 1981 one out of five women in class I was organized. This was the highest frequency of organization for any of the categories during that year. In the other groups men were overrepresented.

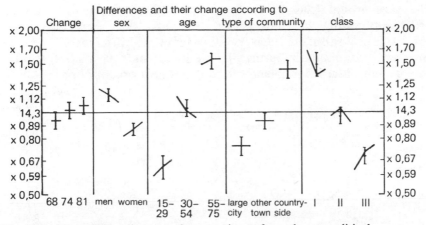

Fig. 11.1   Regression diagram of proportions of members – political organizations

Table 11.5 Political organization, by sex and class. Percentages

	Men			Women		
	1968	1974	1981	1968	1974	1981
Class I	20.5	17.1	18.1	15.0	19.4	20.3
Class II	20.6	20.7	17.8	11.8	13.1	13.3
Class III	13.2	14.0	14.5	6.4	8.3	10.0
All	16.3	16.6	16.0	8.9	10.8	11.9

Against the background of the above description of political organization in different categories of the population, it is not surprising that farmers — a group which lives in the countryside and is characterized by male overrepresentation and a relatively high median age — show a very high level of organization (table not shown here). Even if the degree of organization of this group is lower when sex and age are constant, the political organization of farmers is still extremely high. This can be interpreted in different ways. One possible explanation is that farmers consider political decisions to be highly relevant to their own situation and that the Centre Party, which most farmers probably look upon as their political representative, has been especially successful in mobilizing its supporters.

We found a somewhat different pattern when we analysed the development of participation in political meetings (Figure 11.2). At the beginning of the period the differences between various age groups regarding meeting participation were almost non-existent. Towards the end of the period, however, participation in meetings was highest in the oldest age group. Class I clearly had the highest share of meeting participants during the entire period. The differences between classes were stable and substantial. On the other hand, the differences based on sex tended to diminish during the period, which is similar to the development observed in membership of political organizations.

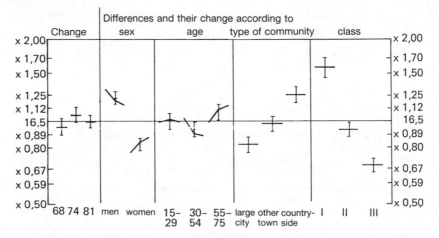

Fig. 11.2   Regression diagram of proportions of participants in political meetings

The foregoing discussion hardly confirms the picture of a continuing 'older male' domination of the political organizations which is often presented in public debate. Rather, the social and demographic structure of political organizations seems to have undergone a change with the result that women and younger people have increased their relative shares of the membership. The trend regarding participation in political meetings is, however, less clear.

Opinion shaping activities

Under this heading we have placed the activities which an individual can undertake to draw attention to an issue and attempt to influence the opinions of others and the decisions of the authorities. To save space opinion shaping activities have been summarized to an index. Participation in these activities is still given the widest possible interpretation. People who have at some time spoken at a meeting, written to a newspaper, or participated in a demonstration have been classified as active. As noted earler, participation in each form of activity increased during the years studied. The share of people who at some time participated in at least one of these activities increased from 34 per cent in 1968 to 38 per cent in 1974 and to 47 per cent in 1981. The regression analysis (Figure 11.3) shows that the relative increase in activity was highest among women and the youngest age group. We even noted a certain evening out of the activity level between different community types. On the other hand, the differences between classes remained stable. Furthermore, the analysis indicates that sex differences in the level of activity are highest among the oldest age group and that class differences are greatest among the youngest group (not shown in the figure).

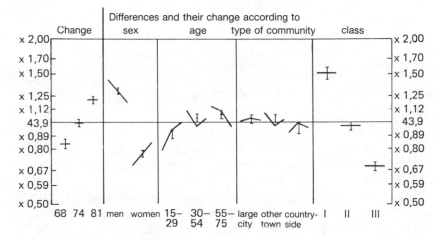

Fig. 11.3   Regression diagram of proportions of participants in public activities

In Table 11.6 the percentages of active people according to sex and class is shown. Differences based on sex decreased in each class. However, men in class I were still the most active in each of the years studied.

Table 11.6 Participation in opinion shaping activities, by sex and class. Percentages

	Men			Women		
	1968	1974	1981	1968	1974	1981
Class I	79.7	81.3	86.6	38.0	52.3	63.1
Class II	51.9	57.0	62.8	25.7	30.0	45.2
Class III	38.9	40.5	44.3	16.6	21.2	28.1
All	47.0	50.4	55.9	21.1	26.4	37.1

The various forms of activity which make up the index are somewhat different in character. They place different demands on the individual's commitment, qualifications, and ability to co-operate. However, the pattern change we were able to observe, which is shown in the figure above, was substantially similar when the different variables were examined separately. Possibly the most conspicuous deviation from the pattern was the difference in class participation in demonstrations. During the first survey period demonstration participation was clearly highest in class III and lowest in class I. In 1981 the order was reversed and the differences between the classes were smaller. One possible explanation of this tendency is that many of the demonstrations arranged during the 1970s involved issues which were not directly related to class structure nor the classic left–right political dimension, as well as the substantial increase in demonstration activity among students.

Membership and activity in trade union organizations

The major purpose of trade unions is to protect the economic interests of employees. However, the union movement does not act only as a body in the labour market looking after employee's wages and working conditions, but also takes up positions on other important societal issues and thereby exercises influence on society.

In this section, the changes in the degree of union organization and in participation in union activities from 1968 to 1981 are reviewed. The review covers the entire population studied within the scope of the Level of Living Survey, employees as a whole and employees classified according to certain demographic and socio-economic variables.

An overview

The degree of union organization is an important indicator of the propensity of employees to act collectively (Korpi 1983, chapter 3). A high level of employee organization can also be seen as a sign of a developed class consciousness (von Otter 1973, 22).

The Swedish union movement is characterized by a strong sense of unity, powerful central organization and a well-developed local organization (see, for example, Kjellberg 1983, chapter 8). Each of these factors seems to have contributed to the high degree of union organization in Sweden by comparison with other countries. During the period covered by the Level of Living Survey, the degree of organization showed a substantial increase (Table 11.7). In 1968, 45 per cent of all those between 15 and 75 years of age were members of some union. During the next survey period the degree of organization had risen to 50 per cent. By 1981 60 per cent of all the adult population were union members.

Table 11.7 Degree of union organization within the whole population and among employees. Percentages

	1968	1974	1981
Total population (15–75 years)	44.7	49.6	60.0
Employees	69.3	73.9	83.2

This clearly rising trend is only partly a result of the increased level of employment during the period. Table 11.7 shows that the degree of organization among employees has also risen at the same rate which indicates an increased tendency among employees to become union members.[6]

The influence of members on shaping union policy and the maintenance of internal democracy presupposes active participation by the members in union activities. Table 11.8 shows the percentages of people participating in meetings in the whole population (15–75 years old) and among union members. We can conclude that there has been an increase in activity both within the population surveyed as a whole and among union members.

Table 11.8 Union meeting activity (people who have attended at least one union meeting during the previous year) within the whole population and among union members. Percentages

	1968	1974	1981
Total population (15–75 years)	20.7	22.3	27.8
Union members	41.4	42.8	45.4

From Table 11.9 we can also conclude that the percentage of people with union positions (both those who had union position at the time of the interview and those who at some time had held such a position) increased during the years studied. The increase applies to the whole population as well as union members. This should mean that the increase cannot be explained by the increased level of organization. However, on the basis of our data it is impossible to determine whether the increase mainly depends on an increase in union positions, a division of existing positions among more people, or an increased rotation of these posts.

Table 11.9 People holding union positions within the whole population and among union members. Percentages

	1968	1974	1981
Population			
(15–75 years old):			
Has a position	4.3	5.4	7.4
Has had a position	7.3	8.7	10.9
Members:			
Has a position	9.2	10.7	12.5
Has had a position	12.2	13.5	15.0

Degree of union organization among employees in different population groups

To be able to show the variation in the degree of organization between different population groups and different survey years, we have again used the regression approach (figure not shown). In addition to the increase in organization already mentioned, the model indicates a substantial decrease in the differences based on sex as well as a relatively minor decrease in the differences between the various age groups. During the entire period the degree of organization was lowest among the youngest employees. Furthermore, it is apparent that the membership level is lower among people in large cities than in small towns and the countryside. The picture provided by the regression analysis regarding the degree of organization in the different classes is difficult to interpret. It is therefore reasonable to present a more detailed description of the developments in various social occupational categories (Table 11.10).

The frequency of organization increased most rapidly in classes I and II. Class III, which previously had the highest percentage of members compared with the other groups, was overtaken by class II. However, the differences between the classes are small. Table 11.10 also shows that the increase we registered holds for each category of salaried employees. Salaried employees in the public sector have, on average, a higher degree of organization than those who are privately employed.

The increase has, however, been fastest among those in the private sector. Increasing union membership among salaried employees could indicate that various social processes in modern society are changing their position in the labour market so that it is becoming increasingly similar to that of workers. Among workers metal workers, construction workers, and workers in state employment have the highest percentage of organization. Workers in manufacturing show a higher degree of organization than service workers. However, the increase in membership has been faster in the latter category. On the whole it can be seen that those occupational groups which had a low degree of organization in . 1968 have also shown the fastest increases. This is reflected, for example, in the decreasing amount of variation explained by occupation.

Table 11.10 Union membership in various occupational groups. Percentages

	1968	1974	1981
Prof., exec. in private employment	47.9	67.6	70.4
Professionals in public employment	83.1	85.4	93.4
Class I, all employees	65.4	78.6	83.7
Farmers	79.8	83.8	76.5
Small proprietors	49.2	65.0	47.8
Foremen	76.1	91.1	93.2
Private technical and clerical	54.7	62.6	79.0
Public lower salaried	80.8	84.4	92.2
Class II, all employees	67.4	75.1	86.1
Agricultural workers	45.7	46.8	68.5
Metal workers	85.7	87.8	93.1
Other manufacturing workers	83.2	83.3	84.5
Construction workers	88.1	88.6	92.8
Manufacturing workers, all	85.2	86.3	89.8
Workers in commerce	51.7	51.8	70.3
Other service workers	49.3	54.0	72.1
Service workers, all	50.4	52.8	71.0
Workers in local govt.	65.8	69.7	81.4
Workers in state govt.	80.5	85.4	94.6
Workers in public employment, all	70.7	74.0	84.5
Class III, all employees	72.8	73.8	83.5
Population 15–75 years	69.3	73.9	83.4
Proportion of explained variance	0.105	0.094	0.058

The differences between men and women in the different classes are shown in Table 11.11. Differences based on sex are most apparent in class III. During the period, however, there was a fairly strong levelling off of the differences. Of all the groups shown in the table, the organization frequency throughout was highest among male workers and women in class I.

Table 11.11 Union membership among employees by sex and class. Percentages

	Men			Women		
	1968	1974	1981	1968	1974	1981
Class I	61.8	75.8	80.0	69.0	73.8	88.6
Class II	70.8	78.3	86.9	60.5	71.1	83.4
Class III	83.4	83.7	88.4	53.2	58.6	75.9
All	77.4	81.3	86.7	56.5	64.3	79.7

Part-time employees previously had a very low degree of organization. We have also seen, in Chapter 6, how this category increased in size. The degree of organization for this category, between 1968 and 1981 (Table 11.12) increased much faster than for full-time employees.

Table 11.12 Union membership, by working hours. Percentages

	1968	1974	1981
Full-time employees	74.5	79.4	87.4
Part-time employees	42.7	54.7	73.5

To summarize, the analyses above indicate a rapid increase in the degree of organization in most of the categories investigated and that the increase was greatest among groups which had previously had a low degree of organization. The differences between the various categories therefore diminished during the period. The increase was especially conspicuous among those categories which increased in size on the labour market during the 1970s (women, salaried employees, part-time employees) which were also previously characterized by a relatively low level of membership.

Meeting participation among union members

We have so far been able to conclude that the substantial quantitative increase in union membership was followed by an increase in membership activity. This is also shown by the regression analysis in Figure 11.4. The analysis also shows that men, middle aged and older people, and people in small towns and the countryside have a higher rate of participation than women, young people, and people in large cities respectively. This pattern seems to be stable throughout the entire period. It is in the comparison of meeting activity between classes that we have been able to find a change. The figure shows that the differences between classes in meeting activity increased during the years studied. The activity level rose the most, relatively speaking, among union members in class II. Towards the end of the period, the level of activity was highest in class II and lowest in class III.

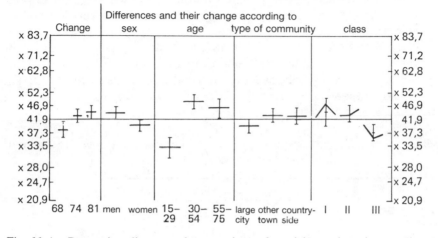

Fig. 11.4   Regression diagram of proportions of participants in union meetings

We can also conclude that the differences in union meeting participation based on sex — on average for the period — were largest among the youngest group (not shown in the figure). This is the opposite of what was seen in the analysis of the degree of organization.

Table 11.13 shows the level of participation in union meetings according to sex and class. The most striking increase for an individual group in the table was among women in class II. Even the rate of increase for men in classes I and II was relatively high. The percentages for women in class I seem to be unstable which could be the result of the small number of individuals in the group. The level of activity for workers, men, and women, was relatively stable throughout the period.

Table 11.13 Union-meeting activity among members, by sex and class. Percentages

	Men			Women		
	1968	1974	1981	1968	1974	1981
Class I	39.5	49.1	48.5	28.6	46.4	38.1
Class II	45.7	49.5	51.4	33.7	39.5	50.3
Class III	44.8	43.8	45.4	34.4	33.7	35.6
All	44.6	46.0	47.7	33.8	37.0	42.4

In addition, it may be noted that meeting participation during the period, on average, was higher among salaried employees in the public sector than among those in the private sector, with the exception of formen (table not shown). Within the different categories of workers, participation in meetings was highest among metal workers and workers in state employment and lowest among construction workers and 'other' service workers.

We will end this section with a review of meeting activity among the members of different central union organizations. The occupational groups which belong to class III are normally organized within LO. The dominant organization for class II is TCO and for class I it is SACO/SR.[7] The results are set out in Table 11.14.

Table 11.14 Union-meeting activity among members in different central union organizations. Percentages

	1968	1974	1981
LO	41.9	41.2	42.6
TCO	41.8	45.4	51.7
SACO/SR	34.6	50.8	46.6
LRF	42.0	45.2	43.5

The results in the table support previous analyses fairly well. Union activity among workers remained relatively unchanged during the period covered by our data. On the other hand, activity in the other groups increased. These groups are characterized, towards the end of the period, by relatively high percentages of participation as compared to workers. Part of these differences could possibly be the result of differences in conditions for participation in the meetings of different unions. For example, certain categories of salaried employees are able to hold their union meetings during working hours.

Union positions

The social mechanisms which affect recruitment to positions within unions have often been the subject of discussion. The desirability of similar socio-economic status between members and their union representatives is often asserted. Table 11.15 shows the representativeness of those holding union positions in relation to the membership of LO, the country's largest central organization, with regard to sex and class. The percentages represent LO members, men and women, in classes II[8] and III respectively who hold elected positions within the union. Men and people belonging to class II are overrepresented among those holding union positions (both the differences based on sex and class are statistically significant). A control showed that the class differences cannot be explained by the fact that some of the people work full time with union issues and have therefore been moved from class III to II.

Table 11.15 Proportion of male and female LO-members in classes II and III[a] who hold union positions in 1968, 1974, and 1981. Percentages

	1968		1974		1981	
	Men	Women	Men	Women	Men	Women
Class II	14.7	0	16.7	11.2	19.0	8.6
Class III	8.6	4.4	10.2	5.7	12.2	6.1

[a] The number of people in class I who are members of LO is too small on all three measurement dates for meaningful calculations.

Although those holding positions in LO may not entirely represent the sex and social class composition of members, it is possible that they may still give proper expression to the member's opinions (representativeness of opinion). That this is the case was shown by Leif Lewin (1977, 157 f.) in an analysis of union democracy based on material collected in 1973. A secondary analysis of the same material (Lewin 1980, 37–51) indicated that the relationship between opinion and class representativeness is not at all simple. In those sections of LO which tried to encourage class representativeness (through quotas, etc.) the similarity of opinion between members and those with union positions was on average lower than in other sections. That we have been able to find shortcomings in one of the system's attributes (class representativeness) does not necessarily mean that there are shortcomings regarding other attributes (opinion representativeness). If Lewin's original results are still valid, about which we cannot express an opinion, then the lack of class representativeness could be considered to be a less serious problem.

The active and the passive

The above findings showed that political and union participation in Sweden increased during the years 1968–81. At the same time we noted that there are substantial differences between various population groups regarding these forms of activity. We shall analyse below the extent to which usage of different channels of political influence vary in relation to one another.[9] Table 11.16 shows the percentage of people who stand completely outside the political process, the percentage who participate in only one form of activity and the percentage who participate in several forms of activity.

For those who have indicated only one form of activity, the table specifies the particular type. The activity increase discussed previously resulted in a definite decrease in the percentage of people who were completely passive. Of those active in only one form of activity, the percentages for opinion shaping activities and union membership increased slightly. Furthermore, the table shows that the percentage of people using several channels of political influence was substantial during each survey year.[10] This percentage increased during the years as a result of the general increase in political activity. Among those using two channels, the most usual combination was union membership and participation in opinion shaping activities throughout the investigation. In the group which used three channels, the most usual combination was union membership, membership in political organizations and/or meeting participation, as well as participation in opinion shaping activities.

Table 11.16 Participation in politics: Cumulative distribution. Percentages

	1968		1974		1981	
Politically passive	36.5	36.5	29.9	29.9	21.5	21.5
Political organization/meeting	4.1		3.6		2.5	
Public opinion activities	9.0		9.3		10.5	
Contact with a public official	0.5	35.0	0.9	37.2	0.5	38.1
Union membership	21.4		23.4		24.6	
Two channels	19.0		21.0		24.8	
Three channels	7.5	28.6	9.3	33.1	11.3	40.4
Four channels	2.1		2.8		4.3	

The next step in the analysis is to describe separately those who participate in three or more channels and those who stand completely outside the political process. The regression analysis (Figure 11.5) shows the statistically significant differences among 'activists' in regard to sex, age, and class. Men, middle aged people, and people in class I are overrepresented. The differences between the sexes decreased during the period while the others seemed stable.

Table 11.17 shows the 'activists' divided by sex and class. We can see that the percentage of people taking part in three or more channels increased quickly in each of the categories, with the exception of men in class III, and that substantial differences still exist between them. The

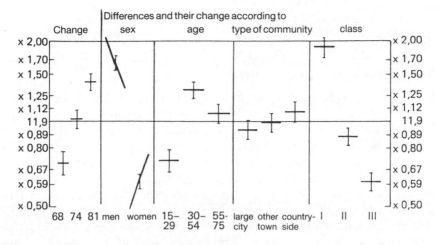

Fig. 11.5 Regression diagram of proportions of 'activists'

increase was most rapid among women, especially those in class I and II. The results of the differences in 1981 can be summed up briefly in the following manner: In 1981 the percentage of 'activists' among men in class I was roughly five times higher than among women in class III.

Table 11.17 People who participated in at least three channels of political influence ('activists'), by sex and class. Percentages

	Men			Women		
	1968	1974	1981	1968	1974	1981
Class I	30.0	31.3	37.3	6.7	12.4	24.8
Class II	17.3	19.8	22.9	3.4	7.3	12.8
Class III	13.5	15.4	16.0	2.2	3.9	6.6
All	16.2	18.5	20.9	2.9	5.7	10.2

Turning to the passive people in various population groups (results not shown) it is fairly natural to conclude that the groups characterized by a relatively high activity level are underrepresented. Men, middle-aged people and people in class I were therefore characterized by low percentages among the politically passive people. In 1981 the percentage of women in class III among the politically passive was about eight times higher than the percentage of men in class I.

To summarize, it could be said that there is a systematic correlation between position in the demographic and social structure and political activity. The definite increase in activity which we have been able to observe for most of the groups investigated has, in a number of cases, resulted in a lessening of the differences between these groups.

Self-defence against the authorities

We shall conclude this report by describing the ability of citizens to defend themselves against the decisions of public authorities. This has been measured as the ability of the respondent alone, or with the help of someone he knows, to write a letter and appeal against the decision of an authority. The percentage of people who believe that they can defend themselves in this way increased during the period. The percentages for each respective year were 44, 54, and 63 per cent. The regression model (not shown here) shows an already familiar pattern. The defence ability was highest among men, middle-aged people and people in class I. The differences between the various categories seemed to remain stable through the years.

Final comment

Politics exist within a field of tension between various group interests and ideologies. In an ideal democracy all citizens should be equal regarding their chances of influencing the political process. Yet there is probably little disagreement that the ideal is far from being fulfilled in any society. The position differs, however, in the degree to which the ideal has been realized. Empirical information about a democratic society's manner of functioning is hardly of the character that it excludes continued disagreement.[11] Empirical studies should, on the other hand, be an excellent means for clarifying the nature of the disagreement.

In this chapter we have examined political activity in the population during the period 1968–81. Our observations could be summarized in the following points:

1. Political participation increased during the period. This increase mainly involves participation in opinion shaping activities and the unions. On the other hand participation in political organizations and meetings seems to have stagnated during the 1970s. The political organizations do not seem to have been particularly successful in recruiting or mobilizing members during the years studied.
2. The connection, between political participation and position in the social and demographic structure is still significant, although to a somewhat lesser extent. The most important result in this context is that differences related to sex have decreased. Class and community type differences have remained stable in most cases and the gaps between these groups remain substantial.

3. Political participation appears to be of a cumulative character. Those who participate in one type of activity also tend to participate in other activities. The percentage of people who did not participate in any channels of political influence at all decreased considerably during the period at the same time as the percentage participating in several forms of activity increased.

The general increase in activity which we have charted here can be related to facts which have been reviewed in earlier chapters. When the educational level of the population is increased and economic security is provided favourable conditions for a sense of community and the release of individual energy which are required for political engagement. The relevance of politics can be assumed to be of special importance to the working population. The increasing political engagement of women is probably a reflection of the gradual strengthening of their links to the labour market. Another factor which may have affected political participation is the decrease in the number of average working hours among employees.

The results presented here could also be looked at from different angles. The increased strength of the unions probably leads to increased influence over the centres of political decision-making which can create problems in the functioning of a representative democracy. Increased participation in opinion shaping activities could possibly be a result of growing dissatisfaction with the political situation. An analysis of the political process and its nature as well as the public's reaction to it must, however, be carried out from points of departure other than those we have used within the Level of Living Survey. The conclusion which one should be able to accept — against the background described above — is that the public became more politically active during the period 1968–81.

Notes

1. The above and similar ideas can hardly be called non-controversial. A number of writers — most often active in the USA — claim that political passivity within large portions of the population fills a positive function for democracy's continued existence. The focal point of democracy is claimed to be the 'enlightened' elites' competition for voters and not the voters' political engagement (for a presentation of the different views in the debate see S. Johansson 1971, Lewin 1970).
2. In 1968 the following two questions were included in the interviews: Did you vote in the local election in 1966? and Are you going to vote in the

national election in 1968. Those who answered that they did not know are classified among the non-voters. A question on the 1973 election was included in 1974 and on the 1979 election in 1981.

3. The borderline between political parties/associations and other organizations is not clear. Different people can place the same organization in different categories. Amnesty International can, for example, be considered to be either a political or a humanitarian organization, depending upon an individual's reasons for joining. We chose to allow the respondents themselves to determine whether or not the organizations they belonged to were political. The respondents also determined if the meetings they attended were of a political character.

4. Answers to questions of the type above are sensitive to the precise formulation of the question. In its continual survey regarding living conditions, the Central Bureau of Statistics (SCB) posed this question to a nationally representative sample of the population between 16 and 74 years old: Have you ever spoken at a meeting? (with a list of different organizations). In 1978, 52 per cent answered the question positively (SOS 1982, 20). The difference between the SCB's and the Level of Living Survey results can probably be explained by differences in the formulation of the question. The results in Table 11.3, therefore, probably shed more light on the change over time than on the absolute level during each survey year.

5. The variable used in the analysis related to participation in the 1968, 1973, and 1979 elections. The first survey asked the respondents if they planned to vote in the forthcoming election. The later surveys asked the respondents if they had voted in the previous election (cf. note 1).

6. Our statistics differ somewhat from those of the central union organizations regarding the degree of union organization. To be able to compare the two sets of data we 'tidied up' our data and removed those people who listed student unions, the Swedish Employer's Union, and non-specified organizations as their union organization. Then, as shown in the table below, our data differs very little from that of the central organizations with the possible exception of 1974. The degree of organization within the population (15–75 years old) according to the Level of Living Survey and the main union organizations (LO, TCO, SACO/SR, SAC, LRF).

	1968	1974	1981
Level of Living Survey	42.7	48.4	57.9
Organizations	43.7	50.2	57.7

The information from the organizations applies to 31 December 1968, 1974, and 1981.

7. However, it is worth noting that about 20 per cent of the SACO/SR membership in 1981 belonged to class II.

8. The following occupational groups belonging to class II have fairly high percentages with LO membership: foremen, technicians, office personnel, and salaried employees in the public sector.

9. The calculations are based on an index which includes the following activities: 1) membership in political organizations/participation in political meetings. 2) Participation in opinion shaping activities. 3) Contact with authorities. 4) Membership in a union.
10. The percentage of people who used several channels was, in each year, higher than one would have expected based on the usage of these channels separately.
11. The Norwegian's 'democracy debate' is a good example of different interpretations of the same idea. See Martinussen 1977, Lafferty 1981 and Hellewik 1983.

12

Family and Social Integration

CHRISTINA AXELSSON

Social relationships in a welfare perspective

The topic of this chapter is social relationships in the Swedish population as revealed in the data from the Level of Living Surveys of 1968, 1974, and 1981. Several studies conducted during this period have stressed the importance of social relationships for the individual's welfare. To begin the discussion, the way in which social relationships are embodied in various controversial concepts of welfare will be illustrated.

The areas of life in which people's conditions are influenced through political means are what is studied in the Swedish Level of Living Survey (S. Johansson 1979). Welfare is defined as the individual's command over resources within these areas. But it is clear that it is only possible to regulate the external conditions of human association through politics. Social relationships thus do not have the same direct political relevance as do education and medical care, for example, Communality among individuals cannot be achieved through political decisions, but may have direct welfare implications. It is assumed that the need for close human relationships is universal.

In his work with the Level of Living Survey, Erikson (1978a) deals with social integration as a dimension of welfare. Accordingly, a lasting relationship between individuals and their social and physical environment is defined as integration. This integration may range from strong to weak, or non-existent. Its most important function is to engender security, but also to constitute a resource for action. There are four distinguishable forms of integration (material, social, local, and cultural), all of which may compensate in part for the others as grounds for security. However, a certain social integration is in all likelihood a prerequisite for the psychological well-being of the individual.

Social integration is defined as the individual's communality with other people, family and relatives, friends, and co-workers. Communality implies a symmetrical relationship which is an expression of friendship or love. Erikson points out that this is an ideal picture, from which there are probably large deviations. Assymmetrical relationships, however, may be crucial if the alternative is isolation.

Social integration is specified according to whether it is primary (family, relatives, friends) or secondary (co-workers, fellow members of organizations).

In the Norwegian Level of Living Survey, it is a description of the results of the individual's activity that is labelled welfare. The point of departure is the notion that the individual has a set of resources to be utilized within different areas of activity. Ringen (1976), in his work with the Norwegian study, also viewed social integration as a dimension of welfare. According to Ringen, the concept of welfare should be expanded to cover also the processes that lead to the results. Activity, joint action, and participation are then assigned an independent value.

According to Ringen, social integration entails active and equal participation within the family, in the network of friends/ neighbourhood, in working life, and in political life. The many-sidedness of social integration can be illustrated by studying the activity within a certain area (for example, political activity) in relation to the integration within other areas (family, network of friends/ neighbourhood, working life). Membership in only one group means the absence of isolation, but in such a case the individual's relationship to the group is one-sided. Ringen views social integration as a source of security, self-esteem, and drive. It further gives rise to a network of contacts and thereby constitutes a resource. Social isolation is seen as incompatible with welfare.

In Allardt's Scandinavian study (1975), welfare is based on the satisfaction of individual needs. Human needs, however, take various forms, which could be defined as Having, Loving, and Being. Welfare is a composite term, encompassing the level of living as well as the quality of life. Level of living, according to Allardt, refers to 'having' as a need for material resources. Quality of life includes 'loving' and 'being', as needs which are satisfied through relationships to other people and to the society.

Social relationships thus occupy a prominent position in Allardt's study. The welfare dimension of 'loving' symbolizes the need for loving relationships between the individual and specific other people. Allardt defines symmetrical relationships of love and concern as communality. A precondition for communality is the ability of people to place themselves in each others' situation, and access to a common language. Communality may be a resource for being able to realize other values, but may also be understood as a goal for the individual. The forms of communality may vary, but some form of it is a fundamental need. As support for this, Allardt points out that mental disturbances can be interpreted as arising from a lack of communality. This communality may be of various kinds: local communality, family communality, and friendships.

Social relationships, therefore, are normally regarded as essential for the welfare of the individual in several respects. Social relationships have the character of an attained goal for the individual, but may also constitute a resource for acting in various contexts. Last but not least, it is assumed that social relationships bring security to one's existence. This is also our general view of the significance of social relationships from the standpoint of welfare. A more precise presentation of our outlook is given in Erikson's discussion (1978a) of welfare from the point of view of integration. The description here will be restricted to primary social integration,[1] that is, the individual's relationships to family, relatives, and friends.

A common notion among the public is that social integration has become weaker, as regards family as well as relatives and friends. The debate during the seventies about the suburbs illustrates the issue of communality and isolation.[2] Through the criticism of suburbs, a picture is conveyed of a society devoid of inter-human relationships, without communality. This wretched picture was often compared with that of 'the good old days' with images of either a farming community or working-class districts. Suburbs thus came to symbolize isolation in today's society, while communality finds its embodiment in bygone days.

The picture of growing isolation has remained dominant in the mass media. Is this a realistic description or a myth? We can throw light on this question partly by describing the development of actual relationships to family, relatives, and friends during the period 1968–1981. The emotional experience of these relationships by individuals is beyond the scope of this discussion. But being socially isolated implies more limited possibilities to form deep relationships with other people. More precisely, we are going to look at social integration primarily by attempting to answer the following questions: Has social isolation increased since 1968? Are there substantial differences in social isolation among different population groups? If there are group differences, have they increased or decreased since 1968?

Family as primary integration

In the late 1960s, divorce rates rose and marriage rates dropped. This could reflect a deterioration in social integration. But it need not indicate either single living or the breakdown of the family. During the same period, it also became increasingly common to live together outside the formal state of matrimony. The family thus proves capable of prospering in new forms. This is seen in the distribution of population in different stages of the life cycle in 1968, 1974, and 1981 (see Table 12.1).

Cohabiting, unmarried couples are counted as cohabiting married couples here in order to give a description of actual family relationships.

Table 12.1 Adult Population, 15–75 years, distribution over different stages in life cycle 1968, 1974, and 1981.[a] Percentages

Stage in life cycle	1968	1974	1981
Single, living with parents, no children			
< 17 years	13.7	11.4	11.0
Single, < 45 years, no children < 17 years	6.6	7.6	9.4
Married,[b] < 45 years, no children			
< 17 years	6.7	7.0	8.4
Married with children < 7 years	17.7	16.6	14.4
Married with children 7–16 years	14.0	14.5	15.1
Single with children < 17 years	1.5	2.4	2.1
Married, > 44 years, no children			
< 17 years	26.9	28.2	27.3
Single, > 44 years, no children < 17 years	12.8	12.4	12.3
Total	100.0	100.0	100.0
Number	5922	6076	6238

[a] The proportion of cohabiting and single old people, like the proportion of children who live with their parents, is less here than in the population as a whole since the sample is limited to 15–75 year olds.
[b] Married = married or cohabiting.

The changes during this interval are on the whole small. The proportion of married and/or cohabiting persons remains largely the same, about 65 per cent. Even the nuclear family (cohabiting and with children) seems to endure. At each measurement date, about 30 per cent of the population are cohabiting and with children. That the proportion of those cohabiting with small children has decreased is probably due to the drop in the size of the birth cohorts from the mid-1960s. One conclusion is that the level of integration in family life remains unchanged from 1968 to 1981.

A qualitative aspect of the development is that the stability in family relationships has changed. A study conducted by SCB (1982b, 32) shows that 16 per cent among the women born between 1946 and 1950 had experienced more than one cohabitory relationship or marriage by the age of 30. The corresponding proportion among women born between 1936 and 1940 was only 5 per cent. In Figure 12.1, the proportion of divorces in marriages entered in 1956, 1961, 1966, and 1971 is shown. Among those people who got married in 1971, 15 per cent, for example,

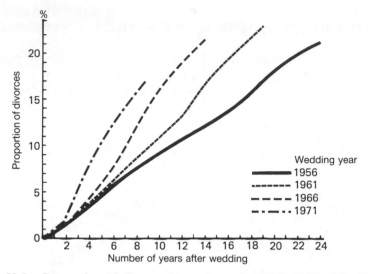

Fig. 12.1. Proportion of divorces in marriages entered in 1956, 1961, 1966, and 1971

were divorced after 8 years. Among those who got married in 1956, 15 per cent were divorced first after 18 years. More recently entered marriages tend to be dissolved after an increasingly shorter duration. To illustrate the welfare implications of a more unstable cohabitation pattern, however, requires an analysis that falls outside the scope of this book.

Individual families therefore, became less stable, while the family as an institution remained stable during the period under study. This indicates that divorces in general are followed by new marriages/cohabiting relationships. It is mainly young people who account for the increased instability in family relationships. At the same time, it should be pointed out that even if divorce has become more common, most marriages do in fact last (see Figure 12.1).

Marital status is inadequate as a measure of family integration. The nature of the relationships will still remain unknown. What we *can* measure here is the occurrence of marital/cohabiting relationships. From the point of view of integration, it is the occurrence itself of such a relationship that is perhaps most significant. But single people (in terms of civil status) do not necessarily lack the kind of integration that comes from living with someone else. Being single is not always the same thing as living alone. The proportion of the population who were single (unmarried, divorced, widow/widower) was 34 per cent, while the proportion of people living alone (one person in a dwelling) was 17 per cent in 1981. Thus, the proportion of single people who live with someone else is also 17 per cent. This is, for example, the case with young people living with their parents, and people who live with others than close relatives. Another measure of social integration, then, is the number of people who live in a dwelling.

Living alone

Living alone is often equated with loneliness. Elderly people in particular are seen as more and more isolated. In terms of integration, an increased number of people living alone can be interpreted as negative even if it need not imply an increased isolation. But, the security and the support one can get from living with someone else is lacking.

It is becoming more common in the population to live alone.[3] The proportion of people who lived alone was 13 per cent in 1968, 15 per cent in 1974, and 17 per cent in 1981. This corresponds to about 750,000 people in 1968, about 890,000 in 1974, and about 1,090,000 in 1981. One of the explanations for this change is that the access to housing has increased during this period.

Who lives alone? Are there great differences in living alone between men and women, among different age groups, types of community, and social classes? In order to present an overall picture of living alone, the regression approach described in Chapter 2 will be resumed.[4]

The diagram shows that increasing numbers of individuals were living alone during the period under study (first square). The averages during the period show that about the same proportion of men and women, and of people from the various classes, live alone. On the other hand, the

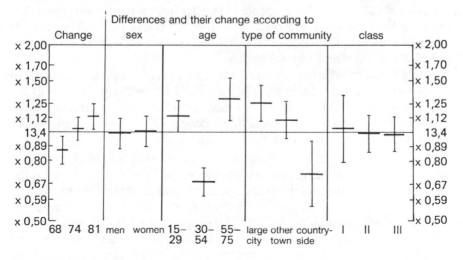

Fig. 12.2. Regression diagram of proportion of people living alone

differences in living alone are quite large among age groups and types of community. It is rarer for middle-aged people to live alone than for other age groups. In the same way, living alone is more uncommon among people in rural areas than in cities. No change in these differences is observed.

The conclusion that the differences in living alone are insignificant according to sex and class is not maintained when these factors are combined with age. Elderly women live alone to a greater extent than elderly men in all classes. This undoubtedly is largely explained by the higher mortality rate for men. Women are also usually younger than their spouses. However, among elderly women, class membership is decisive for living alone. Elderly women in classes II and III live alone more than twice as often as elderly women in class I. The weakest integration, measured by living alone, is thus found among elderly women from classes II and III. Younger men from class I also just as often live alone, but this may be seen as a passing phase in the life cycle.

Class differences in living alone are even more widespread among pensioners. Among pensioners belonging to class III, the proportion living alone was 50 per cent in 1981. Corresponding proportions were 31 per cent for class I and 40 per cent for class II. Among pensioners in class III, there was a significant increase since 1968 in the proportion of people living alone. This development may be interpreted as negative with respect to integration. But this interpretation could naturally be questioned. From another point of view, this development could be seen as positive. That increasingly more elderly people have the chance to live on their own could be a sign of increased independence. According to Sundström (1983), elderly people prefer to live in their own home and manage on their own. However, this does not imply that living alone in all its aspects is positive for the individual. Living alone may be the best alternative while not without problems.

It is unclear whether living alone can be seen as an indicator of something troublesome, especially for people in the higher age brackets. To some extent, this can be studied by looking at whether health problems[5] are more common among people living alone than among others of the same ages (see Table 12.2).

In all age groups, there is a greater tendency towards severely impaired psychological well-being among people living alone than among the cohabiting. We are unable to state whether less satisfactory integration occasions more psychological difficulties or vice versa. The causal relationship is possible both ways. The proportion of people with serious physical disabilities increases with age, but within the higher ages, serious disabilities are more common among people living alone than others. These results support, to some degree, the notion that increased living

Table 12.2 Serious disabilities and seriously impaired mental well-being, by type of living arrangement in different age groups 1968, 1974, and 1981. Percentages

	Serious disabilities			Seriously impaired mental well-being		
	1968	1974	1981	1968	1974	1981
Population						
Living alone	14.0	13.7	11.7	7.7	6.4	6.5
Cohabiting	6.8	6.0	5.9	2.9	2.7	2.3
15–29 years						
Living alone	0.5	—	2.4	1.6	3.1	4.2
Cohabiting	0.9	1.7	2.3	1.1	1.8	0.7
30–54 years						
Living alone	7.5	9.7	3.3	8.6	6.6	6.6
Cohabiting	3.7	3.3	3.5	3.3	2.2	2.2
55–75 years						
Living alone	22.9	22.6	23.0	9.9	7.9	7.9
Cohabiting	18.9	14.7	13.3	4.2	4.4	3.8
Pensioners						
65–69 years						
Living alone	22.0	25.0	20.4	7.5	8.2	4.2
Cohabiting	18.9	19.5	13.8	3.4	5.4	3.7
70–75 years						
Living alone	34.4	28.0	28.9	7.6	8.4	5.8
Cohabiting	30.3	19.1	24.8	7.4	5.3	2.4

alone is partially indicative of a problem, at least for elderly people. As we shall see later on in this chapter, health problems increase when in addition to living alone, a person also lacks contact with relatives and friends.

Social interaction with relatives and friends

Having a large network of social interaction may give the picture of an active and popular person. To be seen as socially isolated is most likely experienced as a failure. This may cause distortion in the answers to the four Level of Living Survey questions on whether individuals regularly visit or are visited by relatives and friends during their leisure. The individual can be asked about behaviour (an interaction) and respond according to his/her perception of or attitude to this behaviour. In such a case, the isolation would be under-estimated. The given alternative responses to the interaction questions are 'no', 'yes, sometimes', 'yes, often'. A further source of error here is that the implication of these responses may be interpreted in different ways, according to age, previous experiences, and so on.

Keeping these general limitations in mind, we will first present simple rates for interaction with relatives and friends in the population between 1968 and 1981 (Table 12.3). What we will illustrate is the individual's actual interaction, in other words, the prerequisites for experiencing communality.

Table 12.3 Social integration and isolation in the population 15–75 years old, 1968, 1974, and 1981. Percentages

	1968	1974	1981
Social Integration			
Regularly visits relatives	87.0	88.8	90.2
of which, often	28.1	29.4	31.0
Regularly has relatives visit	88.4	89.7	90.2
of which, often	26.4	27.5	27.0
Frequent contact with relatives	18.3	21.4	21.5
Regularly visits friends	91.1	94.1	94.7
of which, often	29.8	35.9	39.9
Regularly has friends visit	93.3	94.8	95.3
of which, often	30.2	35.1	38.6
Frequent contact with friends	22.2	31.5	34.7
Frequent contact with both relatives and friends			
('often' on all four questions)	11.1	12.9	14.0
Isolation			
Little contact with relatives	15.8	13.4	11.9
of which, no contact with relatives	6.8	6.9	6.1
Little contact with friends	9.8	6.7	5.8
of which, no contact with friends	4.7	3.7	3.2
Little contact with relatives and friends	9.0	7.7	6.2
of which, no contact at all	1.9	1.0	1.0
Has no relative or close friend that would help out in case			
of sickness			3.8
of need of company			3.7
of personal problems			4.8

Interaction both with relatives and friends has increased since 1968. The proportion of people with little interaction is quite small, and most people interviewed seemed to have the opportunity for forming ties with other people. Support for this is found in that 95 per cent of the population has some relative or close friend with whom they can discuss personal problems. Thus, there is no evidence that isolation from relatives and friends is increasing in the population as a whole. These findings should be interpreted with some caution, since the non-responses may constitute a marginal group in terms of isolation. The non-responses within the group we were able to study (people who participated in 1968, but did not respond in 1981) nevertheless seemed to be randomly distributed in their interactional pattern in 1968.

By using a regression analysis, we shall illustrate which people largely lack interaction with relatives and friends. In terms of integration, this seems to be a problem. Weak integration implies little possibility of getting help from relatives or friends when it is needed. Such help may range all the way from encouragement to getting a job. It has also been stressed before that social integration gives a sense of security in most cases. Isolation from relatives and friends is measured by means of the four interaction questions.[6] How the proportion of people with weak interaction with relatives varies according to study year, sex, age, type of community, and social class is presented in Figure 12.3.

The occurrence of weak interaction with relatives has decreased in the population as a whole since 1968 (first square). The differences in isolation from relatives among different groups in the population are quite large. Those who most often largely lack interaction with relatives are men, younger people, large city dwellers, and members of class I. From the diagram, it can be seen that after 1974, isolation from relatives

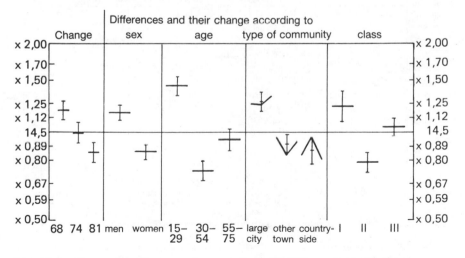

Fig. 12.3. Regression diagram of proportion with little contact with relatives

increases in the cities and decreases in the countryside, in relative terms.

Weak integration with relatives applies to sex, type of community, and class to a great extent in combination with age. In particular, it is younger men, young urban dwellers, as well as young people in class I, who interact rarely with their relatives. Furthermore, isolation from relatives is pronounced among the rural population in class I, and among the urban population in class III. The latter may be due to the fact that immigrants are overrepresented in metropolitan areas and in class III. Greater isolation from relatives among immigrants than among Swedes has been shown in the other studies (Leiniö 1984).

The weaker family integration in class I may perhaps also be explained by the fact that members of this class more often live far away from their relatives. In class I, the proportion who have moved more than 200 kilometres from the area where they were raised was 41 per cent in 1981. The corresponding proportion for class II was 22 per cent and for class III, 19 per cent. Another possible reason for this weaker interaction with relatives in class I, is social mobility; this would be the case if it is so that a change in class occasions a decrease in contact with relatives. Social background varies more among people in class I than in the other classes (see Chapter 3).

The differences in weak integration among population groups are usually smaller for interaction with friends than with relatives. The distribution of proportions who largely lack interaction with friends is depicted in Figure 12.4.

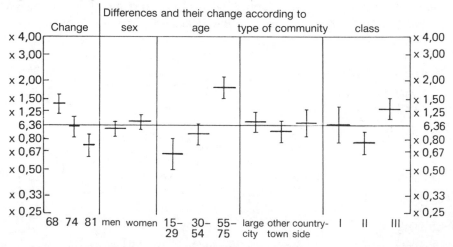

Fig. 12.4. Regression diagram of proportion with little contact with friends

In the population as a whole, the proportion who largely lack interaction with friends has decreased since 1968 (first square). The differences in isolation from friends are insignificant between the sexes as well as among the different types of community. Weak integration among friends, on the other hand, varies sharply with age and the elderly are a marginal group. As was the case with interaction with relatives, isolation is less present among people in class II than others.

Isolation from both relatives and friends has also decreased in the population as a whole since 1968 (table showing these figures not included). Isolation from both relatives and friends is found most often among elderly people, especially in class III. Integration with both relatives and friends is again somewhat weaker in large cities than elsewhere.

Thus, isolation from relatives and friends has decreased since 1968. It is noteworthy that people in class I are more isolated from relatives than are the other classes. Isolation from friends, however, is more common in class III than in the other classes. Moreover, young people are most isolated from relatives, while the elderly are most isolated from friends. On the individual level, it is also the case that people with weak integration in one respect, are not necessarily weakly integrated in the other. Those isolated from relatives often compensate for this lack by interacting with friends, and vice versa.

Isolation from family, relatives and friends

A group of people with absolutely no primary integration are those who live alone and neither associate with relatives nor with friends. This group is defined in the most narrow sense possible, and refers to people who live alone but also answered all contact questions in the negative. According to this criterion, only an average of 0.2 per cent of the population was totally isolated during the study period. Thus, it seems reasonable to jettison the myth of a prevalent and broadening isolation, at least in terms of actual social interaction.

A group with weak primary integration is made up of people living alone who largely lack interaction with relatives and friends. This group remains almost constant over time, at about 2 per cent of the population. Data from Statistics Sweden (1982e, 51) too show that a total of 2 per cent 'has neither the possibility for daily contacts within the family nor regular association with others at least once a week'. How large the differences in isolation are broken down by sex, age, type of community, and social class are shown in Table 12.4. (The percentages are too small for a regression analysis.)

Just over 100,000 people live alone and have almost no interaction with relatives or friends. The differences in isolation among various groups are small, but elderly people and urban dwellers are overrepresented.

Table 12.4 Weak social integration (those who live alone largely lacking contact with both relatives and friends), by sex, age, type of community, and class 1968, 1974, and 1981. Percentages

	1968	1974	1981
Population	1.8	1.7	1.9
Absolute number in 1000s	(107)	(101)	(119)
Sex			
Men	2.4	2.0	2.1
Women	1.3	1.4	1.8
Age			
15–29	1.1	0.6	0.7
30–54	1.2	1.1	1.4
55–75	3.3	3.5	3.7
Type of community			
Large city	2.3	2.4	2.9
Small city	1.9	1.6	1.8
Rural district	1.4	1.2	1.2
Class			
I	2.4	1.0	1.6
II	1.6	1.2	1.5
III	1.9	2.1	2.3

We have previously found some correlation between living alone and impaired health. When in addition to living alone, a person also largely lacks interaction with relatives and friends, the proportion of people with health problems usually increases. There is also a systematic difference in the question of health between people living alone with little interaction and people living with others with much interaction (see Table 12.5).

A dominant pattern is that a greater proportion of people have psychological problems among those with weak social integration than those with strong integration. Previously, it was asserted that mental disturbances can be interpreted as caused by social isolation. But the causal relationship can also travel in the opposite direction. Social isolation may be interpreted as arising from psychological problems. The latter can be assumed to damage relationships to family, relatives, and friends. The correlation between social isolation and mental disturbances is strongest along middle-aged people. The proportion with seriously

Table 12.5 Serious disabilities and seriously impaired mental well-being, by social integration in different age groups 1968, 1974, and 1981. Percentages

	Serious disabilities			Seriously impaired mental well-being		
	1968	1974	1981	1968	1974	1981
Population						
Weak social integration	26.4	31.9	27.9	8.1	13.1	14.5
Strong social integration	4.1	4.0	4.7	2.4	2.8	1.6
15–29 years						
Weak social integration	—	—	—	(5.3)	—	(10.2)
Strong social integration	0.6	2.4	2.2	3.4	2.6	1.1
30–54 years						
Weak social integration	11.1	(18.8)	9.7	10.4	(13.6)	19.2
Strong social integration	2.8	2.3	4.5	1.4	2.2	1.2
55–75 years						
Weak social integration	43.1	42.5	42.3	7.8	14.9	12.5
Strong social integration	11.7	8.6	8.0	3.1	4.1	3.3
Pensioners						
65–69 years						
Weak social integration	(36.9)	(26.1)	(28.5)	(9.1)	(16.7)	(7.1)
Strong social integration	(7.4)	10.2	10.7	(3.9)	2.3	—
70–75 years						
Weak social integration	(53.6)	(45.4)	53.2	(4.3)	(6.7)	3.7
Strong social integration	(13.3)	(7.9)	(13.4)	—	(4.0)	—

Note: Weak social integration = people living alone who are isolated from relatives and friends. Strong social integration = cohabiting people with a great deal of contact with relatives and friends.

impaired psychological well-being was 19 per cent in 1981 (an increase of 9 per centage points since 1968) among middle-aged people who live alone and largely lack interaction with others. The corresponding proportion is only 1 per cent among middle-aged people who live with others and have considerable interaction. In the higher age brackets, we find a large difference in the proportion of disabled people according to social integration. Among the elderly who lived alone and largely lacked interaction, the proportion with serious disabilities was 42 per cent in 1981. The corresponding proportion was 8 per cent among elderly people who lived with others and had considerable interaction. Isolated pensioners 70–75 years old are most often seriously disabled, 53 per cent in 1981. The corresponding proportion among pensioners with strong social integration is 13 per cent. To suffer from serious disabilities in higher age brackets is thus much more common among people living alone who largely lack interaction than among those living with others who have much interaction.

After the age of 30, there is a clear correlation between living alone with little interaction, and impaired physical and psychological health. Ringen (1976) has also asserted that there are clear correlations between social isolation and health problems. The conclusion here must be that isolation from family, relatives, and friends can be interpreted as a sign of serious problems.

Primary social integration — Concluding Remarks

In this chapter, the individual's relationships with family, relatives, and friends have been described from the point of view of social integration. Integration is not viewed as something one has or does not have, but rather as ranging from strong to weak, or non-existent. The most important function of social integration is to create a sense of security in an individual's existence, but also to constitute a resource for action. But solid integration *in all respects* may in fact be negative for the individual. This could lead to intolerance and lack of understanding for people who are different (Erikson 1978), and result in a conservatism which would become intolerable for those around us (Allardt 1970). A *certain* social integration nevertheless is seen as necessary for the well-being of the individual.

Social integration is studied with an 'objective' approach in the sense that the individual is questioned about actual relationships and not about his/her experience of these relationships. We think that the occurrence of social relationships is what is most meaningful when assessing integration. It would, of course, be desirable to describe the subjective side of these relationships as well. In other studies, it has been found that there is no unambiguous association between the degree of social isolation and the subjective experience of loneliness (Tornstam, 1983). It has also been asserted that of those married people who experience loneliness, women are overrepresented. According to Tornstam, this may be explained by the fact that in general women place higher qualitative demands on a marital relationship than do men. When a subjective method is used, disparate levels of aspirations will thus be crucial for the results.

We have chosen to illustrate primarily people who more or less lack social integration and thereby have more limited chances to share communality with others. Our major observations are summarized below.

Since 1968, it has become increasingly more common to live alone.

Elderly people and people living in large cities are overrepresented in this respect. Living alone implies a deficiency in one type of integration, but need not imply social isolation. On the other hand, people who both live alone and largely lack interaction with relatives and friends can be considered as isolated. We find that the proportion of socially isolated people, measured in this manner, remains constant over time, at about 2 per cent of the population. Elderly people and urban dwellers are still overrepresented. When we measure isolation as living alone and totally lacking social interaction with relatives and friends, the proportion drops during the period to an average of 0.2 per cent of the population.

Accordingly, there is nothing to indicate that social isolation has increased since 1968. Living alone has certainly increased, and this is often interpreted as increased isolation. But if we distinguish those people living alone who also lack interaction with relatives or friends, the picture changes. Social isolation then cannot be seen as especially extensive, but may of course be a problem for the individuals involved. Support for this thesis is received from the unambiguous association found here between social isolation and impaired health. In conclusion, it fortunately seems to be the case that most people seem to have the chance of communality within the family as well as with relatives and friends.

Notes

1. Secondary social integration in the sense of participation in working and associational life is discussed in the chapters on employment and leisure.
2. A detailed account and discussion of the debate on suburbs is given by Franzén and Sandstedt in *Grannskap och stadsplanering* (*Neighbourhoods and Town-Planning*) Uppsala 1981.
3. People living in public institutions have been excluded from the analysis.
4. The regression model describes the main effects and interaction effects up to the second order on living alone.
5. In the Level of Living Survey, different measures for health were constructed on the basis of the interview questions. A scale for physical disabilities was based upon the following questions: Can you briskly walk 100 metres without difficulty? Can you run 100 metres without great difficulty? Can you climb stairs without difficulty?
   Those who answered all three questions in the negative were defined as seriously disabled.
   A scale for impaired psychological well-being was constructed with the help of four questions. The individual is questioned about general fatigue,

nervous difficulties, insomnia, and depression over the previous year. Those answering in the affirmative to all these questions were seen as having a seriously impaired mental state.

6. Weak integration: A totalled index was constructed from both questions on whether the interviewee usually visited or was visited by relatives during free time. An analogous index was constructed by means of both questions on contact with friends. Isolation from relatives as well as from friends was indicated by 2 no-responses or 1 no + 1 sometimes. To measure isolation from both relatives and friends, a summarized index for the four questions was used. Isolation from both relatives and friends was deduced from the following responses: 4 no-responses, 3 no + 1 sometimes, 3 no + 1 often/2 no + 2 sometimes.

13

Leisure and Recreation

MICHAEL TÅHLIN

Introduction

Even before the Low Income Commission's report on the leisure
activities of Swedish inhabitants (Lundahl 1971), the myth of leisure as
'free time' had been discredited from several sources. That the manner in
which leisure is employed is not determined by individual tastes alone,
but is to a large extent the result of one's resources and class, was
asserted in several minor studies in the 1940s and 1950s.[1] The available
information was expanded with the first large-scale national leisure study
in the beginning of the 1960s (SOU 1964:47). However, for various
reasons, it was the 1968 findings of the Low Income Commission that
resulted in more fundamental changes in our ideas about people's leisure
conditions. Even if this breakthrough was far from complete, the time
was ripe for a debate about leisure.

The aim of this chapter is to describe people's leisure habits during the
period 1968 to 1981 using the three Level of Living Surveys.[2] A general
debate during this period[3] led to the notion that leisure should not be
treated as a distinct part of people's lives, since the nature of it is so
strongly influenced by the whole way of life. Most empirical research
approaches still lack a broad view, in which knowledge about a socially
and demographically stratified leisure is in fact used to analyse carefully
and classify the relationship between work, private life, and society.

It is beyond the purpose of this chapter, however, and perhaps also
beyond the scope of the Level of Living Survey, to make an analysis in
such depth. Instead, we shall restrict ourselves here to an attempt to
illustrate how the range and nature of leisure is distributed in the
population. On the whole, such knowledge is available for the present,
but we are now also able to show developments over time.

The first task in an account of changes of leisure is naturally to define
the concept of leisure. Many of the problems linked to such a definition
have been discussed in the debate mentioned above. Since it is not our
ambition to make a theoretically original contribution to the discussion
of leisure, our guidelines will be practical considerations. Parker (1976,
17 f.) makes an instructive distinction between three types of definitions.

The first, and most simple, is based exclusively on the dimension of time. Leisure is a residue, that which remains of the day when work, sleep, and so on are subtracted. The second type of definition, often of a philosophical or religious nature, however, disregards *quantity of time* completely. In its place is the *quality* inherent in an activity or in the person engaging in it. The nature of one's frame of mind is central. A third type of definition is a combination of the other two. Hence, included here is both a quantitative component in the form of time, and an almost normative component that involves the nature of leisure.

This third approach is apparently both practical and fruitful. To consider only quantity of leisure would be misleading, since it is not a matter of course that extensive or even unlimited leisure is a positive good. More likely, leisure can be too long as well as too short. A variant of the combined approach is therefore useful for the outline of this chapter. In a strict sense, leisure will be defined in quantitative terms, but the concept will encompass resources and activities that are seen as important for endowing the available leisure with some meaning.

The discussion of the empirical findings is in two parts. First, an attempt is made to estimate the scope of leisure, especially for the economically active. Then, a description and discussion of the nature content of leisure will follow, in the form of various activities, holiday trips, and stays at summer cottages as well as membership in associations.

Leisure and politics

One of the principal assumptions underlying the Level of Living Surveys is their relevance for political decisions. Leisure, however, is one area where societal measures are not only less effective, but also less relevant than, for example, the spheres of education or housing. In terms of its nature at least, leisure neither can nor should be regulated in detail by external agencies. It is naturally the individual who primarily determines how this leisure is to be used.

At the same time, the individual's use of leisure is dependent on several factors besides personal preferences, such as time, money, education, health, working conditions, and social contacts. To the extent that these elements circumscribe an active leisure, political measures are highly relevant. Naturally, it is difficult to formulate a detailed welfare goal within the area of leisure. Few value judgements will be made here about the qualities of leisure activities; that is, all leisure occupations covered in the material from the three surveys will be viewed as equal in value. On the other hand, we assume that a high degree of activity during leisure is valuable for individuals, in that this will enhance their level of living.

In our opinion, the welfare goal of leisure is thus twofold. First, leisure should be more or less active. Second, each person should enjoy as much freedom as possible in the choice of activities. As regards the latter, a reduction in differences in use of leisure among various population categories (but not necessarily among *individuals*) can be roughly seen as a positive sign. It is doubtful whether a complete absence of systematic differences is desirable, since collective characteristics to some degree lead to entirely natural differences in preference. We assume, however, that decreasing differences in leisure habits among separate groups in the population are largely an expression of increased welfare, according to the goal given above. To link this view to the modern discussion on life styles (see, for example, Zetterberg 1977), the political goal is not the absence of diversity here, but rather a reduction of the dependence of life styles on social and demographic characteristics.

The scope of leisure

The term leisure in a broad sense here will indicate the time that remains of the day/week after time for sleep, personal hygiene, gross working hours (see below), and household work has been subtracted. The residue does not reflect leisure in a narrow sense, since we do not have information on how much time is spent on certain activities that may be regarded as duties: meals, childcare, and the like.

This definition of leisure does *not* imply that work, either gainful employment or household work, is negative. For many people, work is their greatest source of joy and pride. To increase leisure at the expense of work is thus not an unambiguously positive value. In a quantitative delimitation of the amount of leisure, however, it becomes necessary to merge all work into one category, regardless of whether it is satisfying or merely obligatory. Otherwise, the nature of the information on the scope of leisure would be unclear.

Gross working time

Before any attempt is made to estimate the total amount of leisure, the length of gross working time as measured in 1968, 1974, and 1981 will be described. The intention with the concept of gross working time is to find a measure for the total time the individual devotes to gainful employment, which is obviously central in a consideration of leisure. The gross working time therefore consists of net working time (regular working hours, overtime, preparatory time, and extra work; see Chapter 6) plus time for breaks and travelling to and from the job. Information on these different components of working time is available for those people who were employed during the week of the interview. The working time reflects precisely that week, which for most people was sometime during the spring of the interview year.

Table 13.1 Gross working hours per week for employed people 1968, 1974, and
1981, by scope of work, sex, and class. Hours

	Full-time			Part-time		
	1968	1974	1981	1968	1974	1981
Men						
Class I	50.4	47.5	44.9	—	—	—
Class II	49.3	45.8	42.9	—	—	—
Class III	49.7	44.9	43.3	—	—	—
All men	49.6	45.4	43.4	29.1	28.5	28.9
Women						
Class I + II	45.3	42.4	40.7	26.0	26.4	26.7
Class III	47.0	43.6	41.0	23.3	24.3	25.7
All women	46.2	43.0	40.8	24.0	25.1	26.1
Class I, all	50.1	46.9	44.8	36.2	30.6	29.1
Class II, all	47.7	44.4	41.8	25.5	26.4	26.3
Class III, all	49.1	44.6	42.7	23.4	24.4	26.4
All full/part-time	48.7	44.7	42.6	24.6	25.5	26.5
	Full-time + Part-time					
All Employees	44.7	40.7	38.2			

That our average regular working time decreased during the period is
well known, and is also shown in Chapter 6. The decrease is pronounced
for full-time as well as for all employed people. It is therefore not
surprising that we find a similar development for gross working times. In
total, the average working week was $6\frac{1}{2}$ hours shorter in 1981 than in
1968, of which $2\frac{1}{2}$ hours had been cut since 1974. A classification
according to full- and part-time employees is given in Table 13.1. As is
clear, full-time employees decreased their gross working time, on
average, from $48\frac{1}{2}$ to $42\frac{1}{2}$ hours during the period. Despite the fact that
the regular working time had not changed since 1974, two hours of gross
working time were 'gained'.[4] The trend seems to be similar for various
subcategories. Part-time employees follow another trend: two hours
longer gross working time on the average, from $24\frac{1}{2}$ to $26\frac{1}{2}$ hours. It is
primarily women in class III that are responsible for this.

For full-time employees we also took a closer look at occupational
categories, though without finding any noteworthy deviations from the
general pattern. Our data indicate, however, that the decrease for class I
was somewhat slower than has otherwise been the case. When

standardizing for age and sex, their working weeks are about four hours shorter in 1981 than in 1968, compared with a decrease of about six hours for classes II and III.

The overall assessment of the trend between 1968 and 1981 is that the average gross working time clearly declined, at the same time as the proportion with very long working hours dropped drastically (the latter analysis is not shown). On the whole, the changes occurred in all groups, but perhaps even more so in class III. In 1981, it is class I that shows the greatest proportion of people with very long working hours, because many of the men in this social class have long working weeks.

Household working time

The 1974 and 1981 surveys make some measurement of the amount of time that people spend on housework. This material will be used here to illustrate the relationship between the sexes in a leisure time perspective. In order to judge the level of equality between men and women, two things must be taken into consideration. First, the distribution of housework. This may reflect the roles of the sexes in Swedish families. Second, the total division of labour is of interest. Even if a state of inequality prevails between men and women with regard to housework, the total leisure time may be evenly divided. In this case, the level of equality may be high, despite strongly defined roles for the sexes.

Because our main purpose here is to describe the equality between the sexes, the analysis will be limited to married or cohabiting people. (Besides, we do not have data about housework for one-person households.) In order to relate the material to the scope of gainful employment, all those who are neither employed nor housewives are eliminated. So are also all those over 60 since the influence of wage labour on work in the home is the question under consideration.

In Table 13.2 the respondents' estimations of their own input at home are given, expressed in percentage of the total household work,[5] and according to sex and age. What is most striking here is the sizeable difference between the input of men and women. Advances were made between 1974 and 1981, during which period men nearly doubled their share of the housework. This change was relatively rapid when viewed in the long term. However, the lack of equality is still great. The difference between age groups is surprisingly small, even if young men do more work in the home than their older counterparts. All three categories of men have approximately doubled their input during the period, which means that the absolute differences between young men and others have grown.

Table 13.2 Distribution of housework between the sexes 1974 and 1981, by age.
Percentages

	1974		1981	
	Men	Women	Men	Women
– 34 years	9	87	18	80
35 – 49 years	6	90	13	83
50 – 60 years	7	88	11	84
All	7	89	14	82

It is possible to analyse the level of equality on the household level for 1981, with respect to the effect of the distribution of gainful employment on the distribution of work in the home. Information is available on the weekly working hours for spouses. In Table 13.3 it is shown how the man's share of housework varies with the woman's economically active working time.[6] (The table only refers to full-time employed men, since the remaining categories are so small as to make any meaningful estimations impossible.)

Table 13.3 Man's share of household work 1981, by wife's gainful employment. Full-time employed men. Percentages

Wife's working hours/week			
0	1–20 hrs.	21–34 hrs.	35– hrs.
8	9	13	19

From the table, it is clear that the woman's working hours have some influence. Men's share of housework appears to rise with an increased economic activity by the wife. But even in those cases where both spouses are employed full-time, the woman performs the overwhelming share of housework.

Thus the analysis of the distribution of housework between the sexes shows great inadequacies in the level of equality. However, some improvement did take place between 1974 and 1981. Here consideration must be given to the fact that this seven-year period is extremely short in relation to the decades during which the unequal distribution of household labour has been accepted without reflection in most homes. Therefore, attention should be turned to the change that has occurred since 1974, an important change from the historical point of view.

Attempting a total estimation of leisure

The material referred to above on gross working time and housework will now be combined into a total measure of leisure. Such an exercise must be approached with considerable caution. As is evident above, we do not have access to detailed data on the use of time. This means that there is no complete coverage of what might be called duties and that information is lacking on the exact distribution of housework among the different days of the week. Perhaps the greatest deficiency concerns child care which is not covered from the point of view of leisure in a relevant way.[7]

The measure that was selected uses the weekday as its base, that is, those 24-hour periods during which employees are assumed to work. An estimation of the amount of leisure during such a period is obtained as follows: 24 hours — 8 hours' sleep — $\frac{1}{2}$ hour hygiene — (gross working time for the whole week $\div$ 5 — (housework time for the entire week) $\div$ 7. It is important to emphasize that this estimation is a model rather than a reflection of strict reality, even if we disregard the uncertainty in the data. All income earners do not work five days a week. Nor is it reasonable to believe that housework is evenly distributed among the days of the week. The model may still be assumed to reveal something important about the scope of leisure: people who work more than five days a week lose some of their weekend leisure, while others who work less than five days a week have, apart from the weekend, some entire days free, in contrast to most other earners. Such deviations in varying directions have a direct effect on the estimation of leisure that is chosen here, thus contributing to an accurate total picture. The same can be said about housework: one-seventh of the week's total housework must be assigned to each of the weekdays, if the weekend's leisure time is not to be decimated. In this manner, the model adjusts for household chores saved up for the weekend, by showing how small weekday leisure becomes if the weekend's leisure is left undisturbed. The estimations should be understood chiefly as approximate points of comparison, in an assessment of whether the quantity of leisure time in question is great or small in relation to other groups' leisure.

As was the case in the section on housework the main comparison here is between the sexes. In Table 13.4 estimations are given of the amount of weekday leisure time for men and women, by the volume of gainful employment. The assessment of the estimations is two-sided. The table conveys two impressions, whose tendencies directly contradict one another. On the one hand, if we concentrate on people working full-time, the injustices produced are greatly to the disadvantage of women. Full-time employed men enjoy about two hours' more weekday leisure than women with comparable gainful employment time. It must be concluded

Table 13.4 Number of hours of weekday leisure time for employed people and
housewives 1974 and 1981, by sex and scope of gainful employment

	1974	1981
Men		
Full-time	5.6	5.8
All men	5.6	5.9
Women		
Full-time	3.7	4.3
Part-time	5.9	6.2
Working in the home	9.5	10.5
All women	6.5	6.3
Total	6.1	6.1

then that men's potential for active leisure activities is much greater than
full-time employed women's. On the other hand, if we look at all
individuals, it is instead women who are 'favoured'. Housewives in
particular seem to have an ample amount of leisure, according to the
measures applied. (It is possible that data on child care would alter the
picture, but less than half of the housewives have small children.[8]) The
leisure time of part-time employed women only barely exceeds that of
full-time employed men, indicating that leisure time is relatively evenly
distributed between spouses in a high per cent of Swedish families.

Accordingly, equality between the sexes is relatively good in terms of
combined division of labour. Full-time employed women are clearly
worse off than men when it comes to amount of leisure time. Other
women's leisure is at least as great as men's.

The total difference between the sexes decreased since 1974. For all
women, on average, leisure time decreased slightly during this period, as
a result of the falling number of people working in the home, while the
opposite is true for men. All subcategories among women, however, had
more leisure time in 1981 than seven years earlier. For men and women
combined, the quantity of weekday leisure time remained the same. The
entire average decline in working time thus has been compensated by an
increased number of economically active individuals.

An overall assessment of equality, in terms of both aspects treated
above, does not result in any clear-cut findings. For the distribution of
housework, the roles of the sexes are still very strong, even if some relief
is seen after 1974. Concerning total leisure time, on the other hand, the
difference between men and women is small.

The nature of leisure

After the description above of the amount of leisure, its nature will now be the object of study. It seems appropriate here to distinguish between weekday and weekend leisure on the one hand, and holiday leisure time on the other. The former aspect primarily covers different types of leisure activities, while the latter mainly consists of holiday trips and stays at summer cottages. Further, participation in associations of various kinds is relevant within the framework for a discussion of the nature of leisure.

Holiday trips and stays at summer cottages

Many of the leisure activities referred to later are of the kind that do not greatly depend on economic circumstances for participation. The situation is different for two other important features of Swedish leisure time, that of holiday trips and visits to summer cottages. In these cases, the size of the family's economic resources determines narrow limits to participation. The differences among various population categories that we find here, are probably due less to different interests than to varying opportunities.

As is seen in Table 13.5, both phenomena rose considerably during the period under study. However, almost one-quarter of all Swedes are still compelled to remain in their regular dwellings during their holidays.

Table 13.5 Proportion of the population 1968, 1974, and 1981 with holiday trips and with stays at summer cottages the previous year. Percentages

	1968	1974	1981
Holiday trip	52	60	66
Summer cottage	36	41	44
Neither trip nor cottage	34	26	23

Stays at summer cottages show less variation in the population at the end of the period than at the beginning. However, the equalization has mostly taken place among different age groups and types of community, so that rural residents and the elderly have approached other groups in level. The differences among social classes are decreasing more slowly. Concerning holiday trips, no pronounced changes can be said to have occurred between 1968 and 1981, as regards the variation in the population. The elderly, class III, and rural residents still fall behind in this regard.

The most revealing indicator of differences among population groups as to opportunities for variety and recreational change of pace and scenery for long periods of non-work, is the proportion of people who have neither taken any holiday trip nor spent time in a summer cottage. Again, this proportion dropped substantially between 1968 and 1981. But has this general improvement also brought with it less inequities? An answer to this is given in the regression analysis in Figure 13.1.

All the lines in the figure are horizontal indicating that all the categories improved their opportunities for long periods of leisure to about the same extent. The overall decline in the proportion with neither trips nor stays in summer cottages thus does not seem to have led to an equalization among population groups. In addition to the very unequal relationship among the classes, the regression analysis shows marked differences between inhabitants in various types of communities, and among different age groups.

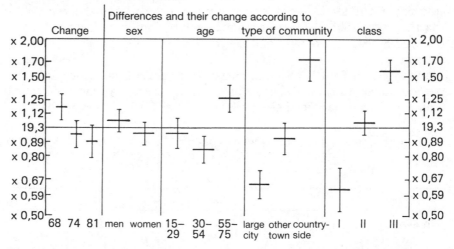

Fig. 13.1.   Regression model of proportion of population with neither holiday trip nor visit to summer cottage

Finally, the conditions of long-term leisure will be located within the social structure in more detail. In Table 13.6 the proportion of the social classes who neither took holiday trips nor stayed at summer cottages is given. A somewhat altered picture emerges here from what is given above. The situation for classes II and III has clearly improved more than that of class I, and this remains the case even after standardizing for the groups' sex and age distributions. A clear equalization has also taken place between the different categories of pensioners, even if the difference between them is still very large. The deviation from the findings of the regression must be seen mainly as a result of consideration being given to the variation among types of community in only one case. The divergence between the two makes some caution in the overall assessment necessary. What is clear, however, is that the difference between classes II and III has not changed since 1968.

Table 13.6 Proportion of the population who neither went on a holiday trip nor stayed at a summer cottage, by occupational category 1968, 1974, and 1981. Percentages

	1968	1974	1981	Standardized for age and sex		
				1968	1974	1981
Economically active	10	5	8	9	4	7
Pensioners	14	14	13	—	—	—
Class I, all	11	9	9	10	9	8
Economically active	26	19	16	25	19	17
Pensioners	47	38	37	—	—	—
Class II, all	27	21	19	26	20	17
Economically active	35	26	23	35	25	23
Pensioners	68	48	43	—	—	—
Class III, all	41	31	28	38	28	26
Population 15–75 years	34	26	23	32	24	21

It is thus clear that considerable improvement was achieved between 1968 and 1981 in terms of holiday trips and summer cottages for the population as a whole. There is still a long way to go, however, before everyone in the society will have an opportunity for a genuine change over long leisure periods. As to the gulfs between the social classes, developments are rather complicated but it seems reasonable to assert that if any equalization has in fact taken place, it has been modest in comparison with the overall improvement in level that is observed for the period under study.

Membership in associations

An important aspect of the leisure habits of the population in Sweden is participation in organizations, or associations. A high proportion of people taking part in such activities is expected to reflect some form of collective leisure pursuit, just as it may in turn reflect the general level of activity in various groups. Here, we will describe how the proportion of people who do not engage in such activities has shifted from 1968 to 1981, as well as its variation among population categories. Included as non-participating in associations are individuals who do not belong to any type of association.[9] Members of unions, however, are classified as non-participants if they have not attended any meeting or held any position in the union during the prior year. The latter procedure was chosen in order to avoid counting more or less trivial ties to the employment level in the population.

After a slight drop in the proportion of non-participants between 1968 and 1974 from 45 to 43 per cent, a great shift downwards took place by 1981, when 31 per cent of the population did not take part in associations as defined here. A regression analysis, however, shows that this increase in participation is followed only to a limited extent by diminishing differences among different groups. Women, large city residents, and people in class III are consistently relatively passive in terms of participation in associations.

Leisure activities

Under this heading, the general nature of weekday and weekend leisure activities will be discussed. Unfortunately, it is impossible to classify these activities accordingly. The questions that were asked in the surveys cover leisure pursuits in a broad sense, regardless of the day of the week. However, in all likelihood, it can be assumed that reported activities play a small role in terms of time, at least for leisure during working days. Studies of the use of time conducted elsewhere have shown rather unambiguously that housework, personal time (meal-times, hygiene, etc.), and media consumption dominate people's short-term free periods (see Blomdahl and Brånell 1981, 13 f. for example).

Before the results are summarized, it may be worthwhile to ask a number of questions without considering the possibility of responding to them. How informative the empirical results are may then be easier to judge, and the limitations in knowledge gained should become clear. Some of the questions that are especially topical in the public debate are the following: Are people becoming more active or more passive during their leisure time? Are leisure activities becoming more enriched or more impoverished? Are the gaps between population categories increasing or decreasing in terms of the nature of leisure? How does the distribution in use of public recreational facilities change among different groups? Is leisure becoming more extroverted and sociable or more private, individual-orientated and isolated?

These questions are rather vaguely formulated and influenced by current fashion, as is often the case in public discussion.[10] Responses to them are seen, in any case, as essential in a study of developments in welfare in the sphere of leisure time. To the degree that we have not succeeded here, it will show the limits of the material's usefulness. We will return to this in the chapter's final discussion. First, some general limitations will be mentioned.

1. Detailed information on activity occasions is lacking. Participation in different activities is judged by means of one of the three expressions 'not at all', 'sometimes', and 'often'. Presumably, every respondent interprets these expressions with personal nuances, depending, for instance, upon childhood experiences, social class, and age. This probably means that the 'real' differences in leisure habits between population categories are underestimated in the survey.[11]

2. Since many of the most usual leisure activities, such as being with family, watching TV, and taking walks, were not included in the interview questions, we are unable to give a thorough description of the leisure habits of the Swedish population. At best, our data reflect how the general level of activity has developed over time, and about which types of activities are practised by different groups in the population.[12]

3. The leisure activities included in the study are often very vaguely specified. Hobbies and reading books are examples of broad and varying activities that are merged into single categories of activity. These rather general groupings probably lead to an underestimation of the association between background factors and leisure habits.

4. Information on the use of public recreational facilities, such as libraries and sports centres, is largely missing. This results in a significant curtailment of the political usefulness of the material.

As we proceed, the reservations mentioned above will be taken for granted. The tone of the description, therefore, will be rather uncritical, but this should not encourage the reader to become more careless. Empirical statements should not be interpreted in terms other than rough indications. In Table 13.7 the level of popularity of the various activities in the population as a whole is given for 1968-1981.

Reading books and weekly magazines, gardening, or practising some hobby, as well as day trips in the car, seem to be especially common recreations. Furthermore, the total activity level seems to have been raised successively throughout the period. Reading books[13] and gardening in particular have increased substantially in terms of the numbers participating. Apart from the five activities named above, a sixth one has become an increasingly integral part of our recreational activities: namely, sports.

Next we shall proceed with an analysis of differences in the nature of leisure within the population, and of the development of these differences over time. To simplify the description a majority of the activities have been grouped into four categories. (The results below are based on regression analyses, not shown here in figure form.)

Table 13.7 Leisure activities, proportion of participants in the population 1968, 1974, and 1981. Percentages

	Sometimes or often			Often		
	1968	1974	1981	1968	1974	1981
Reading books	72	77	78	31	37	44
Hobbies	59	62	62	35	39	41
Gardening	49	56	62	25	33	36
Reading magazines	73	74	69	32	34	29
Sports	26	30	34	13	15	20
Taking a ride in the car	71	72	68	28	24	17
Strolling in streets and window-shopping	40	49	52	9	12	12
Study circles	19	27	32	7	12	12
Fishing	36	39	40	10	12	11
Going out dancing	32	42	45	8	9	9
Playing a musical instr.	14	15	16	5	6	7
Going to theatre, museums, exhibitions	40	45	49	6	6	6
Going to the cinema	42	41	45	6	5	6
Going to a restaurant	36	49	55	3	5	6
Hunting	7	7	8	3	3	3
Bingo	—	8	5	—	1	1

Outdoor activities From an examination of how the proportion of people participating in at least one of the activities fishing, hunting, and sports varies between different categories in the population, differences emerge primarily between the sexes and between different age groups. Women are substantially less active than men, but this relationship has become slightly more equal over time. The elderly (55–75 years of age) are, not surprisingly, considerably less active than the young (15–29) and middle-aged (30–54), a difference that has not diminished since 1968. There are also certain differences among the social classes to the advantage of class I, especially among women. These deviations decreased during the period, however. Type of community appears to be without importance for outdoor activities, as they are measured here.

Entertainment activities Those who participate in at least one of activities such as going to a cinema, restaurant, or dancing, we have called entertainment active people. A background variable that can be expected to be crucial here is age. This is confirmed by the regression analysis. Young people are clearly more active in entertainment than the middle-aged, who in turn are much more active than the elderly. A small equalization of this relationship has occurred since 1968. After age social class is next in importance. The difference between class I and others, which is larger among young people than old, has, however, clearly diminished during the period. The larger the type of community, the higher the level of entertainment activity, is another conclusion that can be drawn. But this tendency is not very strong and has also become weaker over time. The sex differences are only modest, at all points in time.

Cultural activities Under this heading the activity level regarding attendance at theatres and exhibitions, reading books, playing a musical instrument, and participation in study circles is analysed. Here it is reasonable to expect differences mainly between the social classes. Partly because of the high number of activities in the cultural category, the average activity level is very high, which means that differences between groups in the population are quite small. Nevertheless, it is clear that social class is the most influential background variable. The gap between class I and III has, as was the case with the types of activity reported above, narrowed slightly over time. The differences between age groups and types of community are small (young people and large city dwellers being more active than others), but have remained more or less constant since 1968. Women developed a slight advantage over men during the period. As with entertainment activity, class differences are larger among older people than the young.

Undirected activities Finally, we shall see how the proportion participating in at least one of these activities such as reading weekly magazines, strolling in the streets, and day trips in the car varies between different population categories. In view of the rather undemanding character of these activities, background variables are unlikely to be distinguishing factors. Accordingly, the regression model does not show any sizeable differences. Sex seems to be most important, women being more active than men, but not even this difference is more than barely noticeable. It should also be noted that the youngest appear to be slightly more active than others, and that the difference between community types in 1968 (rural dwellers more active than their large city counterparts) had disappeared by 1981. The social classes are not significantly separated regarding undirected activities.

Summary

Our overall impression is that there are two tendencies which characterize the development in leisure habits during weekdays and weekends of the Swedish population between 1968 and 1981. One is a relatively dramatic rise in the activity level, and the other is an equalization of the differences between various population categories. This does not prevent the existence of considerable gulfs on some points. Age is the most decisive background variable with regard to uses of leisure time, closely followed by class. Sex and even more so types of community seem to play more modest roles, according to our findings.

Leisure activities and class

With regard to the social classes, it may be of interest to show in more detail what in the classification promotes differences in leisure habits among the three class categories. Of those aspects of social stratification that are conceivably relevant in the context, two will be briefly discussed here: working conditions and social culture. The former accounts for relatively immediate and concrete differences among various categories in the work process, while the latter phenomenon is an indirect and more subtle difference in experience, knowledge, and interests. One way of distinguishing cultural factors is to compare housewives in the different social classes with each other (cf. Bergman and Olsson 1977, 38 f).

Such a comparison, applied to the four types of leisure activities, produces an almost unequivocal result. The differences between the categories of housewives are at least as great as between the classes as a whole. This is true for all types of activity, and regardless of whether the comparison is made between classes I and III or between classes II and III. With a reservation for the fact that the analysis in many ways is extremely crude, the results seem to warrant the conclusion that it is primarily cultural (or economic) factors that are decisive in the social stratification of leisure. The work environment and working conditions otherwise do not appear to be central in the selection of leisure activities. In the next section, the relationship between work and leisure will be examined more closely.

Work and leisure

After a superficial look at the associations between class and leisure habits, and having found the relationship to be largely determined by culture, it is obviously still interesting to illustrate how leisure activities are dependent upon work.[14] Innumerable suggestions for descriptions of the relationship between leisure and work have been presented over the years. The most well-known is probably Wilensky's distinction between compensation and spill-over (see for example Parker 1976, 72 f. and Wilensky 1960). This distinction has since been complemented with further hypotheses. (For a review of the literature see Staines 1980). In order to give a comprehensive view five hypotheses will be examined here. They are called, in proper order: compensation, spill-over, selection, restriction and resource.

Together with the following discussion of the hypotheses, an empirical examination of them will be carried out. The examination is based primarily on regression analyses, the results of which are given in Table 13.8. The conclusions in the text build on the size of standardized regression coefficients, which express the strength of association between one independent and one dependent variable, when one or more other independent variables are held constant. The coefficients can vary between -1 and $+1$, where the sign is dependent on the direction of the association. The higher the value of the coefficient, the stronger the association. Values close to zero imply weak associations.

The compensation hypothesis is based on the notion that in their leisure time, people try to balance their work in terms of type of activity. People with sedimentary jobs can be expected to favour, for example, physical activity, while people with physically demanding but otherwise unqualified work tasks, would prefer intellectual leisure activity. An empirical indication of the validity of this hypothesis can be given by classifying the economically active according to degree of qualifications needed in their jobs, and see then whether the groups obtained distinguish themselves in recreation.[15] The compensation hypothesis is *not* supported in its entirety. This is so because intellectual leisure activities, roughly defined as going to the theatre, reading books and participating in study circles, are more often exercised by people with intellectually demanding jobs (sex and age held constant). Physically demanding recreations (fishing, hunting, sports) do not vary significantly among the economically active categories.

The second hypothesis is almost a mirror image of the first, and is thus called the spill-over hypothesis. The thought behind this is that work influences leisure, in that the individual applies the same type of behaviour in life outside the work place. Unskilled work leads to less inclination to take part in intellectual pursuits and so on. The association is thus reversed in relation to that of the compensation hypthesis. From the negative outcome for that hypothesis, it follows that the spill-over perspective receives some support in our data.

A third way of looking at the relation between work and leisure is the selection hypothesis. This assumes that people engaged in certain types of jobs 'are selected' from the same population categories as those who exercise corresponding types of leisure activities. Perhaps the most important example of this is the significance of education for both work tasks and recreation. This hypothesis is empirically very strongly supported. In part, the association between level of education and the degree of qualified work is strong, and is also almost constant over time. In part, the difference between low and highly educated people is great for the exercise of so-called intellectual recreational activities. (Sex and age are held constant; for definitions of educational levels, see Table 13.8.)

Table 13.8 Regression analyses of the relationship between work and leisure, 1981. Standardized regression coefficients. Economically active (analysis 1–5) and employees (analysis 6–7)

	Dependent variable	Independent variable	Coefficient	R^2
1.	Physical leisure act.	Qualif. level of work	0.04 S[a]	
		Sex	−0.32 S	
		Age	−0.24 S	15%[b]
2.	Intellectual leis. act.	Qualif. level of work	0.23 S	
		Sex	0.19 S	
		Age	−0.00	9%
3.	Qualif. level of work	Educational level	0.32 S	
		Sex	0.00	
		Age	0.12 S	10%
4.	Intellectual leis. act.	Educational level	0.39 S	
		Sex	0.20 S	
		Age	0.11 S	17%
5.	General leisure act.	Exhaustion from work	−0.03 S	
		Sex	0.12 S	
		Age	−0.28 S	
		Class	−0.16 S	11%
6.	General leisure act.	Gross working time	−0.01	
		Sex	0.09 S	
		Age	−0.26 S	
		Class	−0.21 S	11%
7.	General leisure act.	Pay/hour	0.03	
		Sex	0.11 S	
		Age	−0.27 S	
		Class	−0.20 S	11%

[a] Significant effect on the 95% level. [b] Proportion explained variance.

Definitions: *Physical leisure activity* = summated scale of fishing, hunting, and sports, where no participation receives a value of 0 and participation in all three often receives a value of 6.
Intellectual leisure activity = the same type of scale for going to the theatre, reading books, and participation in study circles.
General leisure activity = the same type of scale for all the activities in table 13.7.
Educational level = 1) Only compulsory schooling; 2) Schooling above the compulsory level, but not upper secondary school; 3) Upper secondary school and above.

Codings: *Sex* = 1) Men; 2) Women. *Class* = 1) I; 2) II; 3) III.

The restriction hypothesis is the fourth conceivable line of reasoning. The interest her focuses less upon particular types of recreational activities than upon the overall level of activity. The assumption is that if work exhausts an individual's energy reserve or claims much of the individual's time, this has a negative influence on the level of leisure activity. Generally seen, however, the restriction theory does not receive much support in our material. Neither people with physically or mentally exhausting work nor those with long working hours are less active than other economically active people (sex, age, and class held constant). Still, this result does not make the rejection of the hypthesis inevitable, but rather emphasizes the need for a more advanced analysis. For example, it is necessary to make a distinction between weekday and weekend leisure time, in order to describe the recreational content of work days accurately. The restriction hypthesis is reasonably valid primarily for these days, whose leisure activities are unfortunately impossible to distinguish in our material.

The fifth and last micro-dimension of the relationship between work and leisure is the resource hypothesis. This is based on the idea that the yield from work constitutes a mediating link between gainful employment and leisure conditions, such as in the form of income. The resources that individuals gain by working most probably affect how their leisure is structured. It is not really possible to make any simple assessment of the validity of this hypothesis. If the reasoning is presented in individual terms, it turns out that the amount of pay is not associated with the activity level during leisure time (sex, age and class held constant). This result is, however, of doubtful value, since economic resources are clearly a household-related concept. On the household level, considerable differences in the general degree of activity in leisure time among groups with varying economic resources are established (measured with the index reported in Chapter 8). Linking this result to the relation between work and leisure nevertheless lies beyond our ambition in this section.

To summarize, the selection hypothesis clearly has the strongest support among those views that could be illustrated empirically. The spill-over hypothesis also seems to have some validity, while the compensation hypothesis seems to be less fruitful. The remaining two theories are left with no final assessment.

Concluding discussion on the nature of leisure

In this final section, we shall return to the questions formulated above, as well as present a short discussion of conceivable explanations for the trends reported.

1. Are people becoming more active or more passive during their leisure time? Despite the limitations in the empirical material, it is reasonable to assert that the level of activity rose between 1968 and 1981. A comparison with corresponding data in the ULF Studies (SCB 1981b), where the precision of the questions is higher, shows a high degree of agreement as to level of activity. It is improbable that the activities omitted from the Level of Living Survey would have decreased so drastically in scope as to alter the overall picture.

2. Is the nature of leisure activities becoming more enriched or more impoverished? There are two possible interpretations to this question: either leisure is seen as a whole, or each of the activities are examined separately. The first question can be elucidated using the Level of Living Survey, on the condition that we place values on the various activities, which would be rather doubtful. One possible point of view would be to regard undirected amusements, that is, reading magazines, strolling in the streets, or day trips in the car, as less enriching than the other types of activities. This notion is not unassailable, but probably corresponds to generally prevalent values. Of interest is that two of these three activities are the only ones among all others to have decreased in volume since 1968. The conclusion from this is that leisure has become more enriched during this period, rather than impoverished. The other interpretation, as regards each of the activities separately, must be left unanswered, as we are unable to judge how the content of, for instance, reading books or hobbies has developed over time.

3. Are the gaps between population categories increasing or decreasing in terms of content of leisure time? The low degree of precision in the frequency of leisure activities makes it almost impossible to accept the empirical outcome as totally certain on this point. As was the case for the general level of activity, however, our results are supported in other studies. The reported differences between age groups, classes, and so on, seem to be real (an excellent summary of different study results are given in Blomdahl and Brånell 1981, 156–180). It does not automatically follow from this that we are also right concerning changes in the differences. It seems likely, however, that the differences between population groups have generally decreased during the period.

4. How does the distribution in the use of public recreational facilities change among different groups? To answer this would be quite easy, provided that the interview questions were designed for this purpose. This is not, however, the case, which is why the information is not available.

5. Is leisure becoming more extroverted and sociable or more private,

individual-orientated and isolated? As with the question on enrichment versus impoverishment, there are at least two interpretations possible here. First of all, is social interaction a more common leisure activity in 1981 than in 1968? We saw in Chapter 12 that this seems to be the case. Second, do people take part in the leisure activities dealt with above with other people, to an increasing or decreasing extent? We know nothing about this latter issue. Therefore, it is difficult to reach any absolute overall conclusions about changes in the social character of leisure. What seems most likely, in any case, is that being alone during leisure did not become more common during the seventies.

Two of the above five questions could, therefore, be answered quite reliably. Another two have been at least partly elucidated, while one has been left completely unanswered. According to the welfare goal that was formulated earlier in the chapter, the responses imply that welfare has increased in the sphere of leisure. The level of activity has risen, and apparently, the freedom of choice between various types of activities has increased. Leisure thus seems to have become more active and more free.

If we accept this conclusion about a welfare increase in leisure, we are left with the task of finding a reasonable explanation for it. Besides the decreased gross working time, which is largely balanced by the increased number of economically active people, three factors emerge as crucial: education, economy, and the nature of gainful employment. A rough description of leisure in Sweden, as we measured it, is that it is becoming more and more like that in class I. As regards years of education, economic resources, and degree of qualification for work, the average level of living rose markedly between 1968 and 1981, at the same time as the differences between various categories in the population decreased. There are strong associations between these three level-of-living components and the nature of leisure, and it is thereby natural that changes in the former result in changes in the latter. It is debatable whether a way of life approximating to that of class I is a positive value in all respects. With the definitions and methods we chose to use in the study, this approximation in any case must be interpreted in terms of improvement, that is, increased welfare. A criticism directed at this type of conclusion must therefore, at least in part, be based upon a critical evaluation of the entire approach of the Level of Living Survey.

Notes

1. Husén 1944, Dahlström 1951, Lundqvist and Segerstedt 1955, Mathson and Åsvärn 1956.

2. The second one, conducted in 1974, has been reported in part elsewhere (Lundahl 1978).

3. Some of the important contributions to this debate are Palm 1974 and Fryklindh and Johansson 1976. Also see Kågeson 1972, Arvidsson and Bucht 1976, Hall 1976 and Blomdahl and Brånell 1981. An international survey of approaches and results is given in Parker 1976. Numerous empirical studies of regional or local character have also been conducted during this period, two of which are Göteborgs Kommun 1970 and Törneman 1977.

4. The decrease since 1974 for full-time employees is not due to a drop in the number of hours per day, but to a drop in the number of working days per week. Neither sick leave nor leave of absence have caused this development. Leave of absence undoubtedly increased since 1974. Most of this, however, is total weekly absence, and in the account of gross working hours above, only those individuals who worked at least one day during the week are included. Increased holiday absence and compensatory leave instead seem to have caused the decrease in working time since the middle of the seventies. If we remove these absences from the 1981 material (which unfortunately is impossible for 1974), the working time increases by two hours, of which holidays account for about one-third. This analysis is thus based on the assumption that partial absence during the week for these two reasons has become much more common since 1974. Underlying such an assumption is the expansion in number of holiday days since 1978, as well as the raised standard of living that probably attracted more and more people to take out the balance of their working time in time off rather than in pay. This behaviour may also have been influenced by the level of marginal tax rate.

5. The questions about housework consist in part of how many meals (mealtimes × people) are prepared and washed up on an average day in the household, and in part of how many hours of the week are devoted to washing clothes, cleaning, shopping, and maintenance of clothes. The respondents were asked to state the total household input as well as his/her own input. In order to obtain a comprehensive measure of time, the information on meals was converted as follows: 1 meal cooking/day was judged as corresponding to 1 hour's work/week (or roughly 10 minutes/day), and 1 washing up after a meal, half as much. This is of course a somewhat arbitrary assessment, but hardly results in serious errors. It should also be pointed out here that people who claimed to work less than 1 hour/day in the home did not answer the detailed questions. These individuals (mostly men) were given the input value of zero in the calculations, which obviously implies some underestimation. The importance of this is probably not appreciable in the whole. Another source of underestimation of primarily men's input is that no questions were asked about traditional male domestic chores, such as repairs, cutting grass, shovelling snow, etc. We assume, however, that this source of error does not disrupt the trend in the obtained results. It is interesting to note that the sum of men's and women's input, according to Table 13.2, does not exceed

100 per cent. The natural conclusion here would be that neither men nor women overestimate their proportion of household chores. The alternative to such an interpretation is that one of the sexes systematically underestimates his/her own input, a not very likely hypothesis. The findings may rightly be taken as a pretext for viewing the superficially uncertain estimations of the distribution of work in the home between the sexes as quite reliable. (Observe that data in Table 13.2 are not on the household level, but are rather averages for male and female respondents, respectively.)

6. In cases where the respondent was a woman, the husband's input was calculated according to the following: 100 per cent minus woman's input minus 4 per cent, where 4 per cent is the estimated average proportion of housework performed by others than the man and woman (such as, by children). The figure was obtained from Table 13.2 by subtracting men's and women's total input from 100 per cent. Table 13.3 consists of average estimations for male and female respondents which differ only insignificantly from one another.

7. Even if some leisure activities can be exercised while watching children, such a supervisory responsibility implies that a person is spatially bound to a limited area. Neither the time nor the spatial aspect of child supervision has been possible to assess within the framework of the total measurement of leisure time as here constructed.

8. In 1974, 45 per cent of the housewives in Table 13.4 had small children (younger than 7 years). In 1981, the proportion was 36 per cent.

9. Specific questions were asked about membership in political, union, sports, temperance, and religious associations. In addition, the respondents were asked whether they were members of an association of a type other than the five named. This latter question had no given alternative responses, and thus is entirely dependent upon the respondent's own notion of the meaning of the phrase 'membership in associations'. It is reasonable to expect that some types of organizations, such as Konsum or HSB (food and housing collectively-owned organizations), have been sifted out by the interviewees themselves. This means that 'non-belonging' should not be interpreted too strictly. The absolute level of 'participation', therefore, is of less interest in this context. What is of primary importance is the developments over time and the differences among various population groups.

10. Several of the questions mentioned above have appeared mainly in the context of the intensive discussion about life in the new suburbs. The fringe areas of large cities have served as negatively charged symbols for the 'new society's' allegedly negative aspects, such as passivity and isolation. (For an account of the suburb debate in the 1960s and 1970s, see Franzén and Sandstedt 1981, 17–53). In the way that we posed the debate questions here, they deal with the welfare development of leisure in general, without any connection with the character of the housing areas.

11. The rough frequency rates imply that, strictly speaking, we can only state how the *proportion* of participants in different activities shift between different population groups. Another important way of describing leisure

habits is to compare the volume of *activity occasions* among various groups, a very instructive method of reporting as it takes into consideration a greater amount of information. In this way not all participants are judged equally active but rather differences in activity rates within the group of participants are also considered. Such a description is not possible here.

12. Even when disregarding the common forms of activity that were mentioned, several leisure activities are missing from our material. All the same, we see it as probable that the available questions capture rather well the types of activities that are relevant for a description of the welfare development within the sphere of leisure. The assumption is thus that an alternative set of questions about different types of activities would give a picture similar to the one given in our material, as regards changes in level of activity and differences among population groups.

13. It may surprise the reader that people are reading books to an ever increasing extent, but this is confirmed by statistics of sales and library book-loans. See Svenska Bokförläggareföreningen 1982, and SCB 1982e, respectively.

14. A thorough assessment of the relationship between work and leisure, based on data from the 1968 Level of Living Survey, is presented in Robert Karasek's doctoral dissertation (Karasek 1976). When we, in this section, attempt an analysis of the same problem with data from 1981, the level of ambition is considerably lower, due to limits in space and time. The analysis here is quite simple, but should nevertheless provide an indication of the associations between the nature of work and the nature of leisure. Karasek's results from 1968 indicate stronger associations than we found for 1981. A more systematic comparison between the two points in time would be of great interest, but is not attempted here.

15. We have used the same classification here as in Chapter 7. Unqualified jobs include those which demand a maximum of two years' vocational training while also being monotonous (according to the interviewee). Jobs that are claimed to be mentally demanding as well as non-monotonous are labelled as intellectually qualified.

14

Coexistence of Welfare Problems

ROBERT ERIKSON and MICHAEL TÅHLIN

Introduction

The concept of welfare that underlies the Level of Living Surveys is formulated in individual terms, that is, as the *individual's* command over various resources. However, the total life situation of these individuals is not reflected in the previous chapters. Instead, the discussions focus on how different population groups vary in terms of the proportion of their members with poor finances, impaired health, overcrowded housing arrangements, and so on. Little has been said about whether low-income earners also suffer from health problems, or whether people with sub-standard dwellings also have poor finances. The purpose of this final chapter, therefore, is to describe the associations between the various components.

Apart from the obvious desirability of examining more closely the individual view when describing welfare trends, there are two reasons for studying the coexistence of separate components of the levels of living. One is of a theoretical/causal nature. If seemingly unrelated problems tend to exist simultaneously, there is reason to seek a common underlying cause. If this is the case, an attempt could be made to identify and isolate one or more general factors giving rise to problems within several spheres of life. If, on the other hand, there is no coexistence between the problems, the search for such general problem-generating factors can be set aside for the time being.

The second reason is more of a social policy character. As pointed out by Hansen and others (1980, 734), the measures taken by society to support and help citizens in need of assistance should be designed in different ways when there is a relatively extensive coexistence of problems than when the problems seem more independent of each other. In the former case, the measures should be designed to lift individuals out of generally undesirable circumstances. In the latter case, measures can be especially designed for more specific problems.

The approach used here for the analysis of the internal association between components is based on the delimitation of negative conditions. A simple dichotomy of conditions is established for the components—problematic versus non-problematic. Much of the information on individual differences in level of living is hereby lost. The purpose of the analyses in this chapter, however, is to examine how different problems are linked to one another and not how the coexistence of more or less favourable circumstances comes about.

There are three main questions that we will attempt to answer in the following discussion:

1. Do problems in one area tend to accompany problems in other areas, or do the different types of problems tend to appear independently of each other?
2. Did the scope and character of the coexistence change between 1968 and 1981?
3. Are there some population groups in which members are more than usually afflicted by deficient resources and multiple problems, or are these hardships distributed relatively evenly among groups?

In the first section, an overview will be given of the scope of the individual problematic conditions in the period 1968–1981, as they have been defined here. After that, the associations among the components will be discussed where an attempt will be made to distinguish between dimensions in the distribution of social misfortune. In this section, we shall also discuss whether the associations between various problems changed between 1968 and 1981. Finally, the existence of accumulated problems in various population groups will be examined, as well as how this accumulation developed over time.

Occurrence of problems: Overview 1968–1981

For the different level-of-living components, 'problem groups' must be defined.[1] This procedure provides us with the opportunity first to summarize welfare trends, component for component, based on changes in the size of the problem groups. Second, we are able to determine whether the same individuals reappear in problem groups for different components, or whether the compositions of these problem groups tend to be unrelated. The primary interest in this chapter is with the latter analysis, and we will return to it later on. First, however, the scope of different problems in the population is presented in Table 14.1 for the period 1968 to 1981. (The delimitation of the groups is given in the appendix to this chapter.)

The main impression from the table is that substantial improvements have occurred in several areas since 1968. The exceptions are health, social relationships, and working conditions, where the size of the problem groups has remained about the same. Clearly, the greatest

Table 14.1 Scope of problematic conditions in seven Standard-of-Living Components 1968, 1974, and 1981, in the population as a whole and among the economically active. Percentages

Problems concerning:	Population			Economically active		
	1968	1974	1981	1968	1974	1981
Physical well-being	16	17	17	10	12	12
Mental well-being	15	14	12	11	11	9
Health, total	24	25	24	18	19	18
Economic resources	19	13	11	14	9	7
Space standard	24	12	6	24	12	6
Equipment standard	31	17	5	28	15	5
Form of tenure	6	3	2	6	3	2
Housing conditions, total	48	27	11	46	25	11
Social relationships	6	6	7	6	5	5
Leisure activities	20	12	10	16	10	8
Political participation	36	29	21	22	18	10
Mobilization	19	14	9	15	10	6
Political resources, total	44	36	26	32	25	16
Labour market integration	—	—	—	2	2	2
Nature of work	—	—	—	7	7	8
Working conditions, total	—	—	—.	9	9	10
Number of observations	5,711	5,900	6,041	3,647	3,985	4,191

improvement is in the field of housing. The widespread problem conditions in this area were reduced by about four-fifths during this period.

Fairly consistently, economically active individuals show lower percentages with problems than the general population. This is entirely reasonable, especially in light of the difference in age composition of the two categories. Wage-earners and proprietors, moreover, are to some extent selected categories, as people who are sick or otherwise low in resources find it difficult to assert themselves on the labour market. Furthermore, an important effect of gainful employment is naturally the economic returns in the form of income, and gainfully employed people also have more chance to make social contacts.

The picture which emerges from Table 14.1 accords well with the findings in other chapters. The substantial advances in finances, housing, leisure and political resources, are clearly reflected in the reduction of the size of the problem groups. The unchanged physical health and the improvement in mental well-being accord well with the deeper analyses made in the chapter on health. The same measure of agreement is found in the information on working conditions. In contrast however, the outcome here for social relationships partly contradicts what was found in Chapter 12. On this point, the general improvements in the population regarding the proportions with slight versus extensive social integration, did not result in a reduction of the size of the problem group, as defined here.[2]

Changes in the magnitude of the problems thus give a fairly accurate picture of the welfare development between 1968 and 1981, at least as reflected in the level-of-living study material. For work and health, the problem groups did not decrease in size, but otherwise the period witnessed advances in welfare.[3] In some respects, we may be witnessing the end of an era, in that some problems are facing almost total extinction. In the future, studies on welfare may need other criteria than those adopted two decades ago. Measured with the now traditional social indicators, welfare has in any case reached a very high level. The central question for this chapter, however, has still not been answered: how great is the coexistence among problems of different types?

Dimensions in the distribution of welfare

The extent of the coexistence of problems of the various welfare components is shown in Table 14.2. As can be seen, it is not only individual problems that have been diminished, but also their simultaneous presence for the same individuals. This is not particularly surprising, but it underlines an important aspect of developments in welfare. There has been a substantial reduction in the number of people hardest hit, with problems in three or more categories, since 1968. This trend holds for economically active people as much as for the population as a whole. The segment of the population without problems, as they have been defined, more than doubled by 1981, while the seriously afflicted group declined to just over a third of its original size.

The proportion of individuals with multiple problems thus does not seem to be alarming. Furthermore, it is decreasing over time. One measure of the 'degree of accumulation' could be the proportion of all individuals with at least one problem who belong to the group of seriously afflicted, with at least three problems. This percentage declined during this period from 28 to 15 per cent of the general population, and from 22 to 12 per cent among the economically active. Accordingly, the overwhelming share of afflicted people have problems in a clearly limited number of areas (which of course need not prevent their situation from

Table 14.2 Number of problems 1968, 1974, and 1981 in the population and among the economically active. Percentages

	Population			Economically active		
	1968	1974	1981	1968	1974	1981
0 problems	21	33	45	26	39	52
1–2	57	54	47	58	52	42
3–	22	13	8	16	9	6
Total	100	100	100	100	100	100

being quite serious).

We shall turn now to the nature of the coexistence, for which two approaches will be used. First, a description is given of various related problems, without considering variations among the categories of the population. Then, it will be emphasized how the problems are related to the background factors of sex, age and social class.

For the first task, the strength of the association among various problems is calculated using so-called gamma-coefficients.[4] Their values may range between -1 and $+1$, high positive values implying that the problems in question tend to befall the same people at the same time. Values close to zero indicate the absence of a systematic link between the different problems. In Table 14.3, the average value of the correlation with the other components is given for each component.

Table 14.3 Average gamma correlations among different problems 1968, 1974, and 1981, in the population as a whole and among the economically active

	Population			Economically active		
	1968	1974	1981	1968	1974	1981
Health	0.31	0.33	0.32	0.20	0.20	0.22
Social relationships	0.36	0.45	0.41	0.24	0.30	0.23
Leisure activities	0.38	0.38	0.44	0.25	0.22	0.25
Economic resources	0.47	0.48	0.50	0.37	0.40	0.44
Housing conditions	0.30	0.33	0.29	0.24	0.28	0.30
Political resources	0.29	0.30	0.33	0.22	0.20	0.24
Working conditions	—	—	—	0.21	0.23	0.28
Average	0.35	0.38	0.38	0.25	0.26	0.28

First and foremost, it can be stated that the strength of the average correlations between different problems remains almost constant over time. Practically all individual correlations (not given in the table) are relatively stable. Thus, an important conclusion is that despite the considerable downswing in the number of individuals with multiple problems, the mechanisms underlying the coexistence seem to have operated in the same manner in 1981 as in 1968. In other words, the relative difference between those who have a certain problem and those who do not have it, concerning the risk of experiencing a specific other problem, was just as great at the end of the period as at the beginning.

In Table 14.3 one type of problem in particular is linked to others, namely, limited economic resources. In the population as a whole as well as among the gainfully employed, this component has the strongest average correlation with other types of problems at all points in time. The central position of finances can be seen in Figure 14.1, where the relationship of various problems is depicted graphically. The stability of the correlations over time makes it possible to summarize the entire study period in a single figure.[5]

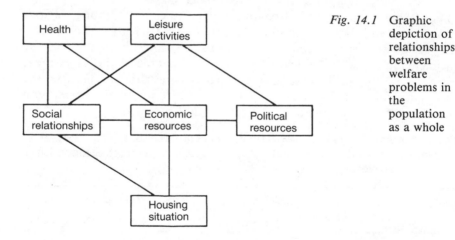

Fig. 14.1 Graphic depiction of relationships between welfare problems in the population as a whole

As can be seen, no problem is totally isolated from the others, which means that the coexistence is quite general in nature. This does not rule out the possibility of certain groups of problems within which the internal correlations are relatively high. If such groups are made up of problems which all have a relatively high correlation to all other problems within the group, three categories result. They are:

A.   Finances–social relations–health–leisure
B.   Finances–political resources–leisure
C.   Finances–social relations–housing conditions

Financial problems appear in all three groups. Social relations and leisure appear in two each. Problems in health, political resources, and housing conditions appear in only one group each. Interpreting this coexistence is complicated because of our incomplete knowledge of the causal relationships among the various problems. By measuring the three problem groups against three key concepts relevant to welfare, we might gain some clues to a possible interpretation.

Group A (finances-social relations-health-leisure) could be understood in terms of physical vitality and agility. Failing physical mobility obviously prevents an abundance of social relations and some leisure activities. Health and finances do not have an unambiguous causal relationship to one another, but the fact of their coexistence is hardly surprising. Their association may be somewhat overestimated here, however, owing to the construction of the measure for finances. In part it measures consumption, for what a certain amount of activity and vigour is undoubtedly required. The measure is therefore, in itself, to some extent dependent upon health.

Group B (finances-political resources-leisure) may be linked to resources in the form of knowledge and education. The size of income as well as the ability to communicate in writing are related to the level of education. This is not as clear in the case of the level of activity during leisure, but such a linkage has appeared for several common leisure activities.[6]

The third problem group, C (finances-social relations-housing), is perhaps easiest to tie to limited economic resources. That bad housing conditions might result from these is not surprising. Bad finances and bad housing conditions in their turn hardly facilitate good social relations. At the same time, one aspect of living alone, that of not being part of a family, leads to non-acquisition of certain assets (boat, summer cottages, detached house) that are contained in the measure of finances.

As for economically active people, the associations among the problems are generally weaker (see Table 14.3). Regardless of this, the pattern is relatively stable over time, making it possible to summarize it in a single diagram (see Figure 14.2).

In an attempt to distinguish groups of at least three problems, as in the analysis above, only one such group emerges, that of Finances-social relations-housing conditions. That the pattern differs from the one previously discussed is probably related to the fact that economically active people are a selected category in some ways, as indicated in Table 14.1. The selection would be especially tough for people with multiple problems, which leads to a reduction in the correlations. That health and physical mobility do not seem to affect the results here, might thus be due to the fact that the percentage of the old and sick is low, especially where

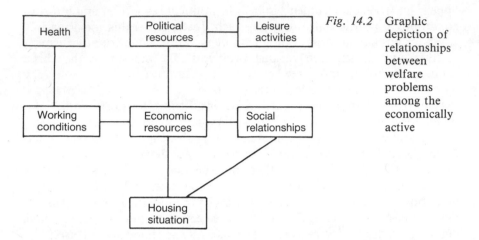

Fig. 14.2 Graphic depiction of relationships between welfare problems among the economically active

this percentage is linked with other problems. In similar fashion, it is conceivable that the resources concerning knowledge and skills vary less among the economically active, as does faith in one's own ability to perform certain tasks. This is probably due less to the smaller variation in education than to the experiences of the gainfully employed to their jobs. The importance of finances, however, is striking even for the economically active, despite the relatively weak links with health and leisure.

Of special interest here is the relationship between working conditions and other components. Impaired health and bad finances appear to be the problems most strongly related to problematic working conditions. That people with bad health have more difficult working conditions than others is explained in part by the fact that many of them are exhausted by work tasks that would present no problem for normally healthy people. Furthermore, it is conceivable that many people with health problems have difficulty obtaining and holding onto jobs. It may also be that bad working conditions and employment give rise to impaired health.

Individuals with problematic working conditions are relatively often in a bad financial situation. It is hardly surprising that the lack of secure employment leads to financial difficulties. But it is also likely that hard working conditions accompany relatively low wages. The strength of the correlations discussed above is largely constant over time.

Problem dimensions in various population categories

By using factor analysis, separate dimensions of problems will be distinguished for different population categories. Here it is reasonable to expect that the previously described pattern changes somewhat in character. In the analysis below, not only are the various problems

Table 14.4 Factor solutions of six problem components and three background variables 1968, 1974, and 1981. Factor loadings after varimax-rotations

1968	I	II	III
Health	0.59	0.05	0.24
Social relationships	0.30	0.28	− .13
Leisure activities	0.69	0.18	− .01
Economic resources	0.17	0.60	0.21
Housing conditions	0.02	0.65	− .07
Political resources	0.06	0.28	0.74
Age 1[a]	0.80	− .08	− .04
Age 2[b]	0.02	0.45	0.06
Class [c]	0.05	0.62	0.05
Sex [d]	0.01	− .09	0.84
1974	I	II	III
Health	0.54	0.07	0.28
Social relationships	0.41	0.31	− .08
Leisure activities	0.61	0.17	− .08
Economic resources	0.11	0.60	0.18
Housing conditions	0.07	0.64	− .15
Political resources	0.09	0.28	0.69
Age 1	0.78	− .19	0.03
Age 2	0.05	0.49	0.07
Class	− .01	0.50	0.10
Sex	− .03	− .07	0.83
1981	I	II	III
Health	0.51	0.12	0.34
Social relationships	0.48	0.17	− .17
Leisure activities	0.63	0.16	− .17
Economic resources	0.21	0.58	0.00
Housing conditions	0.06	0.44	− .39
Political resources	0.13	0.49	0.46
Age 1	0.73	− .22	0.19
Age 2	0.05	0.50	0.10
Class	− .06	0.63	0.00
Sex	− .07	0.08	0.79

[a] Coding: 15–29 years = 0, 30–54 = 1, 55–75 = 2
[b] Coding: 15–29 years = 1, 30–54 = 0, 55–75 = 1
[c] Coding: Class I and II = 0, III = 1
[d] Coding: Men = 0, women = 1

considered, but also the background characteristics sex, age, and social class. The results of the analysis are presented with so-called factor loadings, which can vary between − 1 and + 1. These are measures of the degree of the correlation between variables (in this case, problems with different components as well as the three background characteristics) and statistically established underlying dimensions, *factors*, that can be seen as axes in a coordinate system. In Table 14.4 the factor analyses 1968–1981 are presented, based on data for the entire population[7].

Problems in the various components are quite well-ordered in relation to the background variables. Health, social relations, and leisure activities are correlated mainly with age so that the aged have problems more often than others. Unsatisfactory conditions concerning finances and housing are related mostly to class (III), but even to a certain degree to age (the young and the old more often have problems than the middle-aged). Limited political resources are principally associated with sex (women).

As for developments over time, some change in the nature of the dimensions seems to have taken place. Political resources are included in the class factor in 1981, but are still contained in the sex factor. Furthermore, the association between housing conditions and sex seems to have increased, so that women now have fewer problems than men. Overall, however, the three-dimensional pattern is stable throughout the period.

A comparison between the results of the factor analysis and the previous analysis of the correlations between various problems in the population as a whole (see Figure 14.1) yields some differences in outcome. The problem groups in both cases are three in number, as they are defined, but appear to be more or less different in character. The problem group linked to physical mobility in the first analysis is also found in the factor pattern, with the difference being that economic problems are not included as a part. The interpretation of its nature should stand, however, especially in light of the strong link with greater age.

The group of problems interpreted in terms of knowledge and skills does not recur in the same manner as a dimension in the factor analysis. Limited political resources are linked here to sex, for which an interpretation similar to the one above can be made. Women have less knowledge and experience of broadly defined political and union activities through working life than men. This is a consequence of the fact that fewer women are gainfully employed than men, and when they are, work in more subordinate jobs than men. Therefore, this factor may be interpreted in terms of sex roles.

The problem group that has been interpreted in terms of economic resources also recurs as a dimension in the factor analysis, albeit in somewhat modified form. Problems with finances and housing conditions are here linked to class, which makes it reasonable to interpret this factor again as an expression of limited economic resources.

Altogether, the introduction of background characteristics into the analysis of the association of problems has brought about some changes in the pattern that has been discerned. This means that there are no factors or groups of problems that are *clearly* distinguished from each other. There is a general coexistence of problems, and somewhat varied pictures of their nature are obtained by applying different approaches. The two approaches chosen in this chapter have both yielded what appear to be fully interpretable results.

The findings can be summarized as follows: the coexistence of problems is relatively *general and constant in nature,* but *moderate and diminishing in scope.* Overall it is exceptional for different types of problems to lack any correlation with each other at all. The strength of this correlation varies to some degree, however, and it is this variation that makes it possible to distinguish the problem groups. When we apply the two approaches in the analysis, different segments of the correlations' variation stand out. The principal conclusions can be summarized in three points:

1. Economic resources occupy a special place among the components, to the degree that such problems appear simultaneously with problems of other types to an unusually large extent.
2. If we disregard how the different problems are related to sex, age, and social class, there are three groups of at least three problems with relatively strong internal correlations. Besides financial problems, which are found in all groups, the first group consists of health, leisure, and social relations; the second group, leisure and political resources; and the third, social relations and housing conditions. These three groups are interpreted in terms of physical mobility, knowledge, and economic resources.
3. When studying the way in which the problems are related to background characteristics, the following pattern emerges. Health, leisure, and social relations are associated with age — older people have more of these problems than others. Political resources are linked to sex — women have fewer resources than men. Finances and housing conditions are primarily linked to social class — people in class III have problems more often than others. These three factors are interpreted in terms of mobility, sex roles, and economic resources.

These three points refer to the population as a whole. The picture is not as unambiguous for economically active people, primarily because of generally weaker associations among the problems. The unique position of finances, however, is also clear in this category.

Accumulated problems within population groups

After this overview of the factors in welfare distribution, we will take a closer look at the scope of accumulated problems in specific population groups. Sex, age, and social class are the background characteristics used. Gainfully employed, or economically active, people will be treated separately. Regarding one of the problem categories, leisure activities, we consider the delimitation to be more arbitrary than in the other cases. This problem category, therefore, has been dropped from further analysis since we will now treat all categories as being on a par with each other. The differences among population groups are influenced only slightly by the omission of leisure problems.[8] Basically, only the average range of the coexistence will be affected.

In Table 14.5 the proportion of the total population and gainfully employed people with at least *one* problem is shown, by sex, social class, and age.

Table 14.5 Proportions with at least one problem in five and in six level-of-living components 1968, 1974, and 1981 in the population as a whole and among the economically active, by sex, class, and age. Percentages

	Population			Economically active		
	1968	1974	1981	1968	1974	1981
Men	68	55	45	66	52	41
Women	84	74	59	79	67	50
Classes I and II	66	54	42	61	49	37
Class III	84	73	60	80	67	54
Young[a]	79	68	54	75	62	48
Middle-aged[b]	69	54	41	66	51	43
Elderly[c]	84	75	65	72	61	45

[a] Population: 15–29 years;   Economically active 15–34 years.
[b] Population: 30–54 years;   Economically active 35–49 years.
[c] Population: 55–75 years;   Economically active 50–75 years.

Women have problems more often than men, and class III more often than classes I and II. This is true both for the total population and for the gainfully employed. The differences show no appreciable signs of changing over time. Middle-aged people least often have problems. In the total population, it is the elderly who most often have problems, while the corresponding category among the gainfully employed is the young. This is probably because the oldest adults, those over 65, are only seldom wage-earners or self-employed, and because older people who do work form a positively selected group. The difference between middle-aged people and others seems to have increased slightly since 1968 for the total population, while the opposite is true for the gainfully employed. Despite the fact that six level-of-living components are included for the economically active versus five for the total population, the proportion with problems is lower among the former.

The above discussion gives some information about the general occurrence of problems, but only slightly reveals their cumulative tendency. To this purpose, the distribution of accumulated problems is analyzed, where accumulated is defined as at least three types of problems. The relations between the sexes, social classes, and age groups are given in Table 14.6.

Table 14.6 Proportion with at least three problems in five and in six level-of-living components 1968, 1974, and 1981 in the population as a whole and among the economically active, by sex, class, and age. Percentages

	Population			Economically active		
	1968	1974	1981	1968	1974	1981
Men	11	7	4	9	6	4
Women	22	13	7	17	9	4
Classes I and II	8	5	3	7	3	2
Class III	23	14	8	17	11	6
Young[a]	12	7	3	12	8	4
Middle-aged[b]	10	6	3	9	5	4
Elderly[c]	29	18	11	16	8	5

[a] See Table 14.5
[b] See Table 14.5
[c] See Table 14.5

Compared with the presence of at least one problem, the differences among the various population groups often stand out here as greater. The pattern in the relationship among the groups is nevertheless identical. It is men, members of classes I and II, as well as middle-aged people who are least afflicted by accumulated difficulties. The situation for the oldest group in the total population is striking, as it deviates markedly both from that for the young and for the middle-aged. There is no counterpart to this among the economically active, undoubtedly because only older people with larger resources are gainfully employed. The change in the differences among the different groups is not clear cut. The absolute distance between advantaged and disadvantaged categories decreased in each case during this period. Among the gainfully employed the relative differences between the sexes declined, as well as among the age groups. In the total population, the relative differences among categories were constant or even growing.

It is thus obvious that problems are accumulated unevenly in the population. The groups that in general tend to be subjected to problems more than others, even deviate markedly from the rest concerning accumulated difficulties. It can be assumed that some extreme categories are concealed behind the information discussed above, namely, those that combine decisive background factors. This is illustrated in Table 14.7 for the population as a whole.

On all three measurement dates, middle-aged men in classes I and II are the most free of problems, while older women in the working class are the most afflicted. Other groups with a high concentration of problems include older men in class III and older women in classes I/II.

The absolute differences among the twelve subcategories decreased substantially during the period, and as for the relative change, the proportion with problems was more than halved in all groups. In 1981, it is primarily the three groups already designated as having many problems that deviate markedly from the others. For that year, one in six in the most afflicted group has problems of at least three kinds. For several other groups, accumulated problems in this sense seem to have been almost eliminated.

The background variables interact with each other in such a way that relations among the sizes of the problem groups for different values on a background variable are not independent of the values for other background variables. The relative difference between the sexes for multiple problems is the greatest among the elderly in classes I and II. Another outcome of the same interaction is that the relative differences among the classes as to the proportion with multiple problems is greatest among older men and least among older women.

The relationships have not changed over time. Even if the proportion with multiple problems decreased in all groups, regardless of which combination of background variables they represent, the relationship between these proportions in the different groups is about the same in all three surveys.

The effect of the different background variables is summarized in

Table 14.7 Proportions with at least three problems in five level-of-living components in 1968, 1974, and 1981 in twelve subcategories of the population as a whole. Percentages

1968		Per cent		N	
		Men	Women	Men	Women
Young (15–29)	Class I/II	5	13	309	374
	Class III	11	23	528	420
Middle-aged	Class I/II	3	5	587	536
(30–54)	Class III	11	20	590	665
Elderly (55–)	Class I/II	8	20	330	297
	Class III	28	47	494	581

1974		Per cent		N	
		Men	Women	Men	Women
Young	Class I/II	2	5	318	365
	Class III	6	12	536	449
Middle-aged	Class I/II	2	2	646	584
	Class III	8	11	588	608
Elderly	Class I/II	4	16	362	347
	Class III	18	28	502	595

1981		Per cent		N	
		Men	Women	Men	Women
Young	Class I/II	2	2	253	326
	Class III	3	4	565	442
Middle-aged	Class I/II	1	1	753	695
	Class III	4	6	576	602
Elderly	Class I/II	2	11	388	386
	Class III	10	17	473	582

Figure 14.3. As was suggested earlier, the proportion with multiple problems has declined over time, men have multiple problems less often than women, older people have most problems and the middle-aged the least, and social class III has a greater proportion with multiple problems than the other classes. It is also clear from the figure that the differences as to people with multiple problems among types of communities is insignificant. On the other hand, there is a tendency for this proportion to have declined more rapidly in the countryside than in the big cities. As mentioned above, the relationships among the groups for the remaining background variables have not changed over time.

Table 14.8 Proportions with at least three problems in six level-of-living components in 1968, 1974, and 1981 in twelve subcategories among the economically active. Percentages

		Per cent		N	
1968		Men	Women	Men	Women
Young (15–34)	Class I/II	6	13	308	276
	Class III	10	22	512	240
Middle-aged	Class I/II	2	6	352	200
(35–49)	Class III	11	21	334	250
Elderly (50–)	Class I/II	7	9	368	146
	Class III	19	27	393	268

		Per cent		N	
1974		Men	Women	Men	Women
Young	Class I/II	4	6	358	365
	Class III	8	16	551	318
Middle-aged	Class I/II	1	2	360	248
	Class III	9	9	297	263
Elderly	Class I/II	3	5	354	188
	Class III	10	13	392	291

		Per cent		N	
1981		Men	Women	Men	Women
Young	Class I/II	1	1	333	376
	Class III	5	7	530	376
Middle-aged	Class I/II	2	1	456	371
	Class III	5	8	307	288
Elderly	Class I/II	2	4	357	222
	Class III	7	6	303	272

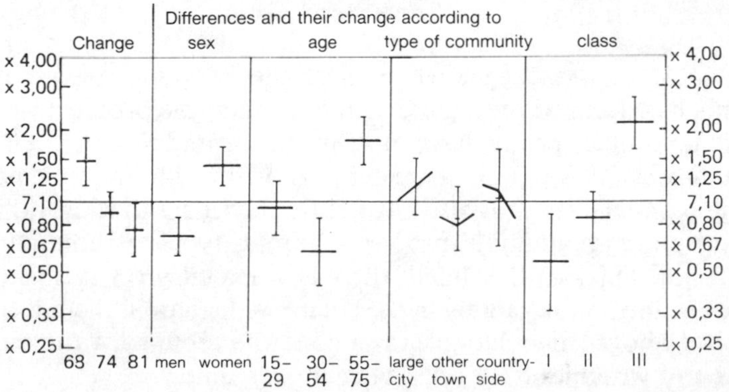

Fig. 14.3 Regression model for proportions with three or more problems in the population as a whole

The relationships among the twelve subcategories among the gainfully employed, or economically active, are given in Table 14.8. Here a somewhat different picture emerges than for the population as a whole. Within the latter, older people in class III are subjected to problems to an unusually high degree. This is an afflicted group among the gainfully employed as well, but does not deviate there as much as in the total population. This is probably because few of the extremely aged are economically active. If this is the reason, it supports the notion that problems are especially striking among the oldest people in social class III. But the selection of the economically active also may have an effect here. It is quite possible that the selection is more rigorous in class III than in the other classes, which would produce such a result.

The relationships among different groups of the economically active closely resemble those for the total population. Women tend to have problems more often than men, and members of class III more often than members of other classes. Again, middle-aged men in classes I and II seldom have multiple problems.

As for the significance of the other background variables, the relative difference between the sexes for the proportion with multiple problems is greatest among the young, while the relative difference among social classes is least among the young and greatest among the middle-aged. The difference between the sexes decreased slightly in relative terms, from 1968 to 1981. During this period, the group of middle-aged economically active people also approached the other two age groups in terms of the proportion with multiple problems.

Discussion

In the introduction three questions were posed which were to be answered in this chapter. They concerned 1) whether problems of different kinds tend to coexist or not, 2) whether the scope and nature of any coexistence changed between 1968 and 1981, and 3) whether it is particular population groups that suffer from limited resources and multiple problems. We found that there is a moderate coexistence that declined in scope over time, that the coexistence remained unchanged in nature, and that old people, women, and members of class III face multiple problems more often than do younger/middle-aged people, men, and people in classes I and II. The group that has multiple problems most often is older women in the working class, while middle-aged men in classes I and II very seldom have multiple problems, as defined here.

Financial problems were shown to play a central role; they exist relatively often together with other problems. It is easy to imagine several causal mechanisms: that limited economic resources underlie other problems, such as bad housing standards; that economic problems are caused by other problems, such as bad health; and that one underlying factor explains the occurrence of several specific problems. For example, bad education, a problem not taken up in this chapter, may lead both to bad finances and to limited political resources. Regardless of how the causal relationships take shape, the findings clearly reflect the central role played by economic resources in people's standard of living. The probability is relatively high that a person with financial problems also has problems in other level-of-living components.

In the introduction, two reasons were given for studying the coexistence of problems. One concerned the occurence of more general problem-generating factors, the second the form of society's social policy measures. Our findings indicate that there may be one or more factors underlying the various problems, although only of moderate strength. Were we to search for a general factor, we might expect it to be linked to economic resources. That problems mainly appear separately makes it less reasonable to focus social policy measures on generally problematic conditions; measures should instead be specifically intended for individual problems. The central role of finances in the problem structure, however, indicates that economic support would probably alleviate many of the different problems which occur.

The proportion of the population with problems in several level-of-living components dropped sharply between 1968 and 1981. This is due to the fact that the frequency of some of the individual problems was reduced. On the other hand, the coexistence of problems is of approximately the same character and strength in 1981 as in 1968. This means that the risk of a person with one problem also having another problem, exceeded the corresponding risk for a person without the original problem to the same degree in all survey years. In other words, the mechanisms or processes leading to problems seem to have operated in much the same way in 1968 as in 1981, even if the number of people with multiple problems decreased considerably. The risk of a person, for example, with financial problems also having problems in terms of political resources was about three times greater than the same risk for a person who did not have financial difficulties, in 1968 as well as 1981. Simultaneously, the absolute differences in the proportions with problems decreased. For both those with and without financial problems, the proportion with limited political resources decreased, and this decrease was greater among those with financial problems.

The risk of suffering multiple problems is relatively high for women, the aged, and members of class III. The fourth variable used consistently in this book for characterizing the population, type of community, was, however, shown to be relatively insignificant for the risk of being faced with many problems.

When men from class III and women grow older, the risk factors seem to pile on top of one another causing a pronounced increase in the risk of multiple problems. On the other hand, when men in classes I and II grow older, the risk of multiple problems does not increase proportionately as much.[9] One possible explanation for this is that men in these social classes have command over such extensive resources that the resource reduction which accompanies old age only exceptionally leads to more than isolated problems.

One of the consistent findings in this book has been that the situation and resources of women are improving. In contrast, we find in this chapter that only the risk for economically active women improved concerning multiple problems relative to that for men. For all women, we cannot demonstrate any change in the relationship, that is, the risk seems to have decreased proportionately as much for men as for women. However, it is not unimportant that the differences are decreasing among the gainfully employed. An increasing proportion of women are economically active; if their conditions have improved relative to men's, it is of great significance for the distribution of problems between the sexes.

That no equalization has been found between the sexes over time may be due to the fact that the test used is not sufficiently sensitive to reveal any decrease in the differences. If the data from 1974 are excluded, that is, if the information from 1968 is compared only with that from 1981, the probability of finding such an equalization is greater. If such a test is made, there is actually a reduction in differences between the sexes, especially between young men and young women.

It is therefore likely that a rather weak equalization has taken place between the sexes as to the risk of multiple problems. The equalization seems to have taken place primarily among young people, so that the previous differences between the sexes largely remains in the other groups. In the future it is, of course, possible that the differences will decrease in all age groups.

However, the same tendency is not found for the social classes. That is, the proportion of people with many problems decreases in all classes, and proportionately to about the same degree. But, as maintained above, this means that in percentage points the proportion has decreased the most in class III.

The same analysis of the values for 1968 and 1981 that revealed a slight equalization between the sexes, also showed changes in the relations between age groups. But it is not so much a question of a general equalization as of a relative improvement in the position of young people.

Welfare problems thus are unevenly distributed in the social structure. Women, the aged, and members of the working class are affected more than others. From 1968 until 1981, however, welfare problems decreased in scope overall. An equalization between men and women seems to have occurred, at least among the young and the economically active. In absolute terms, the problems have decreased the most in class III, but in relative terms, the relationship among the classes has remained unchanged.

Notes

1. Education is not included in this discussion, since a problem category can hardly be designated within this component. The number of individuals with less than compulsory schooling is extremely small, and classifying people who have gone through compulsory schooling as a problem group does not seem reasonable. What would be more satisfactory, theoretically, and most fruitful for policy making, would be to identify people with insufficient knowledge and skills for today's society. However, we have no such information. Security of life and property is also excluded since this component was not contained in the 1968 survey.
2. The size of the 'totally isolated' and 'isolated' groups in Chapter 12, however, is constant. These categories were delimited according to the same principle as the problem groups in Table 14.1 above, but by applying stricter standards. It is thus when consideration is given to *both* interaction and solitary living that the scope of deficient social relations does not seem to have decreased since 1968.
3. It may be worthwhile to state that classic indicators of misfortune such as criminality and alcoholism point in a direction different from our data. These phenomena, however, are still of a relatively marginal scale, for the adult population as a whole (see Tham 1980, 68–70).
4. The construction and characteristics of the gamma measure are given in, for example, Blalock (1972, 298 f., 421 f.).
5. The connecting lines between components indicate relatively strong correlations, at least 0.35, on average, during the period. The lines do not indicate any causal directions, only covariation. The same is true for Figure 14.2 where the correlation between different problems for the gainfully employed is described. In the latter case, however, one connecting line also marks an insignificantly weaker correlation than 0.35 (0.34), between political resources and leisure activities. The figures should not be given any interpretation other than that they are meant to illustrate and facilitate the continued discussion.
6. See for example SCB 1981b, 78–81.
7. Factor analyses for the gainfully employed yielded a result which was difficult to interpret. The factor pattern was not especially well structured,

and moreover was unstable over time. Therefore, it has not been used. The findings may be attributed to the relatively weak correlations among the problems in this category. As regards the relation between problematic working conditions and the three background characteristics, the outcome was unambiguous in any case. Class is much more strongly related to working conditions than sex and age, so that people with occupations in class III are more affected than others. Concerning the factor analysis as method, the dimensions can be established in several ways, depending upon the technique used. The factors in Table 14.4 have been produced via the so-called *varimax-rotation*, which is the most common technique in this type of material. This means that we are striving to maximize the variance within each factor, so that the loadings are either high or low. Attempts to avoid medium-high loadings in this manner facilitate interpretations of the content of the factors. Moreover, a varimax-rotation is *orthogonal*, which means that the factors are forced to be uncorrelated with each other. This also facilitates interpretations. Compared with the previous analysis of gamma correlations, the factor analysis is thus dependent on the relationship of all the different variables *simultaneously*. To use the earlier simile, the factors are the axes in a coordinate system. The gamma-analysis, on the other hand, is based on the simple correlations one at a time. One possible consequence of the differences in method is that the different welfare problems in the factor analysis will be included in fewer dimensions than what could be expected from the pattern of individual correlations. The factor analysis should thus be seen as a schematic simplification of the actual conditions, for the purpose of elucidating certain tendencies in the empirical material.

8. Some reservation should be expressed here about the association between accumulated problems and age. By disregarding the problems of leisure, that are experienced primarily by older people, the differences among the age groups become somewhat less in terms of problem accumulation. There is, however, no change in the *tendency* of the differences.

9. In a strict sense, we have not observed any differences in changes over the life span among different categories. Our conclusions on this point are nevertheless supported by the fact that older men in classes I and II deviate from the remaining age groups to about the same extent on all measurement occasions.

Appendix: delimiting the problems

1. Health

(a) Physical well-being: People have problems here either if they have seriously impaired mobility (cannot run 100 metres, and cannot either walk 100 metres relatively briskly without trouble or go up/down stairs without difficulty) or if they have had any of the following problems during the past 12 months: severe pain connected with mobility (according to the index consisting of aches in shoulders, back/hips, and joints)/ serious difficulties in circulatory system (according to index consisting of chest pains, weak heart, high blood pressure, varicose veins, swollen legs, breathlessness and dizziness)/ serious stomach difficulties (according to index consisting of stomach ache, gall bladder trouble, indisposition, vomiting, and diarrhoea)/serious eyesight impairment/serious hearing impairment/ serious bronchitis (asthma)/serious goitre/serious tuberculosis/serious heart attack/serious ulcer/serious weight loss/serious cancer/serious diabetes/serious organic nervous disorder (CP, MS, polio, etc.).

(b) Mental well-being: People have problems if during the past 12 months they have suffered either from a mental illness (slight or serious) or otherwise clearly impaired mental health (according to index consisting of general tiredness, sleeplessness, nervous troubles, depressions, and over-exertion, where milder difficulties were given weights of 1 and serious ones 3, and the delimitation was set at 3 totalled points minimum).

2. Economic resources

People who have access to not more than one of the following six assets are classified as having problems: Private home (detached house or co-operatively-owned dwelling)/cash margin (able to obtain a certain amount of money, 5000 SEK in 1981, within a week)/car/boat/summer cottage or caravan/holiday trip (previous year).

3. Housing conditions

(a) Space standard: People have problems either if they live more than two people per room within the household, kitchen and living room excluded (that is, crowded in the traditional sense), or live alone in one-room dwelling without space enough to eat in the kitchen.

(b) Equipment standard: People have problems if they lack any of the following conveniences: Water (cold and hot)/sewer drainage/shower or bath/toilet/central heating/modern stove/refrigerator/washing machine (on the premises).

(c) Form of tenure: People have problems if they do not fulfil any of the following conditions: Own their dwelling (house or co-operatively-owned dwelling)/rent an apartment as the main leaseholder/live in apartment owned by employer/do not have control of own dwelling (live with parents, or the like).

4. Social relationships

People have problems who live alone and do not fulfil any of the following conditions: visit friends often/have friends visit often/visit relatives often/have relatives visit often.

5. Leisure activities

People have problems if they do not perform at least two of the following 13 activities often (or correspondingly, that is, at least 1 often and 2 sometimes, or at least 4 sometimes): Fishing/hunting/going to the cinema/going to the theatre (including concerts, museums, exhibitions)/going to restaurant/dancing/reading books/reading weekly magazines/strolling (walking around on the streets and in shops)/study circles/playing a musical instrument sports/hobbies.

6. Political resources

(a) Political participation: People have problems if they do not fulfil any of the following conditions: member of union/member of political group/has demonstrated at least once/has contacted person politically accountable/spoken at a meeting at least once/written in a newspaper at least once.

(b) Mobilization against authorities: People have problems who do not fulfil either of the following conditions: are able to write an appeal against a decision by an authority oneself/know someone able to help with such an appeal.

7. Working conditions

(a) Integration on the labour market: People have problems who *either* have been unemployed sometime during the past year and fulfil one of the following conditions: are presently unemployed (week prior to the interview)/have insecure conditions of employment (anticipate being fired shortly or already have been), *or* have a farm or business that will soon be closed down.

(b) Nature of the work: People have problems who *either* have physically exhausting and at the same time monotonous work *or* have mentally exhausting as well as monotonous work.

Components 1, 3, 6, and 7 are given a comprehensive measure by placing all individuals with problems in at least one of the included parts in an overall problem group. Component 7 is used only in an analysis of the gainfully employed.

One problem of a technical nature that is possibly serious, is that the measurement errors are, as it were, enlarged by this adding together of several indicators. For the seven problem groups that are demarcated here, one must thus expect a relatively large number of erroneous classifications of individuals. There is some chance to correct the errors in analyses of the correlations between different problems, but we have refrained from doing so mostly because of the greater degree of complexity brought about by such a method. The correlations given in the presentation are therefore largely underestmated in relation to the findings one would have obained if the measurement errors were corrected. Since priority was given to describing change over time in our analysis, we must make an important assumption about the size of the measurement errors: *that these are not different for the separate measurement occasions.* Possible changes in strength over time as to the correlations between different problems are thus assumed to reflect *real* changes, and not fluctuating sizes of measurement errors. However, no detailed examination of the differences in errors of measurement has been performed.

Appendix A: Sampling and data collection

LEIF ANDERSSON

The Level of Living Surveys are based on data collected on three occasions: 1968, 1974, and 1981. Most of the data were obtained by conducting interviews with a large number (approximately 6000) of randomly selected people about their life situations. Data that both for the interviewees and for us were simpler to gather via registers than via interviews, were obtained from relevant registers upon proper authorization. This mainly applies to information on income, but also to registration for domicile, immigration and emigration, as well as causes of death. Practically all data collection was conducted in co-operation with Statistics Sweden, but some information was obtained from The National Social Insurance Board. Almost all processing (checking, coding, and keypunching) was performed under the auspices of Statistics Sweden (SCB).

The sample in 1968 consisted of a random sample of the adult population between the ages of 15 and 75 years. Everyone in this sample who was living in Sweden in 1974 and under 76 years old, was selected for inclusion in that year's sample. In order that the sample should be representative of the Swedish population within the same ages as 1968, the original sample was augmented with a sample of young people between 15 and 20 years old, and immigrants who had come to Sweden between 1968 and 1973. Similarly, the 1981 sample consists of all surviving and remaining people under the age of 76 years from the 1974 sample. Again, the sample was augmented with young people between the ages of 15 and 21 years, and with immigrants who had come to Sweden between 1974 and 1980; thus, this sample also became representative of the Swedish population 15–75 years old.

The initial sample from 1968 was taken from a larger random sample of people previously interviewed by telephone for the so-called Low Income Investigation in 1967. The initial sample encompassed 6,524 individuals. The interview work got underway in the middle of May 1968. By that time, two preliminary studies had already been conducted that spring. The interviewers (Statistics Sweden's local representatives) were first briefly instructed and then they conducted a test interview, which was reviewed and judged by the project supervisors.

Most of the interviews were conducted in the period ending at midsummer. Completed interviews were sent to SCB for checking, coding, and keypunching. After the summer holidays in August 1968, the missing data levelled off at about 14 per cent. The follow-up of the missing data that was then begun, resulted in a reduction to just over 9 per cent, as is shown in Table A.1.

The final interview was returned to SCB on November 10, 1968, and in

Table A.1. Proportions of missing data in the Level of Living Surveys

	1968	1974	1981
Interviews	90.8	85.2	82.4
Missing data	9.2	14.8	17.6
of which: are sick	0.2	0.3	0.6
unavailable	1.4	1.7	1.9
refuse	7.0	12.6	14.7
hospital, prison	—	0.1	0.2
other	0.6	0.1	0.2
Net sample	6524	6593	6865

December of the same year, all the interview information was coded and put in mechanically readable form on magnetic tape.

The 1974 study was planned and conducted as a replication of the 1968 study. The same interview forms were in large part used, and the majority of the participants from 1968 were re-interviewed about their circumstances. Dropped from the sample were individuals who by 1974 were either too old or had died or emigrated. As mentioned above, the original sample was enlarged with a sample of young people and newly arrived immigrants between the ages of 21 and 75 years. Younger immigrants (15–20 years old) were included in the youth sample. In this manner, the 1974 sample consisted of three groups or strata: young people, the new immigrants, and the panel (interviewed previously). The panel make up about 90 per cent of the total material. The sample probabilities vary somewhat among these strata, as can be seen from Table A.2. It amounts to about 1/1000 in all three groups. In simple terms, each individual in the sample can thus be said to correspond to about 1000 people in the population. In order to compensate for the difference in the sample probability, observations with differing weights are included when the totals and proportions of the population are being estimated.

Table A.2. Estimated stratum sizes and sample probabilities for the Level of Living Survey 1974

Stratum	Size	Sample	Sample probability
Panel	5 296 000	5820	0.0011
Young people	648 000	617	0.0010
Immigrants	135 000	156	0.0012
Population	6 079 000	6593	

The interview phase came somewhat earlier in 1974 than it had in 1968. The initial phase in the Stockholm area and in Norrland took place near the middle of April, and for the rest of the country at the beginning of May. By midsummer, 78 per cent of the selected people had been interviewed. During the summer and until the end of September, a group of specially selected interviewers interviewed those remaining. The staff of telephone interviewers at SCB also took part in this phase. The level of missing data that we finally were forced to accept was 14.8 per cent of the net sample. The increase compared with 1968 was due mainly to the fact that the proportion of people refusing to take part had increased considerably, which can also be seen from Table A.1.

In the application of the 1981 study, basically the same circumstances were present as for the previous investigation. New samples were made in the lowest age groups and a supplementary sample of new immigrants from 1974 to 1980 was added. The panel from 1968 had by this point been further reduced by rising age and deaths or emigration. About 78 per cent of the original sample, nevertheless, was still confined within the population under study. For the 1981 study, therefore, we have five strata versus three in the earlier study. In addition to the three from 1974, which now make up part of the panel in the 1981 study, there is the new sample of young people and that of new immigrants. The stratum sizes and estimated sample probabilities are given in Table A.3 below. Seven strata are treated in the table since Yugoslav youths and immigrants are overrepresented in the sample. For that reason, the sample makes special studies of these immigrant categories possible.

About 85 per cent of the new sample had taken part in the 1974 study, and 74 per cent had even participated in the 1968 study.

Table A.3. Estimated stratum sizes and sample probabilities for LNU 1981

Stratum	Size	Sample	Sample probability
Panel	4 583 000	5076	0.0011
Youths –74	631 000	601	0.0010
Immigrants –74	106 000	123	0.0012
Youths –81[a]	789 000	840	0.0011
Immigrants –81[a]	146 000	162	0.0011
Jugosl. youths –81	3 000	21	0.0064
Jugosl. immigrants –81	6 000	42	0.0066
Population	6 264 000	6865	

[a] Excluding Yugoslav youths and immigrants, respectively. These are included as over-samples and are reported separately.

Since comparability between the surveys was an important consideration when designing the Level of Living Surveys, the collection of the 1981 material was also conducted during the spring and early summer, and the missing data followed up in August and September. As was the case in the previous surveys, SCB was responsible for the field work as well as the keypunching, checking, and correcting of the interview material. Before the work was begun, the staff were again given instruction in how the survey was to be carried out and training in the more difficult sections of the form. SCB's interviewers were committed to another project during the spring of 1981. The interview work therefore did not get properly underway before May. However, 73 per cent of the selected people had been interviewed by midsummer. After the follow-up of the missing data in August-September, this figure rose to 82.4 per cent. The missing data stabilized at 17.6 per cent. The increase in missing data is largely due to the fact that the number of people refusing to participate increased further, as seen in Table A.1.

The processing of the completed interview questionnaires was performed by SCB for all three surveys, primarily involving keypunching and review of the submitted material. The keypunching was conducted by SCB's permanent keypunching staff. For the checking, both permanent staff and temporary employees were used. Incompletely or erroneously completed forms were corrected following contact with the interviewer responsible. As part of the overall organization of the work, comprehensive mechanical controls were applied in the computers. For the 1981 study, each form was checked against almost 1000 such logical control conditions. in this manner, the group checking the forms was alerted to any unreasonable and potentially erroneous responses. After corrections were made, the data were checked for a second time using the computer.

It may be stated here that the work with revising and checking the submitted material did not cease when SCB delivered the magnetic tapes to the Institute for Social Research. Additional checks were made at the Institute, primarily concentrating on manually coded information, such as occupation, education, social class, etc., in order to ensure the high quality of this information.

In order to compensate for differences in the sample probabilities among strata, each individual in the survey was assigned a weight reflecting this difference. In addition to this simple weighting, a further one was made to compensate for the effect of the missing data. The response tendencies vary between sub-groups of the population. Men and women in different types of communities, ages, and social classes, display a slightly varying response tendency. A factor which is part of the weighting system compensates for this in calculations. Another factor is also included that makes it possible for the responding group, after weighting, to have the same sex and age distribution as the target population. Since the choice of individuals is random, the sample does not automatically reproduce the population being studied exactly. Some difference must be expected which is due to chance. This last weight factor now has the consequence that after weighting the responding group has the same distribution in sex and age as the target population.

Appendix B: A Regression Approach, Background and Details

JAN SELÉN

Introduction

The application of regression introduced in Chapter 2 'the regression approach' is intended for summarizing and describing level-of-living data. The typical application is when proportions or averages are obtained through cross-classification of data to a large number of groups. The regression approach can be designed to answer questions concerning the differences in proportions or averages for these groups. The approach can also be used to show how data can be summarized. Third, the method can improve accuracy in the estimates of proportions or averages.

The approach consists of two parts. In the first, a model type is specified, that is, a priorly selected form for describing and summarizing. The model type determines which questions can be elucidated. By means of statistical tests, it is possible to decide how far (parsimoniously) each level-of-living variable can be summarized. In the second part of the approach, the findings from the summary are presented graphically. The diagrams were introduced in Chapter 2, and the procedure that leads to such descriptions should soon be apparent. Norlén (1976) suggested the use of regression adjustments as a means of describing variations in the level of living. The method was further developed into a multiplicative model and a diagram presentation which were introduced by Selén (1979a, b). Continued development has led to a better diagram and a specification of the regression model which makes the estimation procedure simpler, Selén (1985).

Similar methods of analysis, primarily for qualitative variables, are found in the literature; examples are Theil (1970), Goodman (1972), and Grizzle, Starmer, and Koch (1969). The regression approach differs from these mainly in the emphasis on the presentation of the results using Norléns triangle-shaped table and in the graphic presentation.

The underlying model

Formally, the adjustment procedure in the regression approach is regression on dummy variables. The dummy variables take the values 1, 0, and -1 and are of two kinds; in part, a set of simple variables, in part a set of composite variables which are defined as products of the simple ones. With the notations X_{11}, X_{21}, . . ., X_{52} the simple variables are defined in Table B.1 for our application.
There are 162 different sets of values for the X-variables with sex and each of the three age groups, types of community, social classes, and years. For each

set, there is a corresponding population group. The composite variables are products of the type $X_i X_j$, $X_i X_j X_k$, $X_i X_j X_k X_l$ and $X_i X_j X_k X_l X_m$. The index variables i, j, . . ., m take the values 11, 21, ..., 52. In each product, there is at most one X-variable from each factor.

Table B.1. Simple dummy variables

Factor					
Sex			*Age*		
	1	men		1	0	15–29 years
$X_{11} =$			$X_{21} = 0$	$X_{22} = 1$	30–54 years
	−1	women		−1	−1	55–75 years
Type of community			*Class*		
	1	0	large city	1	0	Class I
$X_{31} = 0$	$X_{32} = 1$	other town	$X_{41} = 0$	$X_{42} = 1$	Class II
	−1	−1	countryside	−1	−1	Class III
Year					
	1	0	1968		
$X_{51} = 0$	$X_{52} = 1$	1974			
	−1	−1	1981		

The aim of the regression adjustment is to describe in a simple manner the averages or proportions in the 162 groups for a given variable. Simplicity here means that the independent variables should be few and uncomplicated. An initial attempt at describing can be based on X_{11}, ..., X_{52} and $X_{11} X_{21}$, $X_{11} X_{22}$, $X_{11} X_{31}$, ..., $X_{42} X_{51}$, $X_{42} X_{52}$, that is, all unique products with two X-variables from different factors. With a multiplicative model, then, let us try:

$$Y = \alpha \prod_i \beta_i^{X_i} \prod_{i,j} \gamma_{ij}^{X_i X_j} \epsilon \tag{1}$$

where Y denotes the population groups' proportions or averages. The model's parameters are α, β_i, and γ_{ij}. The error term ϵ summarizes the excluded terms. We can then write:

$$\epsilon = \prod \gamma_{ijk}^{X_i X_j X_k} \prod \gamma_{ijkl}^{X_i X_j X_k X_l} \prod \gamma_{ijklm}^{X_i X_j X_k X_l X_m}$$

where each product of X is unique with X-variables from different factors. With ϵ inserted in 1), the saturated version of the model is obtained. The total number of parameters α, β, and γ is then equal to the number of population groups. The Y-values can be described exactly, and the parameters can be solved as functions of them. The saturated model gives a complete description, but it does not summarize in the sense that the number of information bits is reduced.

Interpretation of the parameters

The parameters in model 1) are interpreted in the following way. β_{11} is the coefficient for the dummy variable for sex and is interpreted as the effect of being a man. The effect of being a woman is $(\beta_{11})^{X_{11}}$ for $X_{11} = -1$, that is, $1/\beta_{11}$. The multiplicative model concerns relative differences and the relative difference between the sexes is the ratio between corresponding coefficients or $(\beta_{11})^2$. The age factor in the model is $(\beta_{21})^{X_{21}}(\beta_{22})^{X_{22}}$. With the different values for X_{21} and X_{22} inserted, we find that the effect of being 15–29 years old is β_{21}, the effect of being 30–54 years old is β_{22} and the effect of being 55–75 is $1/(\beta_{21} \beta_{22})$. The β-parameters for the remaining factors are interpreted analogously. The γ-parameters denote the interaction effects. For sex and age, for example, we get the interaction $(\gamma_{11\,21})^{X_{11}\,X_{21}}(\gamma_{11\,22})^{X_{11}\,X_{22}}$. Corresponding effects with the X-values inserted become $\gamma_{11\,21}$ for men 15–29 years, $1/\gamma_{11\,21}$ for women 15–29 years, $\gamma_{11\,22}$ and $1/\gamma_{11\,22}$ for men and for women 30–54 years, as well as $\gamma_{11\,21}\gamma_{11\,22}$ and $1/(\gamma_{11\,21}\gamma_{11\,22})$ for men and for women 55–75 years.

Observe that the coefficients are standardized. Standardization implies that the products of the effects within one factor are one. Therefore, the effects, to be precise, relate to a hypothetical population of 162 population groups of the same size. Estimation and inference problems thereby become easier to solve; compare the balanced case within analysis of variance. The implications of standardization for interpretation are of little practical significance.

Seen in an analysis-of-variance perspective, the β-parameters correspond to main effects and the γ-parameters to interaction effects of the first order. The parameter α is an average effect.

With the previously mentioned saturated model, the exact meaning of the parameters can be established. It is found that α is the geometric mean of the 162 groups' proportions or averages. The implication of β_{11}, for example, follows from the fact that the geometric mean for the 81 groups with men is $\alpha\beta_{11}$. Accordingly, if β_{11} is greater than one, this coefficient reflects how much the level for men exceeds α; if it is less than one, the coefficient reflects how much the level for men falls below α. The difference from a model that is not saturated, like 1), is that the parameter estimates are the geometrical means of the predicted values, that is, of the proportions or averages as estimated by the model.

Estimation and testing

The estimation of 1) proceeds from a logarithmic version of the model to which the weighted least-squares method is applied. The fit is assessed using a χ^2-test, where the test variable is a sum of squared and weighted residuals. The test indicates whether any of the missing factors should have been included. By means of χ^2-tests, it is possible to assess the explanatory power of the various factors, for example of the age factor or the interaction between age and sex.

The results of the tests can be used to modify the model, so that certain factors are included or excluded. Details concerning the estimation procedure are found in Norlén (1976) and Selén (1979a, b).

Table B.2. Regression coefficients in a comprehensive description of proportions of disabled people

		Main effects	Interaction Effects										
			Sex		Age			Type of Community			Class		
			Men	Women	15–29	30–54	55–75	Large city	Other town	Country side	I	II	III
All		7.96[a]											
Sex	Men	0.79											
	Women	1.26											
Age	15–29	0.41	0.98	1.02									
	30–54	0.84	0.97	1.03									
	55–75	2.93	1.05	0.95									
Type of Comm.	Large city	1.15	1.03	0.97	1.06	1.05	0.90						
	Other town	0.92	0.98	1.02	0.91	1.02	1.07						
	Countryside	0.95	0.99	1.01	1.03	0.93	1.04						
Class	I	0.80	0.97	1.03	1.33	0.90	0.76	1.01	0.91	1.09			
	II	0.94	0.97	1.03	0.97	0.91	1.13	0.91	1.04	1.06			
	III	1.32	1.05	0.95	0.78	1.11	1.16	1.09	1.06	0.87			
Year	1968	1.06	0.94	1.06	0.82	1.15	1.05	0.95	1.00	1.06	1.08	0.97	0.95
	1974	0.88	1.04	0.96	0.95	1.01	1.04	0.99	1.01	1.00	0.88	1.06	1.07
	1981	1.08	1.02	0.98	1.28	0.87	0.91	1.06	1.00	0.94	1.05	0.97	0.98

[a] This coefficient has been multiplied by 100.

An illustration

Let us look at the example of physical disability used in Chapter 2. A summarizing description for this variable with the model gives a X^2 -value of 75. The number of degrees of freedom equals the number of groups (162) minus the number of estimated parameters (42), that is, 120. The description is extremely good (p < 0.01). A rule of thumb for the descriptions to be accepted has been that the test value shall fall below the ninth decile in the X^2 distribution (p = 0.90). The parameter estimates can be presented in triangle form as in Table B.2. The table contains estimates for all levels within each factor.

In the left-hand column of the table is the α - and β -estimates that is, the main effects. The remaining columns contain the γ -estimates, that is, the interaction effects. The main effect for men, for example, is 0.79. An estimate of the effects for men in 1968 is 0.79 times the effect for 1968 (1.06) times the interaction between men and 1968 (0.94 in the second column) which makes 0.79. In the corresponding diagram in Figure 2.1, the y-coordinates are determined for the thick line for men by means of the sex effect and the interaction effects for sex and year. The line's left-hand end point corresponds to the effect for men times the interaction between men and 1968, 0.79 × 0.94 = 0.74. For the line's centre point, the interaction between men and 1974 is used which gives 0.82. The line's right-hand end point becomes 0.79 × 1.02 = 0.81, using the sex effect and the interaction between men and 1981.

The explanatory power for the various factors in the model is seen in Table B.3.

Table B.3. Degree of explanation for different factors in description of disabilities

Factor	Degrees of freedom	p	Factor	Degrees of freedom	p
sex	1	1	sex*year	2	0.96
age	2	1	age*comm	4	0.93
type of comm	2	0.92	age*soc	4	0.93
soc class	2	1	age*year	4	0.98
year	2	0.79	comm soc	4	0.99
sex*age	2	0.97	comm*year	4	0.70
sex*comm	2	0.43	soc*year	4	0.20
sex*soc	2	0.86			

A rule of thumb has been that only factors with p < 0.90 should be considered significant. The interaction effects with year are given in the diagram only when p < 0.90. The results in the table show that it could have been worthwhile to specify a model without the interactions between sex and type of community, sex and social class, type of community and year, as well as social class and year.

The explanatory power for year is also low.

Some interaction effects that are not given in figure 2.1 are significant. The interaction between type of community and social class is an example which implies that the social class differences for the various types of community cannot be described completely with the main effects alone. If the differences are described without the interactions, the implication is that the comparison of the groups is made for a specific population structure with group sizes as implied by the adjustment procedure. The problem is in principle the same in standardization, but with the difference that here we know the importance of the interaction effects.

Bibliography

Allardt, E. (1970) 'Den sociala förankringens problematik.' In E. Allardt, *Förankringar,* Borgå, Söderströms.

— (1975) *Att IIa Att Älska Att Vara.* Lund, Argos.

Arvidsson, P., and R. Bucht (1976) *Fritiden i Sverige — ett sociologiskt perspektiv,* Stockholm, Scandinavian University Books.

Becker, G. S. (1975) *Human Capital,* New York, Columbia University Press (1st edn. 1964).

Bell, D. (1973) *The Coming of Post-Industrial Society,* New York, Basic Books.

Benzel, R. (1952) *Inkomstfördelningen i Sverige,* Stockholm, The Industrial Institute for Economic and Social Research.

Berg, F. (1911) 'Folkskolan såsom bottenskola. Ett inlägg i en viktig samhällsfråga', *Pedagogiska skrifter* 55: 23-72. Stockholm, SAF:s Litteratursällskap (1st edn. 1883).

Bergman, P., and S. E. Olsson (1977) 'Arbete och fritid,' In Å Daun (ed), *Bingospelare,* Stockholm, Tiden.

Bernstein, B. (1975) *Class, codes and control,* London, Routledge and Kegan Paul.

Birgersson, B. O., and J. Westershåhl (1979) *Den svenska folkstyrelsen,* Stockholm, Liber.

Björkman, T., and K. Lundkvist (1981) *Från MAX till PIA — Reformstrategier inom arbetsmiljöområdet,* Stockholm, Arkiv.

Blalock, H. M. (1972) *Social Statistics,* New York, McGraw-Hill.

Blauner, R. (1964) *Alienation and Freedom: The Factory Worker and his Industry,* Chicago, Chicago University Press.

Blomdahl, U., and U. Brånell, (1981) *Fritid — ett idéprogram,* Malmö, The Board of Health and Welfare/Utbildnings produktion.

Bourdieu (1973) 'Cultural Reproduction and Social Reproduction' in R. Brown (ed.) *Knowledge, Education and Cultural Change.* London, Tavistock.

Boudon, R. (1974) *Education, Opportunity and Social Inequality,* New York, John Wiley and Sons.

— (1979) *The Logic of Social Action,* London, Routledge and Kegan Paul.

Bowles, S., and H. Gintis (1972) 'IQ in the US Class Structure', *Social Policy* 3.

Braverman, H. (1974) *Labor and Monopoly Capital,* New York, Monthly Review Press.

Carlsson, G., O. Arvidsson, L.-O. Bygren, and L. Werkö (1979) *Liv och hälsa. En kartläggning av hälsoutvecklingen i Sverige,* Stockholm, Liber.

Dahlström E. (1951) *Trivsel i Söderort,* The City of Stockholm.

Durkheim, E. (1951) *Suicide, A study in Sociology,* New York, The Free Press. (1st. edn. 1897.)

Eriksson, J., and M. Lindquist (1981) 'Utrymmesstandardens fördelning och samband med andra levnadsförhållanden,' Working paper 1981-05-18. National Institute for Building Research. (Mimeo)

— (1983) *Bostäder, hushåll och utrymmesstandard 1970-1985,* Ds Bo 1983.7 (The Ministry of Housing and Physical Planning).

Erikson, R. (1971) *Uppväxtförhållanden och social rörlighet,* Stockholm, Allmänna Förlaget.

—— (1976) 'Patterns of Social Mobility', in Richard Scase (ed.), *Readings in the Swedish Class Structure,* Oxford, Pergamon Press.

—— (1978) 'Social Mooring — an Aspect of Welfare' *International Journal of Contemporary Sociology* 15, 145–62.

—— (1981) 'Om socioekonomiska indelningar av hushåll — Överväganden och ett förslag', Statistik tidskrift 1981:19, 11–23.

—— (1983) 'Change in social mobility in industrial nations — the case of Sweden'. In D. Treiman and R. Robinson (ed), *Research in Social Stratification and Mobility,* vol 2. Grenwich, JAI Press.

—— (1984) 'Social Class of Men, Women and Families,' *Sociology* Vol. 18 No. 4.

ERU (Government Commission on Regional Development) (1982) *Myter om rörligheten,* ERU-rapport 22.

Esberger, S. E., and S. Malmqvist (1972) *En staatistick studie av inkomstutvecklingen,* Stockholm, Allmänna Förlaget.

Fox, A.J., and P.O. Goldblatt (1982) *Longitudinal Study, Sociodemographic Mortality Differentials,* London, HMSO.

Franzén, M., and E. Sandstedt (1981) *Grannskap och stadsplanering. Om stat och byggande i efterkrigstidens Sverige,* Stockholm, Almqvist & Wiksell International.

Fryklindh, P.U., and S. O. Johansson (1976) *En bok om fritiden,* Stockholm, AWE/Gebers.

Goldthorpe, J. H. (in collaboration with C. Llewellyn and C. Payne) (1980) *Social Mobility and Class Structure in Modern Britain,* Oxford, Clarendon Press.

Goodman, L. A. (1972) 'A modified multiple regression approach to the analysis of dichotomous variables', *American Sociological Review* 37, 28–46.

Gouldner, A.W. (1979) *The Future of Intellectuals and the Rise of the New Class,* London, MacMillan.

Grizzle, J. E., C. F. Starmer and G. G. Koch (1969) 'Analysis of categorical data by linear models, *Biometrics* 25, 489–504.

Göteborgs kommun (The City of Gothenburg) (1970) *Fritid och kultur i Göteborg.* Intervjuundersökning om göteborgarnas fritids — och kulturvanor.

Hall, B. (1976) *Fritiden; Funktioner — förutsättningar — framtid,* Lund, Studentlitteratur.

Halsey, A. H., A. F. Heath, and J. M. Ridge (1980) *Origins and Destinations, Family, Class, and Education in Modern Britain,* Oxford, Clarendon Press.

Hansen, E.J. et al. (1980) *Fordelingen af levekårene,* Bind III. Köpenhamn, The Danish National Institute of Social Research.

Hedström, P. (1980) *Förtidspension — välfärd eller ofärd,* Stockholm, Swedish Institute for Social Research.

Hellevik, O. (1983) 'Politisk deltakelse i Norge — begrenset og skjev?' *Tidskrift før Samfunsforskning* 1983,1.

Hirsch, F. (1976) *Social limits to growth,* Cambridge, Harvard University Press.

Holmberg, S. (1981) *Svenska väljare,* Stockholm, Liber.

Husén, T. (1944) *Adolescensen; Undersökning rörande manlig svensk ungdom i åldern 17-20 år,* Stockholm, Almqvist & Wiksell.

Inghe, G., and M.-B. Inghe (1973) *Den ofärdiga välfärden,* Stockholm, Tiden (1st edn. 1967).

Isling, Å. (1980) *Kampen för och mot en demokratisk skola, Del 1: Samhällsstruktur och skolorganisation,* Stockholm, Sober.

Jacobsson, U., and G. Norman (1974) *Inkomstbeskattningen i den ekonomiska politiken,* Stockholm, The Industrial Institute for Economic and Social Research.

Johansson, L. (1970) *Utbildning: Resonerande del,* Stockholm, Allmänna Förlaget.

—— (1971a) *Utbildning: Empirisk del,* Stockholm, Allmänna Förlaget.

—— (1971b) *Den vuxna befolkningens bostadsförhållanden 1968,* Stockholm, Liber.

Johansson, R., and B. Karlberg (1979) *Bostadspolitiken,* Stockholm, Liber.

Johansson, S. (1970a) *Om levnadsnivåundersökningen,* Stockholm, Allmänna Förlaget.

—— (1970b) *Den vuxna befokningens hälsotillstånd,* Stockholm, Allmänna Förlaget.

—— (1971) *Politiska resurser,* Stockholm, Allmänna Förlaget.

—— (1976) 'Liberal-democratic theory and political processes'. In R. Scase (ed), *Readings in the Swedish Class Structure,* Oxford, Pergamon Press.

—— (1979) *Mot en teori för social rapportering, Rapport Nr 2 från levnadsnivåprojektet,* Stockholm, Swedish Institute for Social research.

Johansson, S., and P. Hedström (1979) *Jordbrukares och företagares inkomster och levnadsförhållanden,* Stockholm, Swedish Institute for Social Research.

Jonsson J. (1985) 'Class origin, cultural origin, and the allocation of education in Sweden,' Stockholm, Swedish Institute for Social Research. (Mimeo).

Jonung, C. (1983) *Patterns of occupational segregation by sex in the labor market,* Meddelande 1983, 89. Department of Economics at the University of Lund.

Karasek, R. (1976) *The Impact of the Work Environment on Life Outside the Job,* Stockholm, MIT/Swedish Institute for Social Research.

Kerckhoff, A. C. (1974) 'Stratification Processes and the Outcomes in England and the U.S.', *American Sociological Review,* vol. 39.

Kitagawa, E. M., and P. Hauser (1973) *Differential Mobility in the United States: A Study in Socioeconomic Epidemiology,* Cambridge, Harvard University Press.

Kjellberg, A. (1983) *Facklig organisering i tolv länder,* Lund, Arkiv.

Korpi, W. (1978) *The Working Class in Welfare Capitalism: Work, Unions and Politics in Sweden,* London, Routledge & Kegan Paul.

—— (1983) *The Democratic Class Struggle,* London, Routledge & Kegan Paul.

Kågeson, P. (1972) *Fritidsverksamhet; idéer och mål,* Stockholm, Bonniers.

Lafferty, W. M. (1981) *Participation and democracy in Norway,* Oslo, Universitetsforlaget.

Le Grand, J. (1982) *The Strategy of Equality: Redistribution and the Social Services,* London, George Allen & Unwin.

Leiniö T.-L. (1984) *Inte lika men jämlika. Om finländska invandrares levnadsförhållanden enligt levnadsnivåundersökningarna 1968, 1974 och 1981,* Stockholm, Swedish Institute for Social Research.

Lewin, L. (1970) *Folket och eliterna,* Stockholm, Almqvist & Wiksell.

—— (1977) *Hur styrs facket,* Stockholm, Rabén & Sjögren.

—— (1980) 'Åsiktsmässig och social representativitet', *Statsventenskaplig tidskrift* 1980, 1.

Lindbeck, A. (1981) *Work Disincentives in the Welfare State,* Stockholm, Institute for International Economic Studies.

Linnemann, P. (1980) 'A band matrix solution of the tails in moving average graduation', Working Paper 34, Försikringsmatematisk Institut, University of Copenhagen.

Liljeström, R., and E. Dahlström (1981) *Arbetarkvinnor i hem, arbete och samhällsliv,* Stockholm, Tiden.

Lundahl, A. (1971) *Fritid och rekreation,* Stockholm, Allmänna Förlaget.

—— (1978) *Livsformer i omvandling,* Stockholm, RSFH:s förlag.

Lundqvist, A., and T. Segerstedt (1955) *Människan i industrisamhället,* Del II; Fritidsliv—samhällsliv. Stockholm, Studieförbundet Näringslive och Samhälle.

Lundqvist, L. J. (1981) *Bostadskostnaderna: En fråga om rimlighet och rättvisa,* Swedish Council for Building Research T, 1981, 19.

Marshall, T. H. (1950) *Citizenship and Social Class.* Cambridge University Press.

Martinussen, W. (1977) *The Distant Democracy,* London, John Wiley & Sons.

Mathson, B., and G. Åsvärn (1956) *Fritid i förort: Sociologisk undersökning i Årsta 1954-56,* The City of Stockholm.

Norlén, U. (1976) 'Beskrivning av levnadsnivåvariationer', *Statistisk tidskrift* 1976, 117-134.

—— (1979) *Välfärdsmätning för social rapportering. Meotdrapport från levnadsnivåundersökningen 1974,* Stockholm, Swedish Institute for Social Research.

Otter, C. von (1973) 'Fackligt medlemskap, aktivitet och arbetsvillkor', Stockholm, Arkiv 1973:4.

OECD (1982) *Historical Statistics 1960-1980,* Paris.

Palm, G. (1974) *Bokslut från LM, 2.* Göteborg, Författarförlaget.

Palme, O. (1967) 'Prioriteringsproblem'. In A. Murray (ed), *Det svenska klassamhället,* Stockholm, Prisma.

Parker, S. (1976) *The Sociology of Leisure,* London, George Allen & Unwin.

Preston, S.M. (1970) *Older Male Mortality and Cigarette Smoking,* Population Monograph Series no 7, University of California.

Propositioner (Government Bills)
    1950:70. Riktlinjer för det svenska skolväsendets utveckling.
    1967:100. Riktlinjer för bostadspolitiken m m.
    1974:150. Riktlinjer för bostadspolitiken m m.
    1982/83:100 bilaga 13. Budgetpropositionen.

Retherford, R. D. (1975) *The Changing Sex Differential in Mortality,* Westport, Greenwood Press.

Ringen, S. (1976) 'Den sosiale forankring,' Working paper no. 82, Levekårsundersøkelsen, Bergen.

Roos, P. A. (1981) *Occupational Segregation in Industrial Society: A Twelve-Nation Comparison of Gender and Marital Differences in Occupational Attainment,* University of California.

Sandelin, B., and B. Södersten (1978) *Betalt för att bo,* Stockholm, Rabén & Sjögren.

Sawyer, M. (1976) *Income Distribution in OECD Countries,* Paris, OECD.

SCB (Statistics Sweden) (1969) *Historisk Statistik för Sverige.* Del 1, Befolkning 1720-1967. 2a uppl.

——(1970) Sm Bo 1970:25. Bostads- och hyresundersökning 1969.

——(1975) Sm Bo 1975:3. Småhusundersökningen 1972.

——(1978a) Regional dödlighet 1970-1975. Information i prognosfrågor 1978:6.

——(1978b) Levnadsförhållanden. Rapport nr 14. Utbildning, vuxendstudier och förvärvsarbete 1975.

—— (1980) Sm Bo 1980:10. Bostads- och hyresundersökningen 1978. Del 3: Lägenhets- och hushålsdata för småhus.

—— (1981a) Dödsfallsrgister 1961-1970. Promemorior från SCB 1981:5.

—— (1981b) Levnadsförhållanden. Rapport nr 17. Fritidsaktiviteter.

—— (1981d) Arbetskraftsundersökningarna 1970-1980, Statistiska meddelanden Am 1981:33.

—— (1982a) Bostads- och byggnadsstatistik Årsbok 1982.

—— (1982b) Kvinnor och barn, Information i prognosfrågor 1982:4.

—— (1982c) Sm Bo 1982:12. Bostads- och hyresundersökningen 1981.

—— (1982d) Socioekonomisk indelning (SEI). Meddelande i samordningsfrågor, 1982:4.

—— (1982e) Levnadsförhållanden. Rapport nr 33. Perspektiv på välfärden 1982. Översikt.

—— (1983a) Levnadsförhållanden. Raport nr 35. Utbildning och utbildningseffekter.

—— (1983b) Inkomstfördelningsundersökningnen 1981:2, Inkomstutveckling för anställda åren 1973 till 1981. Statistiska meddelanden 1983:4.2.

—— (1983c) Inkomstfördelningsundersökningen 1981:2. Inkomstfördelning för hushåll. Statistiska meddelanden 1983:4.3.

——(1985) Higher education 1977/78 — 1982/83 UZO SM 8501.

Selén, J. (1979a) 'Val av regressionsmodell vid beskrivning av levnadsnivåvariationer', *Statistisk tidskrift* 1979, 17-34.

—— (1979b) *Tre bidrag til välfärdsmätningarnas metodik,* Stockholm, Swedish Institute for Social Research.

—— (1985) 'Multidimensionsl Descriptions of Social Indicators', *Social Indicators Research,* 435-45.

Spånt, R. (1976) *Den svenska inkomstfördelningens utveckling,* Acta Universitatis Uppsaliensis.

—— (1979) The Distribution of Income in Sweden 1920-1976, Stockholm, Swedish Institute for Social Research.

SOU (Swedish Government Official Reports) (1948:27) *1946 års skolkommissions betänkande med förslag till riktlinjer för det svenska skolväsendets utveckling.*
—— (1964:47) *Frilufslivet i Sverige.*
—— (1970:34) *Svenska folkets inkomster.*
—— (1971:39) *Den svenska köpkraftsfördelningen 1967.*
—— (1971:61) *Rekrytering till universitet och högskolor* (Bengt Gesser).
—— (1974:17) *Solidarisk bostadspolitik. Betänkande av boende- och bostadsfinansieringsutredningarna.*
—— (1975:90) *Arbete åt alla.*
—— (1977:46) *Pensionsfrågor m m.*
—— (1982:1) *Real beskattning.*
—— (1983:14) 'Barn kostar...' Betänkande av familjekonomiska kommittén.
Staines, G.L. (1980) 'Spillover versus compensation: a review of the literature on the relationship between work and nonwork', *Human Relations,* vol. 33, 111–30.
Stiglitz, J.E. (1975) 'The Theory of "Screening", Education and the Distribution of Income', *American Economical Review,* no 3.
Sundström, G. (1983) *Caring for the Aged in Welfare Society,* Stockholm Studies in Social Work 1, Stockholm, Liber.
Svenska Bokförläggareföreningen (Swedish Publisher's Association) (1982) Branschstatistik 1981/1982. Stockholm.
Svensk författningssamling (The Swedish Statute-book) 1982, 763. Hälso- och sjukvårdslag.
Sveriges Socialdemokratiska Arbetareparti (1970) Protokoll, del II, från SAP:s 24:e kongress 28 september – 4 oktober 1969. Stockholm: Tiden-Barnängen ab.
Szasz, T. (1975) *Ceremonial Chemistry,* New York, Anchor Press/Double Day.
Tawney, R.H. (1964) *Equality,* London, Unwin Books. (1st edn. 1931).
Tham, H. (1980) 'Brottsutvecklingen—indikator på vad?', in S. Marklund and R. Åberg (eds.), *Framtidens oönskade sociala förhållanden,* University of Umeå.
Theil, H. (1970) 'On the estimation of relationships involving qualitative variables'. *American Journal of Sociology,* 76.
Therborn, G. (1981) *Klasstrukturen i Sverige 1930–1980,* Lund, Zenit.
Titmuss, R. (1974) *Social Policy,* London, George Allen & Unwin.
Tornstam, L. (1983) 'Ensamhetens dimensioner — en begreppsdiskussion', *Sociologisk Forskning* no. 2.
Törneman, H. (1977) *Aktiviteter på fritiden,* The City of Stockholm.
Turner, R. (1960) 'Sponsored and Contest Mobility and the School System', *American Sociological Review,* 25, 855–67.
United Nations (1966) *The Level of Living Index,* New York: The United Nations' Research Institute for Social Development.
—— (1982) *Levels and Trends in Mortality since 1950.* United Nations Publication.

Valkonen, T. (1977) 'Excessive adult male mortality in Finland. Its origins and development since 1870', Working paper no. 3. Department of Sociology, University of Helsinki.

—— (1983) 'Mortality trends and projections in cardiovascular diseases', Working paper no. 29. Department of Sociology, University of Helsinki.

Weibull, L. (1983) *Tidningsläsningen i Sverige,* Stockholm, Liber.

Wikman, A. (1982) *Kan man mäta den faktiska arbetsmiljön och andra levnadsförhållanden med hjälp av surveyfrågor?* Stockholm , Statistiska centralbyrån.

Wilensky, H. (1960) 'Work careers and social integration', *International Social Science Journal,* No. 4.

Young, M. (1958) *The Rise of the Meritocracry 1870 to 2033,* London, Thames and Hudson.

Zetterberg, H. L. (1977) *Arbete, livsstil och motivation,* Stockholm, The Swedish Employers, Confederation.

DATE DUE

MR 1 '91			

DEMCO 38-297